HOW TO
Write
WHAT YOU WANT
& Sell
WHAT YOU WRITE

A Complete Guide
to Becoming a Successful
Published Author

SKIP PRESS

BARNES
& NOBLE
NEW YORK

2005 Barnes & Noble Publishing

ISBN-13: 978-0-7607-7233-1
ISBN-10: 0-7607-7233-9

Printed and bound in the United States of America

3 5 7 9 10 8 6 4

Table of Contents

Introduction

BOOKS ABOUT WRITING. BAH! THERE'RE TONS OF 'EM! SOMEBODY get me a shovel. You can't teach anybody to write! Writers are born, not paid. Too many writers are born, matter of fact. Or, should we say, imbeciles who want to be writers. Just ask any editor with red ink in her veins.

Now that we've gotten that baloney out of the way, let's get to the real meat of the matter. Forget every assumption or generality about writing you've ever heard or read. You can teach someone to write. You can learn to write. In fact, you can keep getting better at writing for as long as you're able to think and act rationally and coherently.

I've had students tell me that I was a breath of fresh air, that I saved their writing lives, that they couldn't understand why all their other writing teachers had made it all seem so complex.

I understand why those other teachers stumbled, and so should you. Too often, instructors are more interested in process than in communication. Good writing is simple in concept, though it can be elaborate in execution. What are you doing when you are writing? You're communicating. You learned to talk, didn't you? I trust you learned your ABCs. How about grammar? Did you learn it well? If you didn't, you may need to brush up. Get a copy of *The Elements of Grammar* by Margaret Shertzer. Study it and *The Elements of Style* by William Strunk, Jr., and E. B. White. I also recommend *Eats, Shoots & Leaves: The Zero Tolerance Approach to Punctuation* by Lynne Truss.

In this book I cannot fix the work you missed in English class, but if you have your basics in order, I'll take you the rest of the way. At the very least, I'll point you in the right direction with a road map to where you want to go.

I have a workmanlike view of the world of writing. No matter how successful I become, I will maintain that basic point of view. What do I mean by workmanlike? When I was just starting out as a professional writer—a career I dreamed of, even counted on, from a very young age— I wasn't picky about what I was paid to write. That's why I put my name to articles about air conditioners, quickest taxi arrivals, and the best pizza in Los Angeles (I chose Numero Uno because I liked their sweet dough). I loved the perquisites that went along with writing those articles, and I learned about the drawbacks. (Sick as a dog on the eighth day of eating nothing but pizza, I didn't go near another pizza parlor for six months.)

No one taught me how to write articles; they simply told me how long they wanted them, and I winged it. I learned each new form of writing "flying by the seat of my pants." I've been holding that basic flight pattern for the last fifteen years. If you do some research, you'll discover that the majority of highly successful writers have, like me, a workmanlike view of writing. They have simply written whatever it took, perfecting their craft as they went along.

Here's another tip. One of the best things I learned early on was this: No matter how good your writing is, if it isn't presented in the proper length, format, and "look," you're immediately branded an amateur.

When I began writing screenplays, there was only one book available which explained the proper format. Wow, how times have changed. The correct format for an audiovisual script was explained to me verbally. The best length for various kinds of short stories—the length acceptable to editors—was explained on a postcard from my agent.

When I needed to know about stage play formats, the way speeches should look on a page, or tricks about article writing, I gleaned inside tips from experts. In Los Angeles, where I live, there are plenty of successful writers at hand. I've found that many successful writers naturally seek out experts, while other hopeful writers do not, even when they live in major metropolitan centers. Will you let fear prevent you from making it as a writer, or will you ask someone who knows?

Since I often secured writing jobs in areas of writing I knew nothing about, if I wanted to keep the job, I had to display total professionalism. So I learned to (1) get it right the first time, and (2) ask a pro if I didn't know. Don't know any pros? Well, you do now. With this book in your hands, in essence you know me.

I'll also tell you where to find other experts. So pat yourself on the back. You just moved ahead in the game. In teaching writing over the years, both formally and informally, I discovered that, although most of my students had a very strong urge to get published, or even become professional writers, they didn't know how to sort out their own desires, capabilities, and strengths. They rarely knew proper formats, or thought to find out about them. I determined that, by explaining in brief detail different writing markets, then providing the proper format for each, I gave my students an advantage. They could then do a minimum of two things: (1) hone in on the form of writing offering them the best immediate personal chance of success; and (2) give their work a professional "look" right from the start.

Beyond that, I told them, one becomes a better writer by: (a) writing, (b) writing, and (c) more writing. Thank you, Mark Twain.

I realized I had a pretty good system when I got the Instructor Evaluation Forms back from my first class at UCLA Extension Writers Program. Most of my students rated me a "9," the highest possible rating. A couple of troublemakers gave me a "7" and a "6." One of my best students thanked me profusely for not presenting another "touchy-feely, thank-you-for-sharing" type of class. She was extremely grateful for my honest, practical, useful advice. Like twenty-five percent of my students from that first class, she got published within a year of taking my course. Twenty percent of the students became full-time writers in a year. I've maintained that twenty- to twenty-five-percent first-year success rate with every course I've given.

This book will tell you what sort of submission is expected for a newspaper "op ed" [opinion editorial] piece, an audio-visual script, a year-end report, a screenplay, or even a nonfiction book proposal. There are other places to get this information, of course. You could buy the entire Writer's Digest catalog, including an entire book about nothing but writing query letters. In contrast, my book is one-stop shopping. In *How to Write What You Want & Sell What You Write*, I've attempted to cover virtually the entire field of writing in practical, workable, proven terms.

Although I've sold darn near every type of writing that exists, my own advice is mixed with that of established professionals in specialized topics. I try to cover all the bases. Over the years, I learned to write economically. Quick and clean writing is particularly important in writing screenplays, and a course I teach on that is (as of this writing) available in over nine hundred schools. So I hope this book flies by like a good movie. I don't spend too much time on any one subject, but I do give you the basics. After reading and applying the principles and formats given here, every single want-to-be writer out there (and those interested in switching fields of writing) should know what basic first steps to take. You'll discover exactly how to get started and rapidly achieve quick, no-nonsense results.

People buy "everything you need to know" books about medicines, cars, gardening, home electronic repair, and taking care of babies. Why not a comprehensive one about breaking into all types of profitable writing? Turn the page, and let your adventures begin!

Chapter One

The
Big Picture

I NEVER SET OUT TO BECOME THE KIND OF WRITER I AM. I'M A generalist, a full-time writer kind of a guy, making a living. It amazes my friends and confounds my enemies, but I am rarely between deals. My burden is usually finding the time to deliver all the writing I've sold while also teaching, but that's okay. I've had worse problems in my lifetime. I'm usually happy typing away, meeting a deadline, and I've made money writing just about everything. I love being interviewed by reporters, appearing on talk shows, and being a guest speaker. I'm one of the busiest writers I know, and I have a mouth to match. You may have correctly guessed that I plan to stay that way. Retirement? Why retire from doing something I love? I'd have to be dead.

Guess what? I can tell you how to have this much fun, too.

From an early age, I always thought I would become the great American novelist, not an all-purpose wordsmith. In wanting to write my first novel, however, I became confused about where to start. I knew that a journey of a thousand miles began with the first step, but I didn't know where to step first. I didn't even know what shoes to wear. How long should my book be? What should it look like on the page? Should it be single-spaced, or double? Coming from a small town in Texas, I had no one to advise me, and no idea where to go to find advice.

Busy being confused, I got distracted. Maybe you've shared some of my wrong turns. Inspired by seeing the legendary British rock group The

Beatles on the Ed Sullivan TV show, I became a musician and songwriter. I had some success as a performer, but I didn't sell a single song. Living in Hollywood, I tried screenwriting, with moderate initial success. To support myself through these endeavors, I did office work to pay the rent. Finally, I got back to my original purpose of writing books, and my creative life began to flourish.

Do those detours sound familiar to your own life path? Did you go to law school to secure financial security, and now that you've got the BMW and the nice house, you'd rather be J. K. Rowling, writing major best-sellers that are turned into blockbuster movies?

Are you an office worker who thinks you can write better training manuals than the ones you try to use?

Are you like me, a person who did not finish college, who did hard labor jobs along the way, all the while convinced that one day you'd write and sell books and films?

As a teacher, have you noticed that the books your kids study are no better than ones you could write?

Or are you simply pulling your hair out, trying to write a good speech for your PTA meeting?

Don't sweat it. You may be right about your literary capabilities. You may be the next Tom Clancy, peddling insurance while you try to sell your first novel, but on your way to owning the majority interest in a professional football team. Where you stand with your writing aspirations at this point doesn't matter. I can help you improve your circumstances. As I mentioned earlier, if you can't use English or grammar well, you're lacking some vital education. You need to handle that; it's not my jurisdiction. If you have the rudimentary skills of writing under control, however, I can offer you at least three things:

- ⤙ Help in improving your overall writing
- ⤙ Proper, expected formats to use
- ⤙ Places to get in touch with people who will buy what you write, whatever kind of writing that might be

The latter may, ultimately, be the most important. I've had foreign (English as a second language) students who were stunned that I was interested in their concepts, not the way they turned an English phrase.

Why wouldn't I be? Cervantes wasn't worried about the Queen's English when he wrote *Don Quixote*. Ideas, ideas, ideas are what matter. Great ideas are independent of language; language is merely a tool we use to communicate ideas to others. That might be why all the world loves the motion picture industry, and why an editor praised me for writing "so cinematically." Inspiration literally means the breath of life. Life breathes in any language, and great ideas can come from anywhere. I simply try to help great ideas germinate, reach full bloom, and make it to market. Since I've made a living doing many different kinds of writing on a regular basis, I assume others can learn to do so also. I may or may not be well on my way to becoming the great American novelist, but I'll at least be able to pay for my kids' college educations. I'm living the life I envisioned from childhood.

I don't mind sharing what I know with anyone, because I've seen it demonstrated repeatedly that good works have a way of coming back to you. I never feel threatened by possible competition. Any time I help someone get their career started, or help boost someone's career, I get some kind of unexpected return dividend.

Always, always, always.

And you know what? I rarely run across a person who, when they learn I'm a successful writer, doesn't express a deep desire to write. That's a big reason why I wrote this book. In talking about writing, doing writing, and teaching writing for two decades, I've discovered that most people have an urge to at least write *something* that matters, even if only to them. Usually, their main problem is not knowing where to start. That's where I was, in the beginning, and that's what this book is designed to handle, for you.

There is only one thing I ask of you, if you find this book helpful. Help someone else. Share the knowledge. Don't get territorial and fall into the trap of thinking there's a scarcity of places to sell your work. With the way media has exploded in the past decade thanks to the seemingly all-pervasive Internet, the big complaint I hear from the people writing checks (you know, those who actually pay for writing) is how hard it is to find good writers. That will not change in our Age of Information, so don't get greedy.

Consider this. If we had an entire society where everyone was able to write professionally, imagine what an amazing, literate culture we'd have. Wouldn't you like to contribute to the formation of such a society? (If you wouldn't, put this book down now and go live on another planet, please.)

So you see, I can't lose by helping you.

OK, my speech is over. Let's get down to specifics. So far in my career, I've written and sold the following: advertising copy; "advertorial" articles (a business pays for an ad, and gets an article written about it); biographies (or "bios") and other public relations materials like press kits; children's stories and CD-ROMs (the computer precursor to a DVD); corporate speeches; ghostwritten books; how-to videos; jokes; magazine articles; marketing materials; nonfiction books; novels; poetry; radio scripts; screenplays; short stories; slide shows; stage plays; technical manuals; technical studies; and television. I probably left something out, but I hope you get the point. If I'm interested, and someone will pay me a reasonable fee, I'll write it.

I've been a member of more professional writing societies than I care to count. I've been a board member. I'm listed in Who's Who books. That's all nice, but none of it matters except to point out that I've seen a bit of the world, from the bottom to the top. I can show you around the territory. Remember, I've always operated by getting the job first, then worrying about how to write it, going straight to the experts when need be. Though I don't claim to personally be an expert at any one form of writing, I know enough to make a living at my craft. I'll share everything I know with you. When I don't know, I'll offer an expert (or several) to tell you what to do. What matters to me is the sharing of useful information with those who need it.

One reason I've been successful is that I'm an outstanding researcher. In this book, I've done a lot of basic research for you. I will show you the generally accepted form for just about any kind of writing you can imagine. When I offer expert opinions, they'll be great ones. Tennessee Williams on play writing, for example. Or, at the other end of the spectrum, a mega-successful TV sitcom producer. If you choose, you'll learn how to write and sell comic books, greeting cards, jokes to your favorite comedian or comedienne (believe me, few of them write all their own material), and every form of script you can imagine. If you want, you'll even gain some insight into White House speech writing (are you reading, Mr. President?). Frankly, I feel you'll end up amazed at what you can potentially write and sell.

Beyond that, my friend, it's you and the blank page, or that blinking cursor on your computer screen.

Here's a warning: after reading this book, you will never again have an excuse for not following through if you say, "You know, I always wanted to write..."

Your Primary Focus

I always try to start as large as possible and whittle down as needed. If you think small, your brain will atrophy. Why not aspire to be the most successful writer who ever lived, in whatever area of writing you choose? You might end up like Stephen King, who started off wanting to be a great writer of Western novels, a la Louis L'Amour or Zane Grey, and ended up being a guy who could write a grocery list and have it made into a Hollywood movie. King did not originally intend to be a great horror master, but he did intend to be a very successful writer. Your success will have to do first with how big you dream, then how hard you work to get there. Anything you can dream, you can achieve. The secret in getting there will be in mapping out a path through the jungle and up to the top of the mountain. Your primary image of your potential success is very important, so let's look at it.

Creating Your Image

A popular business phrase is "worst-case scenario." That is, what is the very worst that could happen, if you took a certain path. Similarly, "creative visualization" has come into popularity in the last couple of decades. Olympic athletes and others mentally picture a desired result, such as coming in first in the five thousand meter race or going out with Miss October, with the idea that their projection will be realized. This isn't a new concept. To Hopi Indians, the idea of creative visualization isn't terribly exciting, because their ancestors have been doing it for, oh, around ten centuries. Hopis call the practice "sitting in pictures," and they use it for practical purposes, like getting it to rain.

Don't laugh. Hopis are the only Native Americans who have never been displaced from their original land. The most peaceful of all tribes, they try to work within the balance of nature. When they "sit in pictures" to improve conditions, it works. Otherwise, they wouldn't have kept doing it for over a thousand years. I like the Hopis quite a bit. Frank Waters' *The Book of the Hopi* is one of my all-time favorite reads. My hero Alexander Cloud, the male half of the teenage detective team in my You-Solve-It young adult mysteries, is part Hopi. I study everything I can about the tribe; I've even been to the Hopi homeland.

Here's why I'm telling you this. When I found out about the Hopi's "sitting in pictures" practice, described in *Blue Highways* by William Least Heat-Moon, a little light went off in my mind. I realized that "creative visualization," supposedly developed by psychologists and New Age thinkers, had actually been around for a very long time. I saw that, as a writer, I'd been "sitting in pictures," and writing about them, for a long, long time.

I'm not much of a fan of psychology, pop or otherwise. I prefer traditional philosophy, both Western and Eastern. I see that, despite what the alarmist media would have you believe, humankind is evolving and getting better. Superficial "new" ideas don't mean much to me, because they're usually not new. Since I tend to look for the true source of ideas, I've learned that most "modern" ideas are derived from very old, even ancient sources. The more I learned about mental pictures, the more it became obvious to me that many people have practiced "creative visualization" since the world began. This includes writers and other learned people who pass things on by oral and written means. All artists do it: actors, dancers, musicians, painters, sculptors, you name it. When someone evokes an emotional response in you, they often evoke a mental picture, good or bad, or at least the communication of a concept (which may be in idea, if not pictorial, form). This is important for any writer to understand.

So now we have a starting point for writing. We know mental pictures exist, as the expression of concepts. Words are a writer's main tool, but toward what end? Good writers use words creatively to effectively communicate concepts and paint mental pictures. These pictures then evoke emotional responses and bring about an understanding. Hopefully, the emotional responses aroused and the concepts communicated are positive ones, with a result of increased understanding of life. Even horror writers can do that, believe it or not. News reporters? Well, I said hopefully, didn't I? It saddens me to see writing meant only to evoke emotional response, with little thought for the end result.

If the above sounds easy, it is, basically. You do the same thing, to some degree, every time you talk to someone. Successful writers simply turn communication into an art form. The best writers communicate so well that they transcend simple communication and move into the realm of aesthetics. Page by rapidly turning page, they "get you going" and keep you going, and you're happy to go along.

Truly great writers create works that have a lasting, beneficial effect on generations of readers, often helping to bring about a sea change of understanding and/or social custom in their own society. William Shakespeare, for example, is more responsible than anyone else for making English the most popular language on Earth. And he was quite successful, I should add, in his lifetime. He did not write from an ivory tower, to be understood a hundred years after his passing. He wrote for the upper classes as well as the "groundlings" sitting on the straw in the front rows at the Globe Theatre in London.

These are the basics of all writing. You should continually work to master the mechanics of how they are accomplished. You will get there by learning simple principles, then staying ever vigilant about continuing to improve your skills. Coasting isn't in my vocabulary, and it shouldn't be in yours, if you're serious about writing professionally.

Choosing the Proper Frame

Now let's get to your personal writing aspirations. I would hazard a guess that fear of the unknown is perhaps the greatest fear you will ever encounter. Even if you're caught in a big earthquake (as I have been), though you might know what you're faced with, the unknown factor of "what happens next?" is what terrifies you.

The problem with the unknown is simply that it's not known. That does not mean it is unknowable. When people get the idea that the unknown is unknowable, they can become immobilized by fear. It's the old deer in the headlights situation. Or they become angry, which is equally unproductive. Either way, they don't get much done toward the realization of their dream in such a situation. Fear is usually the first hurdle I have to get over with any writing student. Once they get over the fear of having their writing rejected, and stop being depressed from taking rejection personally, they get angry, because oftentimes the people doing the rejecting don't offer a better direction. Most beginning writers don't know that editors and others usually don't have time to offer comments. When someone does take pains to explain the rejection, it's usually because they see promise in the writing, and would like to see it improved so it becomes salable.

I'd personally like to strangle the smug little sage who said "a journey of a thousand miles begins with the first step," because he left something out. Before anyone goes anywhere, it's good to know where they're going, or want to go, or should go. If they just take off, it's usually a troublesome circumstance prone to cause ulcers. In beginning to write, how can you be expected to figure out your destination, much less reach it, if you don't know how to get there? That's why I always tell someone specifically what I didn't like about a piece of writing. I solve a lot of angry frustration this way.

Once you calculate your destination as a writer, you can backtrack from there, and map out a plan of action. It's a process of simple deduction. If you've been a dabbler with writing, if it's always been on your "one of those days" shelf, if you've got any spare time at all and haven't at least started writing something you really want to write, you're probably in one of three categories:

1. A delusional dilettante who will never adopt a professional attitude and seriously attack actually writing and selling; or
2. Someone who doesn't know where to start, and therefore is hung up in fear of the unknown; or
3. Someone who is angry because of rejection received in which no one bothered to mention specifically what you "did wrong." (Remember, they may not be "right.")

If you feel I'm in error about these points, let me know. If you send me an e-mail or write me a letter, I'll know that there's hope for you. At least you'll be writing something! Even if you're in category (1) above, we might be able to help you.

Notice I said *we*. Strange as it may seem, I didn't write my first novel until a professional writer told me that the generally accepted length for mainstream novels was 100,000 words. (If you count 250 words to a page, double-spaced 8½"-by-11" paper, that's 400 pages of manuscript.) These days, publishers are generally looking for shorter books (75,000 words or so). When I heard 100,000 words, I finally had a frame within which to work. Since I knew the ending I wanted for my story, and where I wanted it to begin, when I did my outline it was easy to calculate the average length of the parts of my book. I simply broke down the story into what I thought were logical chapters, then divided the number of chapters into

400 pages. After I'd written a chapter or two, I could roughly calculate how many hours and days it would take me to complete my book. The process became reassuring and predictable. It was suddenly something known, which I understood and didn't have to fear!

Does that give you some relief?

Wouldn't you benefit by having a frame to work within? Think about it. How many times in your life have you worked within a framework? Johnny, you'll go to school for twelve years, then you'll get a high school diploma. Four more years, Tina, and you'll graduate from college. Three years, Larry, and you'll get through law school. Twenty years with the firm, Margaret, and you'll get your gold watch.

What if someone had told you, at any point along those journeys, "you'll just go till you get it right"? Would that have been a little discouraging? Darn right. That's why you need to have a writing goal, and some parameters within which to work.

I feel comfortable working within boundaries. Other writers I've known operate more loosely. Some simply get an idea, sit down, and start writing, letting the story flow. More often than not, many are soon flooded with confusion, and the piece never gets done, or perfected. I must tell you that I don't personally know or even know of a single writer like that who is very successful. Quite the opposite: I know one hopeful novelist who writes "on a flow" and hasn't sold a thing, after nine books. The writing gets better, but there is little attention paid to whether what is being written is the type of book currently being bought by the public, or has ever been bought.

What the public will buy is another, more important, writing parameter. It's discussed thoroughly in this book. It took me a long time to realize that writing was a job. A hard job, I might add, with hard-to-please customers. I've dug ditches for a living, been a union carpenter, and labored in a foundry, yet I don't know any harder work than writing. It takes constant discipline and mental alertness, so it helps when I lay down guidelines for myself from the beginning. In interviews with highly successful writers, I've never known a "big name" writer who didn't maintain strict discipline with his or her writing schedule, and have some fairly concrete outline when beginning a new work, even if the story changed as they wrote it. I usually have my next four or five large projects mapped out. When I was younger, I had ten.

If you haven't already noticed, genre books like romance novels and detective thrillers tend to be roughly the same length each time. "Big" books such as the latest epic from Stephen King or Tom Clancy are usually just that, big and fat. You can always count on a Danielle Steel novel to be roughly the same size. There are practical reasons why different forms of writing come in certain lengths and are presented in the same format each time. It always comes down to what is commercially acceptable to a publisher, with the parameters developed over a long time of doing business. Big writers write big books because they can. The readers will stay with them, and will pay more money for the books.

Similarly, Hollywood has very strict guidelines for both film and television. Movie scripts are single-spaced, usually varying in length from ninety to 120 pages. Why? Because on screen film time averages roughly one minute per written page. When a script is 120 pages long, the film will be two hours. When a film is two hours or shorter, movie exhibitors can maximize their number of daily screenings. This means they can sell more popcorn and goodies, which is where they make their largest profits. Television situation comedy (sitcom) scripts, on the other hand, are roughly forty-eight pages long, double-spaced. That works out to 24 minutes of onscreen time, leaving plenty of time for commercials. (We'll get further into the structure of scripts, and how you, too, can chase the Hollywood dream, in a later chapter. The above examples merely illustrate how having guidelines is not only important but expected.)

Yes, girls and boys, it all comes down to the buck and the buying public, but isn't that the way of the world? Would you rather write one book that wouldn't be recognized as brilliant for three generations, or would you like to enjoy the fruits of your labor in this life?

Let's review what I've shared with you so far:

- ➤ Form a big picture of the success you will achieve as a writer, as though you're already living the best dream you can imagine, as if it currently existed. *Write it down!*
- ➤ Conceptualize what you want to achieve with each individual completed writing project, just as you would visualize a story before writing it. Each piece is a step on the way to your bigger dream.

- Calculate, as closely as you can, how long your current project should be.
- Make sure you use the acceptable, established format of the professionals in the field. If you don't know the proper format, find out. Don't guess.
- Once you've established your parameters, write on a regular (hopefully daily) basis.

Does that help you take your first step? A thousand miles or a thousand pages, it should. If you're not more comfortable about embarking on your journey by now, I urge you to read this chapter over again to make sure you fully understand everything I've written. Not that I'm the world's biggest expert, but I'm trying to put in one chapter what I learned in over a decade of practice. Sketch the steps out on paper if need be, or work it out with toy soldiers the way a general mapping out a battle would. No kidding. I don't care if you use wooden blocks, just make sure you can see it in the real world. American scientist Alfred Korzybski stressed the importance of understanding each word in a piece of text, with each one like a link in a chain, hooked to the next. If the chain is broken by lack of correctly understanding one word, the meaning of the entire text may be lost. So make sure you understand each successive concept I give you. Then I'm certain you'll see the big picture clearly.

Getting to the Exhibition

If your work is any good at all, there is someone, somewhere, who will publish it. I'm not talking about vanity presses, those companies who charge you for the delight of seeing your work in print. With enough perspiration and a little bit of inspiration, every hard-working, decent writer can get published somewhere. A warning, however. You might be so far ahead of the market with your concepts that you'll have to self-publish first, sell lots of copies yourself, and then come to the notice of a large national company. That's happened with a number of now-famous authors. One example is poet Rod McKuen, who sold 35,000 books of his poetry in the 1960s before hooking up with Random House. More recently, *The Celestine Prophecy* was a great grassroots success before getting noticed by large publishers. Even more recently, M. J. Rose is a great example of a writer who wouldn't be daunted. In 1988 she self-published *Lip Service* after several traditional publishers turned it down—it didn't fit into any one genre. Her "e-book" (electronic book) was a huge success. She has since gone on to publish four other novels and contribute to magazines like *Poets & Writers, Oprah*, and *The Writer*. She is also the co-author with Angela Adair Hoy of *How to Publish and Promote Online*, and with Doug Clegg of *Buzz Your Book*. See www.mjrose.com for more information and her online hangout for writers called Readerville.

For now, though, let's discuss traditional publishing.

The first thing I ever had published was a short poem. The publisher was in prison, and my poem graced the pages of the inmate newsletter he edited. Hold on, now! I wasn't in prison, just in correspondence with this particular inmate via a "help a prisoner" public service situation. He published not one, but two of my poems, and I was thrilled.

My next multiple publication (and the first time I was paid) was to a publisher of a local giveaway newspaper called *The Piccadilly*. Referred by a friend, I wrote my first piece on a trial basis. If the publisher didn't like it, I wouldn't get paid. My first assignment was to find the best price on air conditioners in Los Angeles. The publisher must have thought my writing was cool, because he paid me twenty-five dollars. I figured I was hot when I got another assignment. (Hey, we're all punny once in a while.) This time, I had to determine the quickest response time and best congeniality of local taxi services. I angered most of the cab companies in Los Angeles when I suddenly "changed my mind" as each cab arrived, but I got another Piccadilly check. The third article came with perquisites ("perqs"). I had to find the best pizza in the City of Angels. This meant, as I explained carefully to the proprietor of each establishment I visited, I had to have a large version of their best pizza. (They got a free newspaper and a promise.) I fed some friends a couple of times for free, ate nothing but pizza for a week (at a time when my finances were very tight), and got my third article published.

Bang! In three weeks, I had three "clips" (so-called because in those days, you clipped out the published article, photocopied it, and used it as a sample of your work). I also had three checks. I gloated on my success while I lay in bed, recovering from my dietary disaster.

So what have we learned? Don't buy an air conditioner without doing a survey, be nice to cabbies, and order salads with your pizza. Seriously,

I hope you see my point. I thought big long-term, but I started small short-term. I was willing to build my career slowly. Every city has a publication where you can get started and acquire those all-important clips. Why do you need clips? One reason is because you don't have a resume like mine, which shows the accomplishments of twenty-five years as a professional writer and leaves out the starvation. Since you have to convince editors you can write, showing them a clip with your name on it helps. Even today, if I wanted to break in with a new magazine, I would send an editor a sample of my work, if asked.

So that's your first assignment: Get some clips.

What? You don't want to write nonfiction? You're a serious writer who will eventually make people forget the name Ernest Hemingway? OK. So sell a story. Do I hear gulping sounds? In case you haven't already figured this out, it's much harder to sell fiction than nonfiction. That rule applies from short local sales all the way up to the big *New York Times* best-sellers.

At some point in any writing career, people begin to take you seriously. It's like you've suddenly earned your membership, survived the hazing, and magically gained entry into some sort of literary fraternity or club. Believe me, that happens a lot quicker when you have published enough words. To some extent, it doesn't matter *where* you've published, including on the Internet. People just seemed to be impressed by volume and persistence. If you publish a book, you're taken a lot more seriously, even if you published it yourself (no one needs to know).

A student in my first formal class, Julie Comins, moved to Aspen, Colorado after finishing up with me at UCLA. She was pretty, charming, an accomplished actress. Los Angeles was the place to be for the pursuit of stardom, but Julie was sick of the entertainment rat race, where the rats wear disguises. She was also a poet, with aspirations of publishing a book of poems, maybe even a novel. Since she knew quite a bit about the celebrity "behind the scenes" aspect of the ski resort of Aspen, I encouraged her to write a Jackie Collins type of novel featuring Julie's own unique humor and point of view.

I was thrilled one day when Julie sent me a thick package containing some of her published work. Before my class, she had never had a thing printed. I saw that she had taken to heart my suggestion that getting some writing published—whatever kind—is better than nothing. Julie had taken an administrative job at the *Aspen Daily News*. One of her duties was typing classifieds, and she barely knew how to type. Then, one day, the editor learned of Julie's theatrical background. It wasn't long before the "In the Front Row with Julie Comins" column began appearing in the paper. Her own column! Cripes, I'd never had my own column! (I have since, but Julie beat me to it.) Not long after that, Julie received a scholarship to the Aspen Writers Conference and spent ten days studying nonfiction writing with Pulitzer Prize-winning journalist Madeleine Blais. Julie is now a professional, and will no doubt write me next from the chalet she's purchased with the money from her first novel.

Similarly, my student Duke Bates wrote dark narrative stories, like a slightly more serious Stephen King. Duke Bates, in contrast to Stephen "My Grocery List Will Soon Be a Feature Film" King, lacked confidence that he would ever be published. Duke had tried many times and failed. When I learned about his day job—computer conversions for businesses— I suggested he find a magazine where he could sell an article about what he did. This idea stunned him, because he'd never considered journalism. Nevertheless, he almost immediately wrote and sold "Seven Easy Steps for a Computer Conversion" to a national magazine. Duke's confidence level went through the roof. The other students were amazed—one of their peers had written and sold an article to a national magazine before the term was over!

I'll go along if you only want to write fiction. I've been that route, and I've published a few stories in my time. At times, I've made the majority of my writing income writing fiction. Consider this, however. For 500-word articles in *Disney Adventures* magazine, I used to get $500, or a dollar a word. No writer gets that kind of money for short stories except from big national magazines like *The New Yorker* or *Esquire*, and those editors usually want your name to be recognized nationally before they'll give your work serious consideration. Or, they at least want to know who you are, meaning your story has to arrive via a literary agent or someone they trust, or you should have at least published a book or two.

I've only known one literary agent who specialized in short stories. The late great Larry Sternig helped break my work in magazines with national circulation. I got lucky; my science-fiction author friend John Dalmas recommended me to Larry. Try finding an agent like Larry these days. One agent I knew at William Morris in New York handled the short stories of all his agency's authors, while also representing novels for his individual clients. Does this tell you anything about the market for short stories these days? Before passing on in 1999, Larry took on a partner, Jack Byrne. After a while, though, Jack decided it wasn't worth the trouble to handle short stories, so he stopped taking them on.

Still, if you're focused on fiction, you can try a local newspaper (or any periodical) for your short story. It might surprise you, because such publications usually don't get a lot of submissions like that. Be prepared to be asked if it's humorous, though. "Hometown" publications for general circulation tend to lean in that direction. "Alternative" papers tend to favor dark, twisted fiction, usually of a psychological bent.

If you'd like to publish on the World Wide Web, that's wide open. I suppose you could even publish your short fiction on a blog (Web log). You might also investigate Usenet newsgroups like alt.writing or misc.writing (but beware, newsgroups are not for the thin-skinned). And don't forget The Short Story Group at www.shortstorygroup.com.

When you're beginning, getting published is about all that matters. I can't stress that enough. The more you're published, the more confident you will be about your ability. Just don't sell anyone all the publishing rights. (More on that in another chapter.)

The Matter of Style

I learned how a writer's style develops in my first year of full-time writing. I didn't get to be a full-time writer by selling enough writing to support myself. Rather, I won a lot of money on a TV game show and went on a temporary vacation from the workaday world. In my year off, I wrote the novel I'd always wanted to write, learned the proper screenplay format and completed two screenplays, sold my first script—a radio play for a science-fiction radio show called *Alien Worlds*—and wrote up a couple of movie "treatments" (expanded synopses of movie stories). I made good use of my time.

My style emerged with all this writing. I saw that I tended toward the humorous and poignant, with a predisposition toward unusual characters and situations. A common theme which materialized was redemption— people seeking or having to prove themselves and/or working frantically to salvage a perilous situation. Guess when I first got a glimpse of my emerging style? After completion of the novel. Or, after my first 100,000 words.

I once calculated that it took roughly four screenplays to equal, word count-wise, a novel. Interestingly enough, the fourth screenplay I completed, co-written with Mike Conley, was the first one I ever made much money on. Matter of fact, we made money on that script three different times. Although we eventually sold it outright for a nice price, it still hasn't made it to the screen! I'll explain in the screenplay chapter.

I've never counted up all the articles I've ever written, but it's well into the hundreds. To conservatively say that each article is about 1,000 words, I can tell you with no hesitation that by the time I'd written my hundredth article my journalistic style was very well-established. Once again, 100,000 words. That's another reason why I advise people to write and publish wherever they can, long before they start worrying about money. Whatever field of writing you choose, you simply have to do a lot of writing before you acquire the professional quality that is always in demand. From my observation, 100,000 words seems to be the turning point. Try that as your first big goal and see if it works. At 100,000 words, you might arrive at the place where you join the "club" I previously mentioned, but don't be surprised if it takes a bit longer to gain membership.

I know, I know. I told you about my friend who wrote all those novels without selling one. Remember what else I said about that writer? Potential marketability wasn't the greatest concern. The style is firmly established, and I happen to enjoy the books tremendously. Unfortunately, the style is not one that currently fits in with broad public taste. Notice I said "currently." The history of literature is rife with books that become best-sellers after the authors are gone. *Moby-Dick*, for example, was a big disappointment during Herman Melville's lifetime.

Artistic Success Before You Die

To try and save you from going down dead-end alleys chasing wild geese that bite, I've written this book. I've taken on the Olympian task of trying to be everything to everyone, when it comes to writing and selling. Maybe it's because I watched too many Italian Hercules movies on TV, but I honestly think I can accomplish my goal. Although we live in a finite world, there is infinite potential.

I wrote from the time I was a small child, though not very much for many years. I let myself get discouraged by teachers who should have known better. Mrs. Reagan in my fifth-grade class in Trenton, Texas, wouldn't let me turn in a twelve-page poem (handwritten, double-spaced) about the charge of Confederate General Pickett at the Battle of Gettysburg. She said "it would embarrass the other children because it's too good." She's probably dead by now. (I hope she is, anyway, so it's OK to tell that story.)

After hearing me read a short story in class about a shy boy who wouldn't go out with anyone because he was secretly a werewolf, one of my high-school English teachers tried (unsuccessfully) to seduce me. That's when I first realized the powerful emotional impact of words evoking mental pictures.

High school and college events distracted and sidetracked me from writing pursuits; then in 1974 I got a job in Los Angeles writing business letters. That lasted almost four years. I won't even try to figure how many business letter words I wrote. One week I put out 1,350 letters to customers, each customized letter typed by me personally, on my own typewriter. (The business didn't have much of a budget, and I was happy to have the job.) Out of a contact I made during that time, I sold my first script. Shortly thereafter, I met the publisher of "The Piccadilly," where I got my first clips. After I won the money on the game show, I didn't write business letters any more.

When I started writing seriously, I couldn't find anyone to teach me the rules of writing. No one handed me a road map, and I didn't want to go back to college. (I'm glad I stayed out of school, given some of the writing teachers I've seen.) I spent years studying at the School of Hard Knocks and Rare Checks. The books available when I was starting out didn't quite do the trick. They only gave me pieces of the big picture. I learned the most by doing, and finding out first-hand what was necessary to sell.

I want to save you from traveling the hard roads. (There's my redemption penchant again.) Mark Twain wrote about *Roughing It*. I want to show you how to *smooth it*. In this book, you'll find detailed descriptions of the acceptable formats for all types of writing, as well as good advice on how to make a sale.

In closing this chapter, let me offer you a step-by-step process which might help you become a full-time, professional writer quickly, or at least help you make your first big sale. There will not be a quiz at the end, but if you want Santa Claus to come to your house this year, you'd better pay attention.

Skip's Process—Not to Be Skipped

1. Survey local publications, particularly community newspapers. Read them and see what they buy. Contact the editor. Comment on a specific fine piece you enjoyed in the last issue. If necessary, offer to write something for free. This is your "foot in the door," and I've rarely seen the process fail. Get some "clips" and start a portfolio. Put up your own Web site, which can be viewed from most civilized places on Earth. I add this caution—don't forget to print out any online piece or Web page, as well as save a screen shot of it, as well as saving the pages in HyperText Markup Language (HTML) for future reference and printout.

2. Try to determine what you most want to write. Narrow down the field. If you like romance novels, find out which ones are on the best-seller list. Read at least three different top authors. Buy a book or two on writing your chosen specialty. If possible in your geographic area, take a course on your chosen specialty from a working writer. Or take a correspondence course from a working writer. In the computer age, that's easier than ever. I've taught people halfway around the world on a daily basis via www.screenwritingcourse.com.

3. Figure out what you will have to write to get 100,000 words done. Draw up a step-by-step plan of what you'll have to do to have the time to write 100,000 words, and do your best to follow it religiously.

4. Join a writing group. If none is available locally, start one. In this day of online forums, it's easy to find kindred souls. The resources available to groups are geometrical in proportion to those available to an individual. If you prefer people you can actually touch (as I do), there's a chapter late in this book on writers organizations and where to find them.

5. Unless you have a very big problem with low self-esteem, stay away from "touchy-feely" classes and groups. You'll be amazed how much your confidence will rise through accomplishment alone. "Thank you for sharing that with us" doesn't go very far in getting you published. Completing a major project does.

6. Buy a current *Writer's Market*, published by Writer's Digest Books, available in any large bookstore. The book is divided into categories, so if you know what you'd like to sell, you can go straight to that category. Even better, subscribe to Publishers Marketplace at www.publishersmarketplace.com. The site will give you your own page that can be viewed by the many publishers, editors, and agents resident on the site, and the member database is searchable to help you find

an agent. You might also read Jeff Herman's *Writer's Guide to Book Editors, Publishers, and Literary Agents* (Prima Publishing). Jeff's book, in its 13th edition as of this writing, offers a CD-ROM as well. Read your reference books and sites, don't scan them, and make notes. Then contact the appropriate editors.

7. Write something every single day, even if only a page. Screenwriter/director John Milius ("Apocalypse Now," "Red Dawn," and others) explained his success by saying that he wrote two pages per day no matter what. In two months, that's a 120-page script. Other writers, like Michael Crichton (*Rising Sun, Jurassic Park*) become virtual hermits while completing a project. When screenwriter David Ayer showed me the first draft of his *S.W.A.T.* it was 238 pages; he'd barely stopped to eat while writing it. You might not have the luxury of such a schedule, so go at it bit by regular bit.

8. In social situations, don't call yourself a writer unless you pretty much make a living at it. The exception is when you are with a group of your peers, as in a writing group or class. I consider all my students to be writers, and say so. At parties, when I tell people I'm a writer, they inevitably ask, "Have you sold anything?" Maybe that's indicative of living too close to cynical Hollywood. When you have sold professionally, and can recite a list of your accomplishments, the people who make that kind of snide comment are taken down a couple of notches, which is its own sweet satisfaction. I offer this advice to save you from sneers. Remember, they're probably jealous.

9. Sell, sell, sell! Set a few hours aside each week (or as much time as you can), in locating and contacting markets. Even if you make a big sale, keep promoting. There are few things more disheartening than being "on a roll" with sale after sale, then forgetting to tell people about yourself, and ending up with nothing to do when commitments are fulfilled. Writers who have the problem of selling too much, or getting a break in paid writing assignments are usually as good at selling as they are at writing. These days, the bulk of my sales come from browsing the Internet and sending email queries. I tell people that if they're not online, they're falling behind.

10. Be true to your personal goals. If you decide you really want to write the great American novel, and only the great American novel, go for it. There is something admirable in that type of focused, persistent integrity, and it will come across in your work. I've learned to build the pyramid from the ground up rather than starting with the capstone, but there are people who get rich quick and make a big name for themselves with their first major creation. You may be one of them.

So there you go, I hope. Like I said, this chapter is a summation, a general direction provider. It won't cover all the bases, but I hope the rest of the book will. I would like you to be so well rounded in knowledge of the writing world after reading this book that you can launch or improve your career immediately. Whether you only read one chapter, or merely a few that personally appeal to you, I want you to be able to confidently approach writing and selling. I will never claim to be the world's foremost authority on the written word. I'll never try to be, but I do have a personal policy of trying to make the path easier for all those who come after me. That's why I've given away a lot more advice than I've been paid for. I believe in working for the common good that Plato espoused, and in the Buddhist principle of cause and effect, more commonly known as "what goes around comes around."

I truly wish that you come around to greatness.

Chapter Two

Who Cares Who Queries?

OTHER THAN THE QUALITY OF YOUR TEXT, THE MOST POTENT TOOL in selling your writing is the query letter. Whether you use standard mail, a fax, or e-mail, a query is a message sent to an editor accompanying and/or describing your manuscript, or sent in advance asking if an editor, publisher, or agent will look at your work. A good query letter convinces the recipients of the potential worth of your writing and compels them to read it.

Even if you produce the world's greatest unpublished manuscript, you still need to include a letter, to say something about who you are, what you have to sell, where you can be found, and why you contacted that person in the first place. Who, what, where, and why; maybe you've heard the phrase before. Anything else is fluff, which makes good editors impatient and prone to slam-dunking your manuscript in the round file under the desk. The only other important element is if you can truthfully say you have been referred by someone your addressee knows and trusts.

You can probably visit your local bookstore or library right now and find an entire book on writing a great query letter. This month's issue of at least one writing magazine will probably feature an article about composing the world's best query letter. None of this will change the simple fact that you will still be inquiring whether the editor or publisher you contact has any need for what you've written and, if so, how much they'll pay you for it (providing they pay). Note that I said the editor or publisher *you* contact.

I didn't say the magazine or publishing company. The first secret to writing a query letter that will sell is to address it to a real person, not just a title. Who might that be? Do some homework. If you can't get the information you need about a magazine in *Writer's Market* or another reference book, study the magazine at the library or go to the local newsstand and buy a copy of your own. Most of the time, you can find the best contact in reference books. If you can't, however, you can study the portion of the magazine known as the "masthead," that column of text on a page near the front which lists where the office of the magazine is located, who publishes it, who works on it, how often it comes out, its circulation, etc. (Usually, you find the masthead of a newspaper on the editorial page.) If you see many names in the editorial department, chances are you shouldn't waste your time writing the publisher or editor-in-chief. They'll probably just give your letter and manuscript to a junior employee, so why waste their time and yours? A large magazine will have an articles editor, a fiction editor, etc. Smaller magazines may have only one person wearing all the "hats" and thus you could write directly to the publisher and get a reply. You know when publications are small because they pay only in copies (and a few copies at that), if you meet their supposedly discriminating standards and they make an offer to put you in print. Call me ambitious, but I've rarely sent my work to anything but paying publications. I adopted this attitude that I'd sold something. Before I was a paid (read: professional) writer, all I wanted were copies of my printed work, and I was thrilled to get them. After I was published, I sent my work to places that paid the most, first. If they rejected me, I'd move to the next one down the line in financially rewarding rank. I eschewed literary journals, which I've never thought mattered much to anyone except the people publishing them.

You may see this as mercenary logic, but I never met a writer who paid the mortgage writing for prestigious literary journals. I believe writers should not only be paid, but paid very well, because writing is the hardest work I've ever known. I advise you to get paid as soon as possible. You'll feel a lot better about yourself as a writer.

If You Got Your Letter

I always advise my students to try and find a common ground with anyone they communicate with. That includes other writing students, readers certainly, and editors particularly. By common ground, I mean you should try and find something you both know or can agree on. You build from that foundation for communication. You've experienced some form of this a thousand times, unless you've been living in a cave. "My fellow Americans," began President Lyndon Baines Johnson. "Friends, Romans, countrymen," said Marc Antony. "Four score and seven years ago," President Abraham Lincoln intoned solemnly, setting the scene for his famous speech at Gettysburg. "Don't make me come in there with the belt!" comedian Bill Cosby's father told his children when they wouldn't go to sleep. You know, tell them something they'll understand, something to show them you're on the same track, before you tell them something new and harder to comprehend.

I'd like you to switch seats now. Travel in your mind to a swank office, high in the lofty stratosphere of Manhattan publishing. You are a successful editor, and your office is filled with cutting-edge technological wonders. Decorated like something out of *Architectural Digest*, your work space is a source of great pride. You have half a floor of room, two secretaries, and hot and cold running drinks. Your lunch is catered and you get a daily manicure. You knock off work at four o'clock, and that's on a long day. It's a short walk to your private elevator. Down below, your chauffeured limousine awaits, ready to sweep you off to yet another night of highly expensive dining and dancing. The hostess brightens on seeing your face, and immediately escorts you to the best table in the house.

Sure, that's what happens. Just like monkeys fly. Explode a little bomb under that mental scenario, because it's a ridiculous pipe dream. Most editors I know are pleasant enough, but they are also harried. They never seem to have enough time, I never get the idea their office would win a "neatest place to work" prize, and I'm certain none of them jet to Bermuda every weekend for a nice little vacation. Most editors are hardworking people. They have stacks of things to read and few have secretaries. If they go out to lunch, it's with an agent pitching a book. In other words, you don't need to give them an excuse to use your manuscript to test the new shredding machine because you start off your query letter telling them how your work is the best thing since sliced pumpernickel. Think about it. If that editor—the real one I've just described—was your significant other, your wife, husband, girlfriend, or boyfriend, what approach would you take to brighten their day? What if they were simply a good friend, or a new acquaintance you liked? Would you make sure to keep your workday communication with them short, bright, and to the point? Hopefully, you would. Would you throw in a bit of humor, to try and help them have a better day? If you wanted to build that relationship, you would. So why not see an editor as a real person, someone you might actually like to get to know one day? Believe me, if you sell them something, you will get to know them, maybe better than you initially imagine. You might end up on each other's holiday card lists, or something even more friendly.

When you query, be friendly and cordial, but get to the point. Don't waste time. As your writing success grows, you'll be surprised at just how small a world it can be, in publishing and in our world at large. You'll also see the true importance of first impressions. Getting to the point in brief but friendly fashion will help your chances of making that great first impression.

A few years back, I added a cartoon to my personal stationery. It's in the upper right-hand corner, a clever caricature done by John Caldwell of Mark Twain sitting at a desk looking perplexed. Several dialogue balloons hover over Twain's head: "Strawberry Finn? Blueberry Finn? Cranberry Finn? Boysenberry Finn?" he wonders. I've had dozens of editors comment on that cartoon when they get in touch. One publisher even made a deal with me to print the cartoon on T-shirts and sweatshirts, with royalties going to both myself and John Caldwell (I bought and therefore owned the original cartoon). You might try something similar with your own personal stationery.

Making 'em laugh helps.

Get your own personal stationery or make some up. In these days of inexpensive desktop publishing and word-processing programs, there's really no excuse not to have it. While some editors feel it's not necessary, if it's simple and classy it might show an editor or publisher that you take your writing seriously and have invested some money in playing the game.

If you use an e-mail query, compose a signature no more than four lines long which says something about you, gives your address and phone number, or lists your Web site, if you have one. If the signature is not too obtrusive, it might help.

Some Samples to Sample

So what do you write in a query letter? Some examples of my own letters follow. As I review them with you, I'll toss in comments (*LIKE THIS*) in the text to illustrate points. These points are NOT something you include in the text of your letter. In your letter, you should try to use as little in the way of bolding, ALL CAPS, justification, and other such fancy text elements as possible. My query letters may not be the most perfect you'll ever see, but they'll get you started.

A Query Letter That Didn't Work

Randy Achee, Publisher
Disney Adventures, W.D. Publications, Inc.
500 South Buena Vista Street
Tower Building, 29th Floor
Burbank, CA 91521

Dear Mr. Achee:

I'm presently writing for *Boys' Life* magazine and have some other freelance accounts. *Boys' Life* has a four-month lead time and as a result it's difficult juggling what will be of interest when the issue comes out. It occurred to me, after looking over your magazine, that I might do "double duty" with my intervies. What's right for you might not be right for *Boys' Life*, etc.

In your February 11th issue, you had a lengthy article on stunts, yet didn't cover Kim Kahana, who has the most famous stunt man school going. Also, the writers got one thing wrong—there was trick photography when Harold Lloyd did "Safety Last." The clock Harold is hanging from was actually on a platform several feet above the roof of a building. If Harold had fallen, it would have only been a few feet. This isn't widely known but better research would have revealed the truth (and copies of "how he did it" shots might have been nice). I try not to miss details like that, particularly when young "Bet I can do that" readers are at stake.

I'm enclosing my resume for you to look over. I would enjoy writing about Hollywood for your magazine.

Best,

Skip Press

Why didn't the above letter work? Like all my query letters (unless I have a justifiable excuse), this letter was one page. I always keep them short and to the point, so that's not the problem. As I said earlier, you shouldn't send a letter to the top dog in a big publication. In the example given, I forgot my own rules. I probably didn't help myself by saying what was wrong with the article I had read, but that wasn't why I got no response. When I did not hear from Mr. Achee, I followed up with a phone call. This is a perfectly acceptable practice, but I waited the time prescribed by the magazine ("replies in six weeks" or whatever). My phone call was at first fruitless, which intrigued me. I glibly assumed that my mention of writing for a competitor of *Disney Adventures* (their biggest competitor at the time) would get some attention, but it didn't.

I subsequently learned that *Disney Adventures* has a historically high personnel turnover rate. Achee was gone as publisher by the time I called. I persisted, and finally got through to Andy Ragan, a nice guy who was then associate editor. I explained everything to Andy. He was intrigued, and we hit it off. That started a relationship which resulted in sales of stories I originated as well as assignments from Andy. My query letter didn't work, but my persistence did.

Persist, persist, persist! From surveys of successful people in the entertainment business, I've discovered that as a general rule it takes 15 years to gain national recognition. Writers without persistence are losers.

A Query Letter That Did Work

Ms. Tina Berke, Editor
Computoredge *(yes, that's how they spelled it)*
The Byte Buyer, Inc.
Box 83086
San Diego, CA 92138

Dear Ms. Berke:

I'm currently writing for three national magazines—*Boys' Life*, *Disney Adventures*, and *Grit*. One upcoming assignment is an interview with and article on Stephen Spielberg. The current cover story (September) of *Boys' Life* is mine (in case you know a Boy Scout who subscribes). I sold a screenplay recently and am working on another one that has been "optioned" by some producers.

I recently wrote a computer business article (my second) and I'd like to do more. Your listing in *Novel & Short Story Writer's Market* says you buy material helpful to first-time computer buyers. I may have something for you.

An article I'm developing is called "Man Over Motherboard," a chronicle of my experiences in buying our first computer and setting it up, which included three trips back to the shop. I've found my experiences are the norm. Here's how it's gone:

I got ambitious. I wanted a fax/modem, so I bought the card and installed it personally. That's one of the reasons I was back to the shop three times. Now, I can fax an article, no problem. Modem? If I get lucky.

I also bought and installed a hand-held scanner, which enables me to scan photos and incorporate them into my articles. Of course, I haven't used it once, and don't know how.

I have Windows, a screen-saver named After Dark, and a virus-checking program that hasn't helped me one bit. I also have twenty-one separate manuals, none of which I've read all the way through. I'm not alone in this, as you probably know.

A "friend" with ten years' experience, knowing everything about "PCs" came over and "just put some simple things which will really help you" on my computer. This caused two of the trips back to the shop. He was amazed that I was reading my DOS manual. In his ten years, you see, he never read it.

I can give your readers a few laughs, and some helpful tips. I'm perfectly willing to write my piece as fact, or fiction. My resume and a sample article are enclosed.

Best,

Skip Press

I know what you're thinking. Oh, right. Look at that first paragraph. If I could toot my horn like that, I could get an editor's attention, too. What a braggart!

Guess what? I could have left out that first paragraph entirely. It really didn't matter. Factually, my opening paragraph probably hurt my chance of selling to that editor, rather than helped. Why does an editor of a magazine care if I've sold a screenplay, unless it's a magazine about the film business? What was right about the above letter, and what got me the job, was the second paragraph forward. My second paragraph showed the editor that I'd done my homework. I at least knew what her listing in *Novel & Short Story Writer's Market* said. Actually, I'd written one of the two computer articles I mentioned for her magazine, *ComputorEdge*, but that was for another editor. Tina didn't know me from blue beans when I first contacted her. Her magazine was the largest of its kind in the U.S. at the time, so she had her hands too full to keep up with everyone who had ever written for *ComputorEdge*. Therefore, I approached her as if both she and the magazine were brand new to me.

Why didn't I send her my old *ComputorEdge* clip? I didn't want to run the risk of alienating her. When there's a new editor, you see, writers are often up against a "new broom sweeps clean" mentality. Some editors want to show they can do a better job than anyone from the old regime. Thus, they use writers they know, or writers who contact them anew. (This mentality is epidemic in Hollywood, but that's another chapter.)

Back to the letter. All of the paragraphs after the second one get right to the point. They walk you through the content of the article, step by step. Any editor could see very clearly what my article was about, and decide on the spot whether or not it was worthy of assignment. If a decision from an editorial board was necessary, all the editor would have to do is copy my letter and distribute it.

In the last paragraph, I put in a pitch for humor. Humor almost always works for editors, unless you want to write for *Mortician's Monthly* (a non-existent magazine, I think). Notice that I mentioned my resume and a sample article last. That way, the editor knew about the other pieces of paper I had enclosed. (Don't assume they'll figure it out without your direction—I try to make everything as crystal clear and easy to comprehend as possible.)

As an aside, I went on to write a biweekly business computing column for *ComputorEdge*, an assignment which began years after I wrote articles for editor Tina Berke. I came across an e-mail post by the current editor, John San Filippo, and got in touch with him, using the same procedure all over again. He had no knowledge of my old articles, but my query worked.

You may be thinking this is all well and good, easy for me to say. I was already successful when I wrote the letters above, and had a resume to prove it. What about a writer just starting out? Here's some samples of the type of letter I wrote in the beginning of my career.

A Sample Query Letter If You Haven't Previously Published

Ms. Baleful Glance
Editor
Local Magazine
123 Main Street
Your Town, USA 12345

Dear Ms. Glance:

I've been following your magazine for several months now. . .

> *(DO YOUR HOMEWORK, STUDY THE MAGAZINE, AND DON'T LIE.)*

. . .and I've noticed that you seem to have a fondness for articles about hog-calling techniques and other aspects of country living.

> *(WOW, SHE'LL SAY, A WRITER WHO'S ACTUALLY DONE SOME HOMEWORK.)*

That's why I thought you'd be interested in my enclosed article, "Peccary Persuasion Along the Orinoco." I was marooned in the Amazon Jungle after a failed love affair some time back, and I found solace among a lost tribe, the Heybuddies, who are the best callers of wild pigs in the known world.

> *(YOU'VE GOT HER, BECAUSE SHE'S PROBABLY NEVER HEARD OF
> THE HEYBUDDIES, AND NEITHER HAS ANYONE ELSE.)*

For example, as a passage into manhood, a Heybuddy male of the age of twelve is led into the jungle by an elder, then abandoned. The young man must then squeal like a pig at the top of his lungs until he either: (1) is eaten by a python or some other animal; or (2) attracts a wild peccary suitable for eating. He is, I should mention, given a week's instruction in peccary persuasion before being led off into the jungle.

My article describes the entire rite in a manner I feel would fascinate your readers. I've noticed that your letters to the editor tend to be most vocal when commenting on youthful topics.

> *(YOU GIVE HER A TASTE OF YOUR PIECE, AND CLOSE WITH A
> SALES PITCH ON HOW YOU THINK HER READERS WOULD LIKE IT—
> IF YOU'VE ACTUALLY READ THE LETTERS SECTION OF HER PUBLICATION
> AND USE THAT IN YOUR PITCH, SHE'LL BE AMAZED.)*

I have provided a self-addressed, stamped envelope for you as requested.

I look forward to hearing from you at your earliest convenience.

Sincerely,

Brilliant Writer (Your Name)

(Remember, if this letter goes on your own stationery, all the better. If it doesn't, don't be surprised when the mail carrier passes your house without stopping six weeks later.)

Obviously, the above letter is tongue-in-cheek. I had a bite of peanut-butter sandwich in my mouth when I was writing it, you see, and... But seriously, ladies and germs, if your proposed article was laid out as in the letter above, you'd probably sell it, if it fit the magazine.

A Sample Query Letter If You Have Previously Published

Mr. See Nitall
Managing Editor
Bigtime Magazine
777 Park Avenue
New York, NY 12345

(REMEMBER, DON'T WASTE TIME WRITING THE TOP EDITOR, BECAUSE HE OR SHE WILL LIKELY PASS IT ON TO A LOWER-ECHELON EDITOR FIRST. BESIDES, LOWER-LEVEL EDITORS LIKE TO BE SINGLED OUT AND NOTICED.)

Dear Mr. Nitall:

After studying the *Writer's Market* listing and the last three issues of your magazine...

(OR)

I've been reading *Bigtime Magazine* for years and recently...

...I concluded that you'd be interested in my article, "Peccary Persuasion Along the Orinoco."

As anyone who has been following the news in recent months knows, pigs are the most popular items of interest to the American public today—if not readers around the world.

(SHOW HIM HOW YOUR PIECE REACHES THE BROADEST AUDIENCE POSSIBLE.)

I came to write this piece after being marooned in the Amazon Jungle by a jealous lover. Reluctant to immediately return to civilization (my erstwhile lover runs the Rhode Island mob), I found solace among a lost tribe—the Heybuddies—who are the best callers of wild pigs in the known world.

(YOU'VE GOT HIM, BECAUSE HE'S PROBABLY NEVER HEARD OF THIS.)

For example, as a passage into manhood, a Heybuddy male of the age of twelve is led into the jungle by an elder, then abandoned. The young man must then squeal like a pig at the top of his lungs until he either: (1) is eaten by a python or some other animal; or (2) attracts a wild peccary suitable for eating. He is, I should mention, given a week's instruction in peccary persuasion before being led off into the jungle.

(YOU GIVE HIM A TASTE OF YOUR PIECE, BUT CUT IT SHORT,
BECAUSE EDITORS OF BIGGER MAGAZINES DON'T HAVE AS MUCH TIME.)

I enclose a self-addressed, stamped envelope, along with my resume.

(IF YOU HAVE A RESUME THAT THE EDITOR WOULD CARE ABOUT,
WHICH IS TO SAY, ONE THAT FILLS AT LEAST HALF A PAGE, SINGLE-SPACED,
WITH YOUR LITERARY ACCOMPLISHMENTS.)

(OR)

I enclose a self-addressed, stamped envelope, along with an article I recently published in *Hog Caller News*, as a writing sample.

(OBVIOUSLY, THE EDITOR WILL WANT TO SEE HOW YOU WRITE BEFORE MAKING
AN ASSIGNMENT. WOULDN'T YOU, IF YOU WERE WRITING THE CHECKS?)

I look forward to hearing from you at your earliest convenience.

Sincerely,

Your Name

I would follow similar formats with e-mail queries, but I would make them shorter. Basically if you can't fit it on a page or a short computer screen, your query is most likely too long for that editor to read.

Should you always follow a letter with a phone call? Or if you queried by e-mail, should you wait two weeks and query again? If you're proposing a major article, it usually doesn't hurt. If you're querying about anything else, however, it could hurt your chances. A book manuscript, for example, or a screenplay will by nature take longer to get a response. In those instances, it will be tougher to discover who to send your work to, but you can find out. The personnel who review your material may be subject to weekly musical chairs, even more so in Hollywood, which can often seem like a morass of mindlessness. If trying to sell something larger than an article or short story, you'll probably be better off with an agent. We'll get into that later. If you don't have an agent, can't find an agent, don't know where to start in finding an agent, don't want to follow my advice about agents, or think you can beat all the odds and sell your manuscript because it truly is the greatest thing since sliced pumpernickel and you simply have to let the right person know, then I have another query letter for you which you might find useful. When I say "unsolicited" below, I mean they didn't ask to see your work. You just picked them, and took your chances.

Do your homework. If you can't find the name of an editor to send your manuscript to, call the publisher and ask who handles unsolicited manuscripts. (You'll probably be told "We don't accept those," but it's worth a call.) If you're trying to sell a screenplay, call the studio and/or production company you want to sell to and ask for their Director of Development. This is the designated reader (not buyer) of scripts. (You'll probably be told "We only deal with agents or lawyers." In other words, they won't accept a submission of your work directly from you, for legal protection purposes. Again, all you can waste is some patience and a phone call.)

Remember what I said about it taking fifteen years to make it big? Well, I've lived around Hollywood longer than fifteen years and it took me longer than fifteen years to actually make a name for myself. Not that I'm a household name, but not many writers have sold several screenplays and as many books as I have. Let me warn you in advance: Selling to New York publishers is, percentage-wise, a lot easier than selling to Hollywood.

Query Letter For An Unsolicited Manuscript

Ms. U. Don't Know Me
Director of Development
Bigtime Studios
1 Bigtime Place
Hollywood, CA 90028

Dear Ms. Know Me:

My enclosed screenplay, "Don't Call Me Red," is about the first Martian to be elected to the United States Congress after we colonize Mars, the Red Planet.

(THIS SENTENCE IS CALLED THE "HIGH CONCEPT" IN HOLLYWOOD TERMS.
IF YOU CAN'T SAY WHAT THE SCREENPLAY (OR BOOK) IS ABOUT IN A SENTENCE
OR TWO, YOU USUALLY DON'T HAVE YOUR PIECE FOCUSED,
WHICH IS TO SAY, NOT WELL WRITTEN.)

I know that in the past, your company has made successful films I've enjoyed like *First Woman in the Moon* and *Saucers from Hell*. I believe my film could be another great success for you, and I picked your company as the first to see it. I enclose a one-page synopsis of my script, along with a self addressed, stamped envelope. I look forward to hearing from you at your first available opportunity.

(IF YOU HAVE A RESUME THAT THE READER WOULD CARE ABOUT, SEND IT.
IF YOUR RESUME DOESN'T MUCH RELATE TO THE SUBJECT
OF YOUR SCRIPT, IT WON'T MATTER.)

Sincerely,

Your Name

Note that, in the example above, I mention a one-page synopsis. It's also called a "one-sheet." I've often included a short synopsis, preferably one page or less, with any large work I send in. Script readers go through dozens of scripts in a week, writing synopses or summaries on each for those scripts they either recommend others to read, or those they turn down. The report is usually known as "coverage" and will be filed for future reference, should another production company at that studio receive your script. It works pretty much the same with book publishers, only they aren't as organized, because the financial stakes aren't usually as high. Some people advise against including synopses of any kind, thinking they should read the entire manuscript or script, and gives a potential buyer an easy chance to turn something down, so it's up to you. Here's my logic:

It might cost in the hundreds of thousands to publish a book, yet even a low-budget film might cost well over a million dollars. (Not a digitally shot movie like *Napoleon Dynamite*, but a normal independent movie.) To save companies time (and see if I really do have my work focused) I include a synopsis with my work, but *only* when I'm asked for one or if I have an instinct to include one. (*You must learn to trust your instincts in selling.*) Although people may get edgy over a letter or document longer than one page, I've never had anyone complain about a one-page synopsis. And even if you send in a completed manuscript, you still need a good letter to introduce it to the reader.

If They Don't Like Your Work, It Doesn't Mean They Don't Like You

I wrote a play once about a despondent writer who thinks of committing suicide, then changes his mind, only to lose his life in an accident a few moments later. He is brought back to life by his guardian angel, who is an apprentice angel plenty mad about the threat to her angelic career that the bungling writer in her charge has brought about with his knuckleheadedness.

One wall of the writer's apartment, when the play was staged, was plastered with real rejection letters.

My own very real rejection letters.

If you sincerely want to make it as a writer, grow some thick rhinoceros skin. If you let the rejections you're almost certain to get affect you personally, you'll drive yourself crazy and feel like the worst person in the world. Even if you write perfect query letters and fantastic manuscripts, you'll still get rejections. I keep a small ceramic rhinoceros figurine on my desk to remind me.

Since I want to do everything I can to help you get a few less stinging darts tossed at your feelings, here's one more tip to help you write a better query letter. As you may have noticed in my first letter above when I referred to *Boys' Life*, many magazines have a long "lead time." This means they plan the theme of each magazine and schedule their articles well in advance.

One article I sold to *Writer's Digest* was published a year later than originally planned, while another to *Reader's Digest* had a similar fate. What this means to you is that you can usually write an editor of a magazine and ask for a publishing schedule. They might call it something else, but they'll know what you mean. This might not be mentioned in their "what we're looking for" description in a book or magazine.

Think about it logically. If you were an editor planning a Christmas issue, wouldn't you want to buy your articles starting in March or so? If you planned on doing an issue that you wanted to be read by every armed services veteran in America, wouldn't it make sense to have it come out on Memorial Day, or Veterans Day?

As a writer, you should consider things like this. If you have a piece about a unique Thanksgiving your family had, don't write the editor in October! You can find out what's on their mind by asking for the publishing schedule. They might not always stick to it, but it's at least what they're planning.

Don't Downplay Your Hunches

Last, but not least, no matter what your homework tells you, if you have a sneaking suspicion that you can sell your piece to an editor despite everything you've read about them, act on it. You'll only waste postage if you're wrong. I once read about *Grit* in a market listing and was intrigued. *Grit*, a tabloid-size newspaper, was geared to families when I was a kid, bringing news and homey advice to rural areas. Kids went door to door selling subscriptions to *Grit*, which featured comics that I didn't see in my local newspaper, like "The Phantom." *Grit* held fond memories for me, and the idea of making a sale to them was a boyhood fantasy. Problem was, the only fiction need they listed was full-length novels for serialization. At the time, I didn't have a completed novel that I thought would be right for *Grit* readers. Still, I had this funny feeling that if the magazine serialized books, they might buy short stories.

So I sent the managing editor my resume and mentioned the short stories I had for sale. My hunch paid off. Mike Rafferty, the managing editor, had just been promoted to editor-in-chief when my letter arrived. No new managing editor had been selected. Mike read my letter and called me. He wanted to do exactly what I had proposed—publish some short stories. From looking at my resume, he said, he thought I might have some good ones. That made my month. I sold Mike several stories that I had already published locally (meaning his national readers had probably never seen them). So I not only sold on a hunch, I made money on something I'd already sold in the past!

Never, ever, discount your own instincts about what you might sell to whom, no matter what my advice, any other person's advice, or conventional wisdom tells you. Often enough, acting on an educated hunch can make all the difference, and give you a big sale that can change your career.

I hope you get something out of my advice about query letters. A big sale, hopefully. When you get your first great response from a query letter, write or e-mail me and let me know.

You'll get another great response!

Chapter Three

Artful Articles and Superb Short Fiction

The Basics

By now you've probably figured out that I have a fondness for journalism. I was a journalist when I began on my road to success, but it's not generally seen as a route to riches for writers. Most of the successful writers I've known or read about, however, put in a lot of hard work at some form of paid writing which allowed them to learn as they went and at the same time made high demands on them to deliver the goods. Journalism, with deadlines and demanding editors, readily offers this opportunity.

I am a fan of journalism because you have to get to the point right up front. You have to grab the reader's attention and keep it. Remember this if you are convinced you only want to write fiction. It's hard to author a novel. It's very hard to write a great one. You have to learn a lot of tricks, some of which I'll explain later. Not many writers write hugely popular works as their first work. They build up to it. You learn to write "page-turner" text the more you write. If you can learn to write and sell articles on a regular basis, or if you get a job writing for a periodical like a newspaper or monthly magazine, it's inevitable that your writing skills will be honed and improved. So if you were looking for a place to start, I'd advise you to write articles, or even get a job working for a periodical. Articles are easier to write and sell than short stories, and the market for them is much bigger.

Did you know that articles have been made into major Hollywood films? It's happened time and time again. Producer Peter Guber developed

Midnight Express from an article he read in the newspaper. In *Esquire* magazine, screenwriter Floyd Mutrux read about modernday cowboys in Houston, Texas. He secured the rights and developed *Urban Cowboy* from it. (He later sold his interest and someone else got screenplay credit.) You can make a big name for yourself by writing articles.

The first thing you need to know about article writing is what it looks like on the page. Once you're past that hurdle, you'll have the editor convinced that you are at least clued in on proper format. You'll probably find someone who will tell you they want a different format than the one I give you. That's fine. This format is one I've used and seen used (minus the recent e-mail listing) for two decades. I'll explain all the parts later. Meanwhile, here it is:

Your Name	About 1,000 words
Your Street Address	
Your City, State & Zip	
Your Phone Number	
Your E-mail Address (if you have one)	

TITLE

by (Your Name)

The text of your article or story begins at least four lines down from your name, and continues double-spaced to...

THE END

Now let's break that down. Your name, address, and phone number go at the top left because that's what someone reads first on a page. Some editors also like to see the following on subsequent pages:

Your Last Name	2 etc. (Page Number)

Some editors like this format on subsequent pages:

Article or Story Title/Your Last Name	2 etc. (Page Number)

(If you have a long title, you'd abbreviate it in this type of header.)

Other editors prefer numbered pages only. I advise you to use the title/last name and number header. Why? Because if your work gets broken apart, it will be easy to put back together. With the necessary information on each page, the whole thing is easy to put back together. This is particularly important for long pieces.

If you have an agent, the agent may instruct you to leave your name and address off, or type their name and address on the page under yours. They might simply paste their label over your name and address. However that happens, the editor or editor's assistant will return the manuscript to the name and address in the upper left corner. If they want to buy your manuscript, they'll call you or e-mail. In the past, people would write a letter informing you, but things move more quickly these days. So why waste paper and postage? Make sure people know exactly how to reach you.

Why "About 1,000 words"? Editors have space constraints in their publications. Small articles are generally 800–1,000 words long. That means they are four double-spaced, typewritten pages of 250 words each. The word count per page is calculated on a twenty-five lines per page, ten words per line average basis. This means you'll roughly have one-inch margins on all sides of the page. If for some reason you don't have a computer and software program that counts words for you, I suggest you get one.

Any time you're researching a listing about what a magazine will buy, you'll probably see a notation about article size. Normal articles used to be 2,500 words or so. Now it's more like 800 to 1,200 words. A 10,000-word article or short story is very large by modern standards but some magazines like 3,000- to 4,000-word major articles. Beginning writers mostly sell short articles, sometimes as short as 450 words. That's why you tell the editor how long your written piece is, in the upper right-hand corner. It's the second thing they look at.

Next is the title, centered. I advise you to put the title in caps. Some editors might prefer a different look, but don't sweat it. Titles are important. Good ones give you the essence of what the piece is about. So put it in the center and make it noticeable. If you send it via e-mail, it will probably default to the left margin, but that is understood.

Below that is the "by-line." Who wrote it, right below the title. Even though you've listed your name in the upper left corner, you still need the byline. Why? Well, maybe you're using a pen name. You could list Joe Smith if that's your real name in the upper left, then put Jack Benimble on the "by" line if that's your chosen pen name. The editor will see the distinction. Maybe he/she will think that Joe Smith is your agent, but they usually know agents they deal with.

Note that the double-spacing begins with the title and continues throughout the article. The exception to this would be if you inserted a block quotation in your text, or a poem or lyric. For example:

> Once when I was a young lass, I read the following poem which made me weep and long for my lost love:
>
> > *Now you're gone*
> > *I'm all alone*
> > *And my, am I so sad*
>
> I completely forgot about this cherished verse of my youth until my twenty-fifth high school reunion. It was there I saw Johnny, the captain of the football team and president of the Poetry Society. . .

You get the idea.

At the end of your writing, put THE END in capital letters, centered. Don't get fancy and use a foreign phrase like "Finis" that you saw at the end of a French film, thinking you'll make a clever impression on the editor. Don't use THE END, OR IS IT? or anything else like that, unless you have a very, very, very good reason to do so and it makes sense within the context of the rest of the piece. You'll run the risk of irritating the editor. That same editor who never gets manicures or rides in limousines, remember?

As I mentioned earlier, having parameters helps me pace my writing. I hope that by having the above format to use, you'll be better able to plot out your articles. Guess what? A short story uses the same format. On top of that, it's my contention that a great article and a great short story are constructed with roughly the same elements. That's what we'll discuss next.

Elemental Essentials

Any piece of writing begins with a premise. By that I mean the concept, the central idea, the thing you want to get across to the reader. The premise should answer the question: Why is this tale so special?

Give that some thought. If you read a book and are thrilled by it, chances are you'll tell a friend. You'll do the same with a movie you like, or someone on TV who catches your eye. You'll talk about a magazine article you enjoy. Along that line, did you know that editors generally consider that three to five times as many people read their magazine as buy it? If the magazine circulation is 100,000, they figure 300,000 or more people read it. No matter how many people find the writing in question to be special, it begins with the person who buys it for broad public distribution in the first place. So you have a double duty. You have to convince an editor that your work is special so it will be bought. That's the query letter. Then you have to convince your reader it is special, and the editor is Reader #1.

This all starts with a premise. In Hollywood terms, the premise is called the "high concept." TV movies turn heavily on this, usually from true life stories. *Police Woman Centerfold* (a real TV movie) tells you immediately what it's all about. Here's a description of a better film: "A learned man is able to turn a poor girl into a cultured lady." That's the premise of George Bernard Shaw's *Pygmalion*, which inspired the musical *My Fair Lady*. Dolly Parton starred in a film which tried to reverse genders and use the same premise. *Rhinestone* didn't work, because Sylvester Stallone couldn't sing nearly as well as Audrey Hepburn, and didn't have half her charm.

Stallone worked just fine with a similar premise, however. "Journeyman ne'er do well boxer gets a surprising shot at the heavyweight championship and triumphs." That premise is the essence of Stallone's *Rocky* and all its sequels.

On a less lofty level, let's look at another premise. "Your fat can make you thin." That's the central concept of an amazing diet regimen by a doctor friend of mine, Calvin Ezrin. It's also a book—*Your Fat Can Make You Thin* by Calvin Ezrin and Kristen L. Caron. He originally wrote a more scholarly book entitled *The Type II Diabetes Diet Book, the Insulin Control Diet: Your Fat Can Make You Thin.* A learned endocrinologist who studied with one of the co-discoverers of insulin, Dr. Ezrin discovered that insulin imbalance brought on by excessive carbohydrate intake was the source of dietary failures. He co-authored an even earlier book which had all the same information called *The Endocrine Control Diet* but it didn't sell that well. Why? Because most people couldn't readily tell you that the word endocrine refers to our glandular system. The title didn't reveal the premise, or give the reader a rough idea what the diet was all about. *Your Fat Can Make You Thin*, on the other hand, reveals the premise. The latest book merely elaborates on that primary idea, showing you how you can cut your carbohydrate intake way back, concentrate on a protein and vegetables diet, and with proper exercise and medical supervision get to and maintain your ideal weight. (As a further but cursory explanation, lacking enough calories from food, the body is forced to turn fat into substances called ketones to provide the extra calories. Thus, your fat literally makes you thin.)

Ezrin was years ahead of Barry Sears, who turned his book *The Zone* into a cottage industry, but Sears got there first with an easily grasped concept. Choose your titles carefully.

Now let's move on to what really matters in your story—and in any story, matter of fact.

What Makes Your Tale Special?

You should always be able to answer this question about your work. What are you doing when you write? I say you are taking the reader to someplace new. It might be a place where they haven't been, or someplace where they've been but have never seen with your unique perspective. In Dr. Ezrin's case, he was revisiting that old diet road that so many people had been down before. Having lost 50 pounds or so on his program in a few months and gotten educated on how to keep the pounds off forever, I was happy to go on that road, because it is my belief that his unique under-standing of the mechanics of the human body saved my life.

Everyone likes to think they are special. When considering life as a writer, people enjoy thinking they fit that old proverb that each person has at least one good book in them. People also like to be able to offer something worthwhile to the world, and spend their time doing worthwhile things. When they take the time to read an article, they want it to be something they can use to make their life better, even if it only entertains them for a while and gives them some relief from the stresses of life. Keep that in mind when you're forming a premise for a piece of writing. Why is your idea special? What does it tell the reader that they haven't seen before? If it travels a path already visited, what's your unique angle?

Another thing to remember is that you, as a writer, are often able to put into words something that other people can only conceptualize. They don't have the vocabulary to fully and specifically express their emotions, their vision, and their philosophy. That's why politicians have speechwriters to tell their constituents what they are all about. As a writer, you'll hear: "You put in words what I've always thought."

With a premise, you usually offer one of the following:

(a) a new reality
(b) a fresh look at modern reality
(c) an examination or reexamination of an old reality

Or a combination of any of these. Remember what I said about finding common ground? If you plan to introduce a new reality to the reader, you need to get on common ground first. You can do that by comparing the new reality you're about to explain with a reality you're pretty sure your reader will understand. Similarly, a look at an old reality usually needs to be grounded in modern examples. If you are reexamining a modern reality, you will still need to compare. Example:

> We've all heard that you starve a fever and feed a cold, haven't we? A doctor in Houston has proven that this old wives' tale isn't always true. (Please note this is just an example, and that I don't know any medical specialists from Texas.)

Got the idea about premises? I hope so. You should take pains to get your premise in order. If someone asks you "What's this about?" you should be able to answer quickly and coherently with no hesitation. It's the old twenty-five-words-or-less approach. Many screenwriting teachers will tell you that, if you can't describe your entire story in a sentence or two, you don't have it fully focused. I agree, and I feel it applies to any type of writing.

A friend of mine, Howard Steninger, dabbled at poetry. He was never very serious about it, but he did come up with one poem that I loved and have always shared with writing students. It is a haiku poem (a Japanese form) of five syllables:

> ### *Watching*
> ### *falling*
> #### *snow*

See why I like it? You can see the snow, the wind, and the rhythm of the falling flakes. It's a perfectly realized premise and execution that conveys Howard's experience magnificently.

The premise is often expressed fully in the title, but not always. The title might merely allude to the premise. It might convey a double meaning, or make you wonder what the story is about. A good example of the latter is a book, *The Adventures of Huckleberry Finn*. Adventures? Great, you know what that is. But what's a huckleberry? Many people didn't know, before Mark Twain wrote that book. He certainly didn't find them in Hannibal, Missouri, where he grew up. He tasted huckleberries for the first time when he moved to the East Coast of the United States. But doesn't that make you wonder why someone would have the name Huckleberry? The word rolls nicely off the tongue, and you want to learn all about a person with such an odd name. And that's what you do when you read the book.

For now, though, just work on your premise. See if your title expresses what it is. Try to make your premise as special as possible. If you treat everything you write as something that might be enjoyed for centuries, you will be far more likely to uniformly turn in work that has a special quality.

Then, like cream, you will rise to the top as though by a force of Nature.

Planning by Parts

As a writer, you'll hear Aristotle's "beginning, middle, and end" over and over and over. These have been the agreed-upon parts of an article, story, or creative work since before the ancient Greeks. They are such a given it would seem we wouldn't need to discuss them, but I inevitably find that my students aren't quite sure what these parts of stories really mean.

Actor/comedian/composer/musician/talk show host Steve Allen once said that you should begin a story where it truly begins. By that, he meant that writers will often ramble around, provide back story (explanation of prior events), and use other devices to begin a story, boring the reader with details. Where does your story really start? What action (note that word) takes place that sets in motion a major event? That's the beginning of your story. For a very basic example of this, take the Book of Genesis in the Bible. Adam and Eve were created in God's image. They were living in Paradise, the Garden of Eden. They were innocent, free of care. Then Eve heard a whisper, said hello to the snake, and decided to chomp an apple of wisdom. God got mad, the angel arrived with the flaming sword, and the first couple had to start working for a living. Where did that story really start?

"Hey, Eve! Tired of being ignorant? Take a look at this!" Hiss, hiss, wag of tail. The apple glistened in the midday sun.

That's where it began. That's where the premise kicks off. There is the action that set everything else in motion.

The beginning of a story provides the following items: (a) point of view; (b) the main character(s); (c) the setting; (d) something happening. In other words, you establish the elements of the entire story. Once you've done that, you're finished with the beginning.

Have you ever thought about the opening scene of a movie? Often, you see a broad panorama, with a character going somewhere. Something is happening, and you're in on it. That broad opening view is called an establishing shot. If the movie begins in New York and then shifts to Chicago, there will be a new establishing shot in the Windy City. You'll probably see the title "Chicago" briefly displayed on the screen, and/or a year such as "1950." Ron Howard spoofed this process in his film *Splash* when he shifted the opening action from the Atlantic Ocean off New England to the Big Apple. "New York," said the title, "This Morning."

Once you know where you are and who is doing what, you can move on to the middle. The middle of a piece of writing usually deals with one theme: transformation. The main character is changing, and/or struggling to bring about change. Often, the hero or heroine is on a literal journey, or quest. In any good story, the main character is embarked on an inner transformation as well. Look at the transformation undergone by Sylvester Stallone's "Rocky." In the middle of that story, he went for it. He put in the hard work, ran the miles, pulled himself up by the bootstraps, and listened to his trainer, Mickey. As we headed into the end portion of the story, we knew all about Rocky except for an unanswered question: Could he do it?

Could he win? We wanted to know. We were dying to know. That question was repeated in four more *Rocky* movies, and we always wanted to know. In essence, the first *Rocky* was the beginning to all the rest, just as *Star Wars* was the beginning to the other five movies in the series of films made by George Lucas.

If you're writing an article, you introduce your subject in the beginning. In the middle, you will describe what you found, how it is special, and how it may affect the world around us, if at all. Even if you're writing a recipe, you'll have a beginning, middle, and end. The middle is how to use the ingredients to prepare the food. Before we retire for dinner, though, let's discuss endings. The end is very important. Usually, I get the idea for something, and I work it. I get the premise in order. Often at the same time I get the main idea, I see the logical progression of the story to its end. So I often start off with a beginning *and* an end in mind. It's much like I discussed earlier in forming the big picture. Like the Greek legend of the goddess Athena springing fully born from the brow of Zeus, I'll have a general idea of the full story as soon as the concept comes alive in my mind. You might find that you have a similar experience. You'll know how you want it to end, you'll figure out how it begins, and get it outlined. Then you start writing, and the fun begins. The middle, where the transformation takes place, will more easily write itself when you have the ending in mind.

This doesn't always work when you're researching an article. You might not know how it will end. Once the research is done, however, you will. You'll know what you want your article to convey to the reader. You can write toward that point. Just as you need to have your premise in good order, you might find it beneficial to work out the end, too.

What does the ending do? What does it tell you? That they kissed and rode off into the sunset toward the castle in the clouds? Superficially, perhaps it does. What an ending really does is tell you whether the transformation was achieved or not. Did Han Solo change the irresponsible ways we first witnessed in *Star Wars*? Obviously he did, because he's right there with the rebel forces in *The Empire Strikes Back* fighting alongside Luke Skywalker and Princess Leia. In *Revenge of the Jedi*, the end of the trilogy, he's transformed completely. When it is revealed that Luke is actually Leia's brother, and therefore not a romantic challenger for Leia's hand, Han Solo gets the girl. Even more to the point, he has changed (transformed) to such a degree that Princess Leia is now perfectly willing to become Han's mate (or maybe that's what she had in mind all along).

Perhaps the beginning, middle, and end could be summed up more simply in the following manner:

(a) What change is imminent or what should change?

(b) What changes are put in motion?

(c) Did the desired changes take place?

Just as Presidents of the United States are often elected by promising change to American voters, I have often observed to my friends that the only constant in most people's lives is change. Change is inevitable, if continually fought. All writing I've ever felt to be memorable is about change, and usually great changes. "It was the best of times, it was the worst of times..." Charles Dickens said in the beginning of A Tale of Two Cities. In other words, it was a time of changing conditions. In that story, enormous change.

Remember this, though. People generally want positive and even permanent changes for the good in any story. In the Joseph Campbell studies of great world myths and religions, the protagonist after great struggles returned home with knowledge that could be shared so that the lives of all could be improved. Great writers offer us routes to positive change.

I would hope that your efforts as a writer help bring about such changes. I would hope your work might also help smooth over the changes of time and circumstance for your readers. Lastly, I would hope that you never stop changing with your writing. By that, I mean I hope you always get better as a writer. I hope you never get complacent, even if you reach the pinnacle of international success. Before your great changes begin, though, make sure to get your basics in order. Then you'll be prepared for anything.

Chapter Four

Genres, Generally

B Y NOW YOU MIGHT SEE A PATTERN IN MY PRESENTATION. I'VE been laying out, step by step, the path I took to success. Since it seems I made every mistake possible in trying to succeed as a writer, I want to steer you away from the wrong turns, detours, dead ends, and traffic tickets I got along the way. Which gets us to the next rest stop: genres. What's a genre? It's a type of writing, a category. A tag a publisher can hang on a title, to explain to bookstore owners what is being sold. After all, those bookstore owners need to section off their stores, don't they?

You might have a favorite genre. Let's say you like "whodunits" (mysteries) or romance novels. Maybe you have an inclination to write children's books. (Curiously, in every class I teach there's at least one person who wants to write children's books. The first book I ever wrote was a children's book, and I've written quite a few titles which are tagged Young Adult, meaning the books are meant for readers ages ten to twenty or so.)

If you can pick a genre to write in, you'll give yourself another useful parameter within which to work. In describing your book to an editor or publisher, you'll be able to more easily tell them what kind of book it is. They'll have a higher estimation of you, because once again you will have shown them you've done your homework and have a professional approach. If you look in *Writer's Market*, you'll see that publishers are divided by genre as well. And if you try to sell a property to Hollywood, you'd better be able to categorize it on first mention.

At this point you might be in a bit of shock. Perhaps you're someone who merely wanted to write an article or short story when you picked up this book, and here I am talking about writing big old books. Get over it. You *should* write a book. Think big or your brain will atrophy. When someone comes to me having written a book, I immediately have a great deal of respect for him or her, whether the book is any good or not. At least they had the gumption to finish a major project. That's admirable. Besides, if you know genres it will help you in calculating what sort of short story or anything else you want to write.

Are you convinced your work transcends genres? Maybe it does, but not likely. I've had beginning writers tell me they didn't want to get pigeonholed. "What's your story about?" I'll ask. "Well, you'll just have to read it," they say. Oh, no I won't! Probably, since they can't tell me what it's about, they don't have a focused story. They've rambled, so I'm not interested, because my rambling days are over. If they said, "It's a whodunit in which the hero discovers he's actually a heroine," they might pique my interest. They might not have something I'd personally be interested in, but at least I'd know they knew their story, and the genre in which it fit.

In Hollywood, you have to put a handle on your story. "It's a buddy movie," you explain, or "It's a road picture," or "It's a buddy movie on the road with a sci-fi backdrop." (An example of a buddy movie on the road would be the old Bing Crosby and Bob Hope pictures, such as *Road to Morocco*.) High concept, it's called.

More on movie categories later. Right now, we're at a rest stop. Grab your favorite beverage, kick off your shoes, and take it easy. Study the following list, but don't take it as gospel. Times change, and genres do, too. Here are the various publishing categories I've found, and where to find more information.

Young People's Books

These range from ages two up to twenty or so. By "twenty or so" I mean they are meant for people who are not yet of legal age, which in most states is the age of twenty-one. I've had plenty of adults read my Young Adult novels and enjoy them, including a Justice of the Supreme Court, but we're talking categories here, not taste.

1. **PICTURE BOOKS.** Aimed at ages two to six. The "Hello Kitty" books are an example. If you also illustrate these books, you'll make more money. In fact, publishers prefer a writer/illustrator in this genre. Otherwise, most of the time a publisher has its own illustrators, so in most cases you don't need to find your own artist. There are exceptions. If you happen to know a superb illustrator, go ahead and let them illustrate your book, but don't be surprised if a publisher (who sometimes has illustrators under contract) uses someone else. These books are generally 300 words or less in length.

2. **YOUNG READERS.** These are aimed at ages six to eight. They have pictures with more text. The same rules regarding illustrations apply here. These books are generally 500 words and up in length.

3. **MIDDLE GRADES.** These are aimed at ages eight to twelve. James Barrie's *Peter Pan* falls in this category, as does *The Wind in the Willows*. These are your classic "children's" books and stories that make billions in Disney animated feature versions. Length varies.

4. **YOUNG ADULT.** As I mentioned previously, these are aimed at ages ten and up. *Flowers in the Attic* by V. C. Andrews or any book by Judy Blume are well-known examples. The difference in this genre and classics like The Hardy Boys and the Nancy Drew series is that the main characters are approaching adulthood and dealing with "adult" problems (though rarely experiencing sex). My "You Solve It" Mysteries with Alexander Cloud and Jilly Adams for Z*Fave, a division of Zebra Books, are examples of this genre. They run 20,000 to 50,000 words and up.

5. **LOWER READING SKILLS.** These books are also called "Hi-Lo" (High Interest, Low Reading Skill) and "Reluctant Readers." They are intended for teenagers, high schoolers (or adults) who have only third- to fifth-grade reading skills. They are mostly marketed to schools and libraries. In fiction, this genre is usually packaged with ten or so novels in a genre such as "fantasy" or "adventure" and each set is accompanied by a teacher's guide. In these books, the characters are teenagers in challenging situations who learn something as a result of the story. This is a good "break-in" category for a writer. They are easier to write and sell than other novels. An example is *The Big Picture*, published by Fearon/Janus/Quercus. These sets are often put together by book "packagers" or book

"producers." I sold *The Big Picture* to a book packager. (You can find a list of book producer Web sites at the Yahoo.com Small Business Directory, and learn more about them at www.abpaonline.org, the site of the American Book Producers Association.) Books like these average 6,000 words and up. The main drawback to writing in this genre is that most manuscripts purchased are "buy-outs," meaning you don't get any royalties, just a one-time fee as a writer for hire. You also surrender the copyright, but you can often negotiate and retain theatrical rights to such stories.

6. COMIC BOOKS AND GRAPHIC NOVELS. Graphic novels are basically expanded comic books, although they are sometimes published in hardcover. They are very popular with kids of all ages (translated: adults, too). The graphic novel sub-genre became important with *The Dark Knight Returns*, on which the first *Batman* movie with Michael Keaton was based. The comic world has been particularly interesting to Hollywood in recent years. For example, the hit movie *Sin City* originated in a comic book that emphasized black and white. (Inside tip: the book's "film noir" look came about because the wife of the creator, Frank Miller, was too busy to do her usual coloring of his book.)

7. YOUNG ADULT TEXTBOOKS. These books are generally created and distributed by companies specializing in textbooks and nonfiction for junior high and high schools. They are often sold in "packages" as mentioned in the "hi-los" above. My *The Importance of Mark Twain* for Lucent Books is an example. It was part of a set about important world figures. These books are generally 20,000 words and up.

8. YOUNG ADULT NONFICTION. The eight volume *Star Families* I did for Silver Burdett Press is a nonfiction example in this genre. They are of similar length to textbooks, usually shorter. They cover a specific area of interest and can be expanded to include more subjects if the initial books are popular. My *Star Families* were about children of famous people who went on to their own fame, such as Natalie and Nat "King" Cole. (If you think I'm plugging my own books here, I'm not. I was paid a flat fee to write these books and receive no royalties.)

Take note: Every genre that exists for adults, by and large has a similar place in young people's literature, usually minus violence and sex. There are exceptions to the no violence and sex rule, particularly in comic books. It will vary by publisher.

- **SUGGESTED READING:** *Writing Juvenile Stories and Novels* by Phyllis A. Whitney, 1976, The Writer, Inc.
- **RECOMMENDED ORGANIZATION:** Society of Children's Book Writers and Illustrators (See listing in Chapter 7.)

Speculative Fiction

This genre is most often broken down into the sub-categories of science fiction, fantasy, and horror. I lump them together because they share a common theme—their stories are far outside the bounds of "normal" life and bear heavily on "what if" premises. In legendary test pilot Chuck Yeager's words, they "push the envelope" of human existence. The length of these books are generally the same as adult fiction. You'll find length guidelines in books on where to find publishers, such as *Writer's Market*. In recent years, 75,000 words (a 300-page, double-spaced typed manuscript) is a general rule, although paperback novels may be shorter in length.

1. **FANTASY.** This is a story that has no "rational" explanation. Magic may be used in the story, or circumstances that cannot be easily explained according to known laws of the physical universe. Classic examples of this genre are *The Charwoman's Shadow* by Lord Dunsany and *The Dragonriders of Pern* (my personal favorite) and sequels about the fantasy world of Pern by Anne McCaffrey. The subcategories:

(a) **Sword & Sorcery.** The name explains it. Step into any comic book store and you'll find a graphic novel in this genre. This has long been a popular fantasy genre. The ancient poem "Beowulf" is an example. Conan the Barbarian, which was adapted into a movie that really put Arnold Schwarzenegger on the movie-star map, is the modern archetype for this type of story. Curiously, the Conan books (which preceded the comic books of the same name) were written not by a world explorer, but a man in West Texas who lived with his mother.

(b) **Action Fantasy.** This genre is amply illustrated by movies like *The Neverending Story* and *Shrek*.

2. SCIENCE FICTION. This story is based on current fact expanded into "what if," keeping in mind our current knowledge of the workings of the physical universe. In other words, the emphasis is on science. Classics of the genre include *The Foundation Trilogy* by Isaac Asimov and *Stranger in a Strange Land* by Robert Heinlein. Science fiction not only predicts the future but inspires it. H. G. Wells basically started the genre, along with his contemporary, Jules Verne. Many of the scientific developments of our modern age were first envisioned in science fiction. For example, satellites were written about by Arthur C. Clarke long before they were orbited. In recent years, fantasy and science fiction have been lumped together as "speculative fiction." That way, the term "SF" can be used for both. Science fiction as a category is still generally used, however. When I say SF I mean science fiction. SF has many sub-genres within its own category. Some examples:

> **(a) Detective story mixed with SF.** A good example of this is "Do Androids Dream of Electric Sheep?" by Philip K. Dick, which was made into the movie "Blade Runner."

> **(b) Cyberpunk.** This refers to outlaw computer geniuses of the future, what current "hackers" (people who break into computer systems over phone lines, often using stolen credit card numbers) may become. This sub-genre, which began with novels like *Neuromancer* by William Gibson, were epitomized in the *Matrix* films starring Keanu Reeves.

> **(c) Action SF.** A quick review of highly successful big-budget Hollywood features of the last decade or so reveals a huge appetite among the public for this type of writing. Recent examples are *Minority Report* with Tom Cruise (from a short story by Philip K. Dick) and *I, Robot* starring Will Smith (from several works by Isaac Asimov).

> • **RECOMMENDED ORGANIZATION:** Science Fiction Writers of America (See listing in Chapter 7.)

3. HORROR. Huge careers are built on this genre, probably much more than SF or fantasy. In modern times, Edgar Allan Poe started it. I say "in modern times," because scary stories told around the fire have been with us for a long, long time. Authors Bram Stoker (*Dracula*) and Mary Shelley

(*Frankenstein*) greatly expanded this genre. Stephen King is the king of current horror authors, with Anne Rice (*Interview with a Vampire* and other titles) the queen. Clive Barker, with his *Hellraiser* and other gloomy tales has also become a darling of horror fans. I don't espouse writing horror because frankly I don't like it much. The sight of a vampire with fangs dripping blood makes me yawn. Maybe it's because I eat so much garlic. In any event, millions of readers absolutely love the genre, so if you're inclined to write it, that's fine with me. By the way, a great many horror movies are made because:

(a) They're usually cheap to make;

(b) People as a general rule love to be scared;

(c) It's often seen as the quickest way for an aspiring director to make a big splash for his/her career.

Here's another curious note. The vampire theme in Hollywood films is far and away the most popular theme of all time, from the early "Nosaferatu" to the long-running TV series *Buffy, The Vampire Slayer* to the 2003 film *Underworld* (where vampires battle werewolves).

- **SUGGESTED READING:** Read the classic books of the genre, much more than any "how-to's."
- **RECOMMENDED ORGANIZATION:** Academy of Science Fiction, Fantasy & Horror Films. See www.saturnawards.org.

4. VIDEO GAMES & GRAPHIC NOVELS. This is a multi billion-dollar industry that rivals the income of Hollywood films. If you can come up with a game that:

(a) has a good plot involving a hero on a quest;

(b) has a lot of action and/or violence;

(c) features colorful characters who also make good toys;

(d) would work as a comic book, a movie and a video game;

you might have the basis for a hot Hollywood property, since the biggest movie audience is males age 18–34.

- **RECOMMENDED ORGANIZATION:** CMP Game Group, www.gamasutra.com, The Art & Science of Making Games.

Mystery, Detective & True Crime

This is a big, big category, perhaps because people like to exercise their analytical abilities. More often than not, when a new detective comes along on television, the public eagerly embraces the character and we see TV movies featuring the same for decades. Peter Falk as "Columbo," for example. Similarly, the proliferation of crime shows in recent years like *C.S.I.* offer a new twist to crime solving, and satisfies the public's seemingly endless thirst for stories in this mode.

The following sub-genres are not about television, but books. Create a great detective character or characters, though, and chances are good you might see him/her/them on film or television fairly quickly. You'll also run a good chance of selling not one book, but a series. Having sold a series of detective novels and then the film/TV rights, I'm particularly fond of this genre.

1. **HIGH-TECH OR SPECIALIZED KNOWLEDGE THRILLER.** This is the essence of many big-bucks novels of the last twenty years. Think Tom Clancy's *The Hunt for Red October* and other novels with his hero Jack Ryan. The tradition Clancy follows was heavily popularized by Ian Fleming's James Bond books. Another example of what I mean by specialized knowledge is the "inside the legal profession" setting of John Grisham novels like *The Firm*. Sometimes these books are written by someone who is a professional in the field, such as Robin Moore's medical setting works. Don't fret if you don't have specialized knowledge. The specialized knowledge often comes from intensive research, which is the case with Clancy's writing. Clancy's research for *Red October* was so thorough (done in libraries) that he was visited by intelligence officers after the book's publication. They wanted to know who gave Clancy the classified information! Last time I heard, he occasionally lectures at the Central Intelligence Agency.

2. **MEN'S ADVENTURE.** This category once rode high with "series" novels including *The Enforcer* series, the *Matt Helm* books, and *The Executioner*. As sexual attitudes changed, sexually transmitted diseases spread, and women's issues became more prominent in our society, a James Bond "playboy" outlook on things was not as popular in books and movies. Nevertheless, Bond movies have continued to be made and the popularity

of men's adventure may be resurrected thanks to books like *Men's Adventure Magazines* by Max Allan Collins, Rich Oberg, George Hagenauer, and Steven Heller (published in October, 2004) which chronicles tales from the heyday of pulp fiction.

3. **CLASSIC DETECTIVE.** This ranges from "hard-boiled gumshoe" books like Raymond Chandler novels (*The Maltese Falcon, The Big Sleep*, etc.) to Agatha Christie's books (the basis for the TV series *Murder, She Wrote*) to a recent flood of Orange County, California novels (all written before the famous California county declared bankruptcy). According to a front-page article in the *L.A. Times* dated Sunday, November 8, 1992: "Over the last decade, Orange County has served as the setting for more than sixty novels ranging in genre from mystery to science fiction to romance to fantasy" including Judith Krantz's glitzy *Dazzle*. Sherlock Holmes books by Sir Arthur Conan Doyle still stand as the standard for all others in this genre. If you can figure out a "new twist" to the detective novel genre and write a good book, chances are good you'll be set for life. Just keep churning out the pages, and publishers will beat a hasty step to your door, bearing checks.

4. **POLICE NOVELS.** "Cop" stories have been a popular theme in films and literature for a long time. In recent decades, Joseph Wambaugh, an ex-L.A. police officer, has written only about police in his books like *The Onion Field*. Perhaps the first such book of this kind, believe it or not, was *Pudd'nhead Wilson* by Mark Twain. Wilson incorporated the then new science of fingerprinting into this turn of the century story.

5. **EROTIC THRILLERS.** The film *Basic Instinct* is the primary modern example. This is a Hollywood favorite, which explains why *Basic Instinct* screenwriter Joe Eszterhas gets multi million-dollar paychecks. These stories sit right on the line between mystery and sex, and combine pornography with analytical detective skills. This was an increasingly popular theme for a time, but it has been satirized (the film *Fatal Instinct* by director Carl Reiner). Satirization by Hollywood sometimes means the genre is declining in favor. In the 1990s, most Hollywood studios are supposedly trying to do less violence and more family films. What Hollywood says and what it does don't always match, however.

6. **Horse racing.** This sub-genre was once the province of Dick Francis, an ex-jockey who became hugely successful by writing about fictional crimes set around the world of horse racing. His *Driving Force* is a good example. Francis's success demonstrates that it is possible to create a genre within a genre. *Seabiscuit: An American Legend* by Laura Hillenbrand, although nonfiction, was so wildly popular it became a major motion picture. Never underestimate the possibilities of a previously untapped major fan base when creating fiction.

7. **True crime.** As you might suspect, these are nonfiction stories. Usually, the more outrageous the crime, the better. In the 1950s, newsstands were filled with true crime magazines. More modern TV movies and "reality" TV shows such as *Hard Copy* eat this theme up. True crime books are equally popular. The first modern true crime book which really made a splash was *In Cold Blood* by Truman Capote, which explored a real-life murder of a family in the Midwest. Other examples are *The Onion Field* by Joseph Wambaugh, which described the murder of some police officers in Southern California. *Rush*, written by a female police officer who got hooked on drugs, was a best-seller. All the books mentioned became films. If you write a great true crime story, you might be on the road to a bloody fortune.

- SUGGESTED READING: Again, read the books that are successful. They are generally entertaining, and you'll learn more than you will by reading "how to" books and articles—but those can help, too.
- SUGGESTED RESEARCH: This genre usually follows well-established formulas. You need an "angle" that hasn't been seen before (or done very well, perhaps) to really make yourself well-known. Jessica in *Murder, She Wrote*, for example, is a mystery writer who comes across real-life murders every single week of her life (you'd think she'd start to wonder why). If you pursue this genre, take some courses in how to be a detective. Visit police stations, or bars where cops hang out after work. The more authentic your work sounds, the more likely the reader will enjoy what you are writing.
- RECOMMENDED ORGANIZATION: Mystery Writers of America, Inc. (See listing in Chapter 7.)

Mainstream Adult

This is a broad, broad category, so if I leave something out don't send me hate mail. Like I said, public taste changes all the time. If there's a big new category in the bookstores that you notice and I didn't, write and let me know. I'll talk about it in subsequent editions of this book (and I might send you an autographed copy).

1. **ROMANCE.** This remains the biggest market in the world for fiction with almost half the published fiction and $1 billion in sales per year. It's not unusual for one author to turn out dozens of books over a few years, often having other people write for them, based on the author's outline, such as the fiction factory of romance legend Barbara Cartland. This category of books is written mostly by women, or men writing under female pseudonyms. It really took off in the 1970s when the genre was broadened in theme by Kathleen Woodiwiss's *The Flame and the Flower*. Roughly, the formula for a romance novel is this: (a) girl meets the man of her dreams, (b) is swept off her feet, (c) then, for some stupid reason, is separated from him for most of the story; (d) she goes through all sorts of troubles, and (e) still manages to end up with Dream Man at the end of the story. Sometimes the heroine doesn't get the guy, if your name is Scarlett O'Hara and the novel is Margaret Mitchell's *Gone With the Wind*. The sequel, *Scarlett* by Alexandra Ripley, wrapped that up nicely. Scarlett and Rhett went through some mighty changes, but got together at the end. Well, fiddle dee dee! If you want to write romance novels, think "feel good" and happy endings. For the official word on the latest in romance novel writing, see the Web site of the Romance Writers of America at www.rwanational.org.

3. **WESTERNS.** The classics are anything by Zane Grey (*Cimarron*, for example), and more recently anything by Louis L'Amour. With the death of Louis L'Amour, there was no "king" of this genre until Larry McMurtry emerged with *Lonesome Dove*. Since he writes other types of stories, the opportunity for another L'Amour to emerge is possible. (And lest we forget, horrormeister Stephen King originally wanted to write Westerns.)

4. **HISTORICAL.** Examples are Barbara Tuchman's *A Distant Mirror*, and *Clan of the Cave Bear* by Jean Auer. This genre is not limited to time period, but the books are generally very thick novels that imaginatively

transport the reader to a world very different (yet factually accurate) from our modern one. They are tough to write if you're not good at research and detail.

5. THE ETHNIC EXPERIENCE. This genre exploded after the smash success of Alex Haley's *Roots*, although movies about Italians—the organized crime version, anyway—have been made since the beginning of Hollywood. Ethnic novels like *The Color Purple* by Alice Walker and *Waiting to Exhale* by Terry MacMillan became best-sellers and movies, too. Amy Tan's *The Joy Luck Club* is another good example. More recently, the debut novel *The Kite Runner* by Khaled Hosseini gave readers a well-told tale of Afghanistan and became a best-seller. It's refreshing to be able to "look into" an entire new world, particularly when you don't have ready access to that ethnic background. This idea—along with good writing, of course—might explain the genre's increasingly broad popularity. The rise of such tales speaks well of the possibilities of harmony among races.

6. HUMOR. These books are often "nonfiction" in name but fiction in truth. Columnist Dave Barry, author and the prototype for the *Dave's World* TV series, is the reigning king of this type of book. A great recent success story in this genre is *8 Simple Rules for Dating My Teenage Daughter* by W. Bruce Cameron, which became a hit TV series on ABC (see www.wbrucecameron.com for information on this clever author).

7. HUMOROUS FICTION. Kurt Vonnegut's *Hocus Pocus* is a fine example, as is the best-seller *Mostly Harmless: The Fifth Book in the Increasingly Inaccurately Named Hitchhiker's Trilogy* by Douglas Adams (author of *The Hitchhiker's Guide to the Galaxy*, which began as a radio show in England). The current king of this genre is Carl Hiaasen, author of *Skin Tight*, *Native Tongue*, *Strip Tease*, *Stormy Weather*, *Lucky You*, *Sick Puppy*, *Basket Case*, *Skinny Dip*, and others (see www.carlhiaasen.com).

8. NONFICTION. This includes everything from biography to commentary to essays. These books are usually written by seasoned journalists even if a celebrity has his or her name stamped on it. If you have sold a number of articles, editors might think you're "ready" to write such a book. Exceptions are when people have specialized knowledge (there's that term again), such as a therapist who discovers (or thinks they discover) a new aspect of the human mental condition, or a salesperson or businessman who reveals their secrets for others to use. There's almost always a market for celebrity books. If Paris Hilton hasn't written an autobiography about how her homemade porno film was released on the Internet, just wait, it's coming. It usually matters most to a celebrity if they can trust you as a writer first, then whether or not you can do the job. If you want to write nonfiction books, you'll simply have to study the market, figure out where you can fit in, and draw up a step-by-step plan of achieving your goal or goals. I also advise you to pick up the latest copy of *Publishers Weekly*. You'll see more categories of nonfiction there than you ever thought existed.

9. MODERN CLASSIC. This is the book every writer ultimately wants to write. I've discovered some common elements of a great many of the books that have become classics in this century and others, which I'll share with you now:

(a) Usually, a first-person narrator tells an intimate tale, often from his or her own childhood. "Coming of age" is a term you will hear used, or "rites of passage." *To Kill a Mockingbird* by Harper Lee (my personal favorite novel) had a tremendous influence on me. The film of the movie was the only one my entire family ever saw together in a theater. *Sophie's Choice* by William Styron is another example, as is *The Prince of Tides* by Pat Conroy. Steinbeck's *East of Eden*, Faulkner's *The Rievers*, and Laura Ingalls's *Little House on the Prairie* are other examples. Stephen King's "Rita Hayworth and the Shawshank Redemption," adapted into the film *Shawshank Redemption* with Tim Robbins and Morgan Freeman, is another excellent example of this wonderful genre.

(b) Although the narrator may be young or very young when telling the tale, the story is more often than not told in retrospect, with the perspective of an adult looking back.

(c) The book may tell a personal story but it usually encompasses the beginnings of a larger social change, such as the Southern attitude toward African Americans and the injustice perpetrated upon them covered in *To Kill a Mockingbird*.

(d) The writer is tremendously poetic in the way he or she tells the story. He or she is simply wonderful with words. As a reader, you are artistically transported to the time and place being described. You're taken on a wonderful ride to someplace you've never known, at least not in the manner the author describes it. It is as though you are personally living the experiences, and you are continuously emotionally moved.

(e) There are very few or no stereotypical characters or places. Every line of dialogue, every description of setting and mannerism, seems perfectly authentic and, most often, unique to the broader society.

(f) Occasionally, there is a literary device used to tell the story. The book may be epistolary—that is, told via letters, such as *A Woman of Substance* or *The Color Purple*.

If you are only going to write one book in your life, I urge you to attempt a Modern Classic. You might come up with something that greatly enriches us all. I must caution you, however, that most of the writers of classics were well practiced as authors before they penned a masterpiece.

Whether you write a classic or a romance novel, I have a simple "Suggested Reading" list that will enhance anything you write. Read the classics. Read as many classics as you can! It is essential, if you want to be a good writer, to have a broad knowledge of human history. Even though it is a daunting undertaking, I suggest you read *The Story of Civilization* by Will & Ariel Durant. I recommend anything by Plato or other ancient Greek philosophers, particularly Aristotle's *Poetics*. Give Shakespeare, or Cervantes (*Don Quixote*) a read or two. You may be surprised at how good they are. Read Joseph Campbell's *The Hero with a Thousand Faces* to get an idea of where we have come from as storytellers. You'll have a better grasp on where we are and where we might go. Campbell's book has to some degree become the ruling story model in Hollywood (particularly for big-budget films), thanks to screenwriting teachers like Christopher Vogler, and filmmakers who swear by Campbell such as George Lucas.

Campbell was the subject of an extensive documentary by Bill Moyers that originally appeared on the Public Broadcasting System in the United States and is available on video. If you agree with Campbell, it might appear that humanity keeps telling the same old story, over and over, with minor variations. Apparently, however, we never get tired of it. Therefore, I advise you to study thoroughly Campbell's blueprint of this recurrent hero myth, which is most thoroughly laid out in *The Hero with a Thousand Faces*. That book, by the way, sprang from a class Campbell taught for decades to students at Sarah Lawrence College in New York. He formed the basis for the class during five years in which he couldn't land a job, so he spent his time studying all the philosophies, religions, and myths of the Earth. He continued that study all the rest of his life.

In summation, it doesn't matter if you find a genre or sub-genre in which to specialize. If a publisher accepts your manuscript, it will be put in a category. Maybe you don't want to specialize. Perhaps you want to write in several genres. I have, but I hope to eventually settle into writing Modern Classics. (Hey, I told you I think big.) If you successfully pick a genre in which you're happy writing, you might find that you'll make a lot more money quicker than you would otherwise, and also gain the time to write that classic you've always wanted to write. That is the way it happened with me. You'll get better, hopefully, every time you put words on the page, as long as you keep expanding your horizons. See if you can find a genre from which to begin.

As I cautioned earlier, I may have left out a few things in this discussion of genres. Well, so what? You need to do personal, extensive research into what the market is doing, and that market changes all the time. You need to get out there and find out. Everything I've given you here is simply a guidepost toward launching your career.

Genre-ally, I hope I've helped you.

Chapter Five

Nonfiction Knowledge and Nonsense

THIS BOOK WAS TURNED DOWN BY THE FIRST PUBLISHER I SENT IT to, and I'm glad that happened. Why? Because the publisher who accepted it had no titles like *How To Write What You Want & Sell What You Write* when I sold them this book. That was important to me. The first publisher who seriously considered my manuscript already had a truckload of books on writing in its catalog. Since that publisher specialized in books about writing, it seemed like the logical place for my book. Then an editor there wrote to say that, although I had a very strong book in mind, it wasn't a "niche" book, the kind they'd been successful with.

See what I'm getting at? If you wrote a book on horses and sent it to a publisher of nothing but horse books, you might be accepted, but you'd probably be just one more title in the catalog. Sure, they would know where to market horse books, but would they put much financial backing in promoting your book? Or would they simply feature it in the catalog? You could get lost in the shuffle. If you place your book on gardening with a publisher who has only one book on gardening—namely, yours—chances are good that publisher will put more "juice" into contacting every gardener possible to tell them about your book.

Sometimes, this reverse logic doesn't make sense. In the case of art books, those big coffee table things you see in the rooms of people's homes that they enter only on special occasions, there are only a few publishers. The books are expensive to produce and these publishers (such as Harry

Abrams) have the market fairly well sewn up. But back to selling your book. We'll get into agents, marketing, and public relations later. There was another reason my book proposal was bought after another publisher turned it down. Can you guess?

The secret was format.

My agent for *How to Write*, David Andrew, looked over the proposal I'd sent out and asked me to rework it. (I signed on with David some time after my first submission and subsequent rejection.) I had always been under the impression that all you needed with a nonfiction book proposal was the first three chapters and an outline of the remainder. You wrote a good query letter, you put in a copy of your resume and/or curriculum vitae, and that was it. The rest was up to the fickle whims of puzzling publishers. I sold a number of books using that simple guideline. In retrospect, I now realize that the books I sold were not mainstream adult. The competition was not as fierce in the genres in which I formerly worked. When I moved into the big leagues, I had to learn what was expected of me as an author all over again. What I was mainly missing was an effective format.

Just as you need to submit stories, screenplays, and manuscripts in an acceptable format, you need to do the same with book proposals. With most writing sales, you need to write the entire manuscript to make a sale. What I like most about writing nonfiction books is that, in contrast, you don't always need to write the entire manuscript to make the sale. You need to provide proof that you can write, which is what the chapters do. Usually, three is enough, but not always the first three. Sometimes you can get by with less than three. With the proposal for this book, for example, I sent the publisher an introduction, Chapter 1, and Chapter 18. (I wrote a bit less than one chapter and an outline to sell a three-book young adult series, but that's fiction. Right now I want to tell you about selling nonfiction.)

I'll clue you in on what else was in the proposal for *How to Write* shortly. Before I do, let me add this: if you intend to write a book about a technical subject, you'd better have someone to back it up. Note I said "someone," not "something." If you want to write a book about "Alaska on One Salmon a Day," it could be about your personal experience. If you want to write "The Salmon Diet," however, a book about losing weight by eating mostly salmon, you'd better have a roomful of doctors, or at least one very good one, as your recognized expert in the field. Why? Because publishers don't want to be sued by readers who feel they've been defrauded. You can write about a technical subject and have no certification in it whatsoever, as long as you find enough people who are recognized experts to back you up. This applies with article writing as well as with books. Now do you have an idea why I advised writing articles early on? If you establish yourself as a journalist and have a thick sheaf of clips to send an editor to whom you want to sell your first book, it can only help to prove your credibility and professionalism.

As with all things, there are exceptions to this rule. I'm too busy to try being an exception, so I always like to know where the experts are and what they can tell me.

What are nonfiction books? Animals, autobiographies, beauty, biographies, business, celebrity profiles, cooking, current events, diet and nutrition, entertainment, health and fitness, how-to (instructional), history, hobbies, humor, men's issues, parenting, philosophy, photography, psychology, self-help, sports, travel, and women's issues are just some of the categories of nonfiction books. Is it any wonder that nonfiction books are, as an overall category, about equal with fiction in sales? In this Information Age we're supposedly in, nonfiction can only expand. Here's some even better news for beginning writers: Percentage wise, it is generally much easier to sell a nonfiction first book than a novel.

This fact has its drawbacks. One woman I know of sells a lot of books on love. She was once married to a former friend of mine, who stopped being my friend when I discovered he was a liar, scoundrel, and tax criminal (which is a lot worse than tax cheat). This woman dedicated three books to her lover. The man's ex-wife told me repeated horror stories of this self-styled pop psychologist/author and her behavior. Yet the public continues to lap up her printed posturing. Why? Because, I suppose, any information on relationships—which sounds good whether it works or not—is better than nothing.

This example gives you some clue as to how much credence publishers give college degrees. I've met enough Ph.Ds to know that many of them are good at going to school, but their degree doesn't mean they are geniuses. Still, if you want to write about things technical, you'll need an expert on your side unless you are yourself an expert. Most publishers expect it.

So let's get into what goes into your proposal. A nonfiction book proposal is like a movie trailer (preview). Just as a reader might pick up your book in a bookstore and read a few pages before making a decision on whether or not to buy, you will "hook" a publisher with your proposal or not. That means it needs to be good, quickly.

Overview

The first item in your proposal is a description of the book. The introduction you read in this book is a combination of the overview and the introduction of my book proposal. Once I'd sold the book, I adjusted language in the overview intended for publishers to make it more appropriate for the mainstream public. In rereading my introduction, you see, I decided it didn't say all I wanted to say. So I borrowed from the overview that had pleased my publisher.

The overview should fully describe what you hope to achieve with your book. Remember my advice about "why is this special?" The overview will state why it is special, hopefully in a number of pages less than a normal chapter in length. For me, a chapter is usually around sixteen to twenty typewritten pages. My introduction in this book was about six double-spaced typewritten pages long. Over the years, I've learned to say what needs to be said in as short a space as possible. I'd advise you to do the same. Brevity is beautiful, as far as I'm concerned. A number of editors I know feel the same way.

Of course, your manuscript will be double-spaced. Ever wonder why? It's simply easier to read. In addition, an editor can make marks in red ink between the lines. (You'll learn about red ink when you are about to be published, believe me!) Since your introduction is the lead-in to a manuscript, it should be double-spaced as well. Number the introduction with small Roman numerals (I did), but it's not that important. No one will reject your manuscript because they don't like your numbering, although they might not read it if you fail to number the pages at all. (If they dropped it and the pages got out of order, then what would they do?)

The Marketplace

If you spend twenty dollars or more on a book, aren't you a bit discriminating about how that money is spent? If you don't have to watch your finances, good for you, but most people aren't in that situation. Most people comparison shop. They look over a number of books, perhaps in a number of bookstores, before they spend their hard-earned money. Who can blame them? You should think about that when you approach a publisher. It costs a lot of money to hire a staff and get a book manuscript in shape to be printed, then shipped. Public relations campaigns must be mounted, and book catalogs must be mailed. Publishers are not, as strange as it sounds to some writers, endless fonts of finance. They want "bang for the buck" just like you do. When they buy your book and take it seriously—that is, if they think it might be a big moneymaker for them—they consider the competition. You can help them decide in your favor by doing as much of their competition survey as possible. I call this section of the proposal "The Marketplace." Here's the opening paragraph of my marketplace section in the proposal for this book:

"Beginning writers have these alternatives: (1) seminars, workshops, and classes at the local college; (2) correspondence schools; (3) advice from writing magazines; (4) joining writer's groups; (5) winging it; (6) finding a personal mentor. *How to Write What You Want & Sell What You Write* delivers all these."

I then went on to list five other books which were available in major bookstores at the time. These books were, unlike mine, niche books. They were all about only one segment of writing, such as writing articles or technical writing. I told my potential publisher that no book then on the market offered all the basic formats and advice on any field or type of writing in one book. At the time, that was true. I said that my book would not be loaded down with theory. It would offer concise, easily understood advice, for both writing and marketing.

I did not shy from venturing into hyperbole, either. If I was shy about what I thought my book could do, how could I expect a publisher to tout it as something great?

"My book can become the bible of all writing how-to books," I proclaimed. "Delivering all the goods, it's aimed at every wanna-be writer in the English-speaking world. How many is that? The UCLA Extension Writers' Program, where I teach, has a mailing list of 250,000 people! It's the largest program of its kind, but certainly not the only one."

Okay, so that's some hyperbole but remember, this section of a proposal is a sales pitch. It follows your overview. You've said hello, and now your foot is in the door. You're getting the potential publisher to at least listen to all of your sales pitch, whether you'll close the sale or not. If they've read this far, you want to keep them, so you'd better be passionate in your convictions. Here's the rest of what I said in "The Marketplace" section of my proposal:

"In the most recent *Writer's Digest* listing of writer's workshops for all fifty states, there were almost 1,000 entries. With 500 video channels coming and exploding multimedia and interactive needs, writers are needed more than ever before. The next decade could be the Golden Age of Writing, no kidding. Expansion of cable, video, and computer offers something we didn't have in the beginning of the TV Age. We're used to broadcasting, but for years now we've had narrowcasting. That means it can be cost-effective to make a cooking show for people speaking Tagalog (the language of the Philippines, #3 in California). Someone has to write that show. Technology has reached the point that, within five years, a person will be able to film scenes, dump them into the computer, edit their own movie, use that in creating an interactive game, upload that to a publisher via modem, and bank the profits the same way.

"When a person can do all that, will they want to access fifty books, even on CD, to find out how to write various items necessary for the complete package? What if they want to spin off greeting cards, or transmit quotes from their work to be used in a speech? Or turn their screenplay into a stage play, or a camera-ready article via desktop publishing.

"Or will they want one book that covers it all, like *How to Write What You Want & Sell What You Write*?

"The answer is obvious. When this book is published, I will immediately embark on seminars around the country. It will be published, and I'll keep making writers. Hopefully, you'll help me do that."

Let's analyze my pitch, if you'll indulge me. Was it passionate? It was. Were you convinced? Would you be moved to check out my claims? If you did check them out, you'd find they were true. For example, I knew that Tagalog, the language of the Philippines, was #3 in the State of California because at the time I was in the middle of writing my *Awesome Almanac: California* (one of fifty on each of the various states). I knew about narrow-casting because I'd written and produced how-to videos in the past. The rest of my summation was simply something I had personally observed.

When I acquired a computer with a CD-ROM player, the idea of being able to plug in a disk and access whatever I needed to know in an encyclopedia was much more appealing than getting up, finding the right volume, and looking up the information manually. It stood to reason, I felt, that people would also like to find basic information on writing and selling any form of writing in one book.

Obviously, my publisher agreed with me!

About the Author

If you have one degree, or several, no doubt you studied long and hard to get those credentials. Similarly, you might have put in many years to acquire the information you want to share in a nonfiction book. If you propose to profile a celebrity, you might have years of experience writing about celebs for magazines. Should you be modest and simply provide a neat copy of your resume?

I think you know how I'll answer that. No! You need to do everything possible to explain to the publisher why you are qualified to write about your chosen subject. Sure, you can show them a copy of your resume, but it's not much good without explanation. I would advise something else as well—a one-page narrative about you told in the third person. "Skip Press has received national recognition in almost all forms of media…" my "About the Author" began. I went on to relate how the first how-to video I put together sold over 100,000 copies, how another won the Silver Medal in the New York International Film Festival, how a corporate slide show of mine became a video and sold 100,000 copies (and also won an award), and all the other diverse areas of writing in which I'd been successful. I mentioned how I had sold seventeen book titles in three years, as well as two screenplays. In closing, I listed all the writing societies I belonged to or had once belonged to, and spoke of my teaching at UCLA Extension Writers' Program. As a final touch, I said, "His happiest accomplishment in the whole wide world is helping other writers get started."

It wasn't bragging, just sharing the facts. I also meant every word about my happiest accomplishment. One year, I interviewed Steven Spielberg for *Boys' Life* magazine (the magazine of the Boy Scouts of America). That same year, I sold my first four books and a screenplay.

None of these feathers in my cap meant as much to me, however, as something else I accomplished. I was asked to judge a short-story contest of some fifth graders in Beckley, West Virginia. That's where my ex-wife was from, and the school kids were students of her aunt, Jewell Graybeal. One of Jewell's students, Billy Hopkins, wrote a clever, hilarious story called "My Homework Ate My Dog." I not only chose it as the winner, I sold it for Bill to a national magazine called *The Children's Album*, which was written and illustrated by kids. The editor (an adult) not only published Bill's story, but hired me to write the advice page in the back of the magazine in which Bill's story appeared.

When I went back to visit my ex-wife's family the next year, Bill's accomplishment was written up in the local paper. A picture of us grinning side by side accompanied the article. Nothing in my professional writing life had ever made me feel more proud.

My entire "About the Author" pitch was one page. I didn't list every single writing society I had ever belonged to, or all my accomplishments. My resume and a letter from my agent accompanied my book proposal, but was not included in it. I told the publisher just enough about the author to give them a sense of security that I could deliver the goods.

If you're uneasy writing about yourself, get someone to do it for you, then edit it. I'd advise writing it yourself, however. Otherwise, you run the risk of disturbing the voice of your proposal, which should be uniform throughout.

Table of Contents

This is as simple as it sounds. List the chapter titles on a single page. (If you can't get all the chapter titles on a single page, you're writing an encyclopedia, not a book.) You don't have chapter titles? Well, many books these days don't have them, but I always use titles. It gives me a chance to catch the attention of the reader with a catchy, possibly humorous phrase that gives at least a hint on what the chapter is about. Also, if I can come up with a good chapter title fairly easily, I'll know that I have my chapter focused. If you want examples, look at the chapter titles in this book. Just remember what I said about keeping 'em turning the pages. I'm in favor of catchy chapter titles. If you have page full of dull line after line titles, you run the risk of losing the reader.

Outline by Chapter

Which would you rather read?

> **Chapter One.** This chapter is about...
> **Chapter Two.** In this chapter, I...
> **Chapter Three.** This is the chapter where...

OR

> **Chapter One:** Life with the Oinkers. I relate my beginnings on the
> Arkansas pig farm, and how I acquired the nickname Porky...
> **Chapter Two:** A Sizzling Education. When my father was appointed
> Ambassador to Colombia, I had never even drank coffee, much less
> raised it. Here I describe my Central American school days, and...
> **Chapter Three:** Bacon and Eggs. How I got in the diner business...

That's a further example of why I suggest you use chapter titles in your Table of Contents. If your book proposal is boring, you're dead. You won't sell the book. Your Table of Contents is followed by a description of the chapters. This chapter-by-chapter outline (which I called "Chapter Descriptions" in my proposal) will cover each chapter in one paragraph. A rough guideline is half a page, double-spaced, per chapter. That means two chapter descriptions per page. I averaged four chapter descriptions per page, but I've had a lot of experience at saying what needs to be said in a short space. You may need more room.

The chapter outline is no time to get dry, boring, and technical. Remember, the publisher or editor still hasn't seen a fully written chapter. You're still selling. You don't have to sound like a used-car salesperson, but you should maintain the overall tone and style of the book you propose to write.

Writing Sample

And now to the meat of the matter! The proving ground, the showdown, the true test. This is where you show what you can do. Following your chapter outline, you provide an introduction (if you plan on having one, as most nonfiction authors do). The introduction (which you may choose to call a preface or foreword) is usually followed by Chapters 1 and 2 and sometimes 3. As I mentioned earlier, you might have a reason to include a chapter that appears later in the book in lieu of an opening chapter. Just make sure you include Chapter 1, because that's the opening to your book, and crucial to keeping the reader turning the pages. Beyond that, the chapters you include are your call, and perhaps that of your agent or representative, if you have one. In the case of this book, I included the introduction, Chapter 1, and Chapter 18 in the proposal. The first chapter, "The Big Picture," fully covers my broad view of writing. Chapter 18 is about my experiences with and advice on writers' groups, so I thought it was particularly pertinent to the overall proposal. After all, part of selling my proposal was showing how I had experience with many forms of writing and writing groups.

In another book that I ghostwrote, the proposal included the first five chapters. In that case, the main supporting character of the book, a companion who walked with the author across North America, did not figure prominently in the book until Chapter 5. Since I considered this character critical to the book, I needed to have the first five chapters in the book proposal. My agent agreed, so that's how the proposal went out.

Supporting Evidence

Think of this section as the "show and tell" portion of your proposal. My agent calls it "Photographs and Exhibits." In the proposal for this book, this section was titled "A Partial List of Suggested Experts." Note I said "Suggested." Since I don't claim to be an expert on all types of writing, I made sure my potential publisher knew that I would consult experts in various areas of writing as necessary. Most of the experts I listed were friends or acquaintances. The majority of them get our family newsletter. In some cases, however, I didn't know the expert. I merely knew from long journalistic experience that I could get this expert to talk to me once I revealed I wanted to include their expert opinion in my book.

People have egos, which they like to have flattered. Once, when I found out Tennessee Williams had an apartment in a security building in New York City where a friend of mine lived, I visited my friend, then went and knocked on Mr. Williams's door, unannounced. I showed the famous playwright a copy of a Los Angeles theater magazine that another friend of mine published. I told Mr. Williams I wanted to interview him for the

magazine. He took it from me, looked it over a second, and then agreed to
the interview. He was one of the most gracious interview subjects I've ever
had. He even pulled a copy of his *Memoirs* from a shelf, autographed it,
and gave it to me. It was a calculated, educated guess on my part that he
would grant me an interview. After all, wasn't this the man whose character
Blanche DuBois had proclaimed in his play *A Streetcar Named Desire* that
she had always depended on the kindness of strangers? I mentioned this to
Mr. Williams, then asked him whom he patterned Blanche after. Was it
Blanche Cutrere, a girl from his youth?

"No, no!" Tennessee laughed. "It's like Flaubert said, about Madame
Bovary. 'C'est moi!' Blanche is me, young man."

One of my so-called friends carped that Mr. Williams gave me the
interview because he liked tall, blond young men, but that wasn't true.
Like the majority of the highly successful people I've met, he was extremely
gracious and quite willing to share knowledge with me. After all, there was
something in it for him.

So I knew that, when pressed to consult experts for my book, I would
be able to deliver. If the ones I listed didn't work out, I could find others
just as good that would. And that's precisely how it worked out. You'd be
surprised how the doors fly open when you ask for someone's expert opinion for a book you're writing. If you're doing an unauthorized biography or
some similar book, a different reaction is likely. But when you want their
opinion about something having to do with their area of expertise, *yes* is
the predominant answer.

I found a number of experts via the online service Compuserve (since
swallowed up by America Online), in various writing and entertainment
business forums. Now that I've moved onto the World Wide Web, the
possibilities seem endless. What an amazing thing, doing interviews via
computer with people you've never met or talked with, or searching
through whole books without having to leave your chair. The Age of
Information has its benefits.

In my book proposal, I listed all the experts with a brief description
of their expertise out to the side. For example: Stan Lee—Creator of
Spider-Man and other comics. You don't need to go into excruciating detail
about listed experts, unless they are the primary source(s) of information
for your book.

In closing this section, I briefly explained my relationship with or access to the experts I had listed. A word of caution: Don't overdo it. If you intend to write a book about the history of real estate in New York City, don't list Donald Trump as a potential contributor to your book unless you have a very good idea that he'll participate. You run the risk of getting the publisher thinking that Trump is locked in. When you turn up later and say Trump declined, it could cause problems.

A list of experts may not be necessary for your specific book proposal. Instead, you might have a package of photographs or drawings to include. If so, you should own them, or have an agreement with their creator. Previously unpublished photos are quite desirable to a publisher, which is understandable. When most people pick up a biography, they open the book to the photo section, particularly if there are never-before-seen pictures there. If you've had newspaper articles written about you, and/or about the subject of your book, include them in this section. Anything that might be pertinent as an exhibit of the value of your book should be included. If you're writing a true-crime book and have obtained photo-copies of applicable items from the public record—marriage certificates, court filings, etc.—put them in. This part of the proposal is the "close" of your sale. Drive home how important your book will be, and how much the public will like it. If possible, get your publisher thinking that people will be lining up outside the bookstores at six A.M. to get a copy of your amazing book.

People Are Talking

Along the lines of the previous section, support your proposal with quotes from others. This was an addition to my proposal that came from David Andrew that, I feel, really put me over the hump with the proposal for this book. It was fine for me to make the pitch about my book. My "What People Are Saying…" section provided quotes from other people, declaring why my book was worthwhile, and needed to be published. I contacted former students, recognized experts, even the head of the UCLA Writers Program for quotes. I told them why I needed a quote, and got letters from them. (That way, I could show the letter as evidence if ever necessary.)

For the sake of brevity, I excerpted quotes from these people on two pages of paper, single-spaced. I could have provided copies of their letters, but that meant my publisher would have had to flip through many more pages of paper. Depending on what your nonfiction book is about, you'll have to determine how many testimonials you think you'll need to support your pitch.

So how can anyone give a quote on a book that isn't finished? Good question. Some of my supporters knew my work and trusted that I would turn in a superior product. In other cases, they talked specifically about work I had done with them. In one case, I wrote the quote for a screenwriter friend who was busy. I showed it to him, and he signed off on it with a "Yeah, that's about what I would have said." (After interviewing and writing about people for years, it isn't hard to write something that sounds like it came directly from their mouth.)

This is support material, remember, not the *Congressional Record*. No one lied about me, or my proposed book. Here are a few examples of the quotes I used. Note that I followed each quote with an identification about the person quoted.

> "*I cannot tell you how much I adored this instructor—I've never been given so much help, confidence, and practical advice in any classroom situation before. Skip is the kind of writing teacher everyone should experience. He took the fear away and helped us laugh.*"
> UCLA STUDENT OF SKIP PRESS

> "*When I started in the film business, I not only read books about the process, I outlined them so I could remember all that I read. With his book, Skip Press has successfully outlined the path to success in all fields of writing. I highly recommend it.*"
> ROBERT BONNEY
> SCREENWRITER
> "*THE NIGHT THE LIGHTS WENT OUT IN GEORGIA*"

> "*Skip Press's UCLA Extension class, 'How To Write What You Want And Sell What You Write,' was an unqualified success with our very demanding, educated students.*"
> LINDA VENIS, PH.D.
> DIRECTOR, DEPARTMENT OF THE ARTS, UCLA

The quote from Linda Venis was about my class, not my book. That way, Linda spoke only about what she knew about, and preserved her integrity. Since the class I taught at UCLA Extension Writers Program was somewhat of a jumping-off point for this book, it was appropriate to have a quote from her. Subsequent to the time I taught that class at the program, Linda received a well-deserved promotion from Executive Director of the Writers Program to the position listed in the quote.

Do not make the mistake of including letters or quotes, however, from people whose aim is to proclaim what a worthwhile person you are. That's egotistical and a turnoff to a potential publisher. If you include quotes, make sure they pertain to your qualifications to write your proposed book. Then it's OK for them to say how great you are! Humility can be a noble quality, but in general meek people don't sell a lot of books.

In this chapter, I purposely did not discuss the content of writing nonfiction articles. That ground has already been covered. Besides, if you aspire to be a journalist, you should try to write a book, sooner or later. People in all walks of life then tend to take you much more seriously as a writer. Authors of nonfiction books are often asked by magazine and newspaper editors to write articles. They'll come to you, instead of vice versa. My friends Adrian Colesbury and Brass McLean were amazed at the doors that opened up after the publication of their first book, *Costa Rica: The Last Land the Gods Made*. Done in conjunction with a well-known photographer, the book got a great review in the *Los Angeles Times* Sunday edition travel section, was mentioned in the Auto Club magazine, and won the award for "Best Travel Narrative" in 1994 from the Publishing Marketing Association. Adrian and Brass's phone started ringing and kept ringing. Among other things, they were invited to write about a film being shot in Costa Rica. Those invitations might not have come if they hadn't written a book.

"Oddly enough," Brass told me, "we wrote the book as a last-ditch effort. Our journalism careers were at a standstill. Nobody was returning our calls. The book was a boon for us right out of the starting gate. Now, our pitches are accepted immediately, and we've gotten several unsolicited assignments from editors who have seen the book."

So write something big. Write a book. Write a big book, why don't you? If it's nonfiction, the good news is you probably won't have to write the whole book to make the sale. Now you know how to write that proposal, so you have no excuse in not getting your book sold. I hope I get to read it some day.

Chapter Six

Novel Means "New"

S O YOU WANT TO WRITE A NOVEL? HERE'S WHAT YOU NEED TO know. Any editor you'll ever contact mainly wants to know three things: (1) if you have writing talent; (2) if you have something they can publish profitably; (3) if you will fulfill the contract they make with you. In short, "Will you give us the book we want?" That applies whether you send them a complete book or part of one.

In the previous chapter, you learned that it is not always necessary to write a complete book to sell it. One can often sell a nonfiction book based on a few chapters and a complete outline. Would it surprise you to learn the same holds true for novels?

Well, it does, in some cases. When I got the contract for my You-Solve-It Mysteries featuring Alexander Cloud and Jilly Adams, I gave the publisher only sixteen pages and short descriptions of the remaining chapters. I was able to do this for two reasons: (1) I had already sold some books and could show the publishers copies of same if necessary; (2) the sixteen pages of actual novel I gave them were (I was told repeatedly) very good. I didn't write three chapters; I wrote just a bit less than one, in fact. The writing was good enough that I got a three-book deal, with my first book becoming the "lead title" (first book in a series).

I subsequently learned that in certain genres this type of sale is common. My You-Solve-It books were mass-market paperbacks. The company that published them prints millions of books annually. They employ thousands of writers. Mystery publishers and romance publishers have similar operations. The writing has to meet a certain criterion of quality; they don't expect it to be great literature, just good entertainment. Since I later sold my books for film and TV, I like to think I provided more than just passable entertainment, but the point is that you realize the parameters of novel writing.

If you're aiming for a big best-seller, a hardcover book with a nice dust jacket, a budget from the publisher for a promotional tour, appearances on talk shows, a big sale to Hollywood and all that, then forget the idea of writing only a few chapters and an outline. You'll simply have to write the entire book. Then, most likely, you'll need to do copious editing. The finished book better be darn near perfect.

When the editor of the century, Maxwell Perkins, received the manuscript *O Lost* from Thomas Wolfe, it was 1,114 pages long, written on onionskin paper. Massive editing was necessary to rescue the book and turn it into *Look Homeward, Angel*. Don't expect to find an editor like that now, either in dedication or talent. Such editors might possibly exist these days, but I haven't met one. Max Perkins knew talent. He worked with Taylor Caldwell, Ring Lardner, F. Scott Fitzgerald, Ernest Hemingway, and many other greats. He was willing to put in the work necessary to turn Wolfe's endless (but very good) writing into a publishable manuscript. These days, editors don't have the time to do that, except for perhaps the most successful authors or notable celebrities. Nor will most editors even consider taking the time for such an effort. In the majority of cases, the manuscript an editor receives is published—if it is published—in pretty much the same shape as received. And the really successful authors usually don't need much editing.

Novel Knowledge

So, once again, let's get some basics in order. How long should your novel be? These days, roughly 75,000 to 90,000 words (300 to 360 double-spaced, typewritten pages). When I first tried writing a novel, in 1978, 100,000 pages was the norm. In 1993, a big best-seller was Robert James Waller's *The Bridges of Madison County*, which is half the size of a normal modern novel. Bridges was quickly bought by Hollywood and turned into a film starring Clint Eastwood and Meryl Streep. Nicholas Sparks's *The Notebook*, published in 1996, was typical of this size of romance-based novel; it became a hit movie of the same name in 2004. Readers' attention spans have shortened considerably since the days of Max Perkins and why? A lot of it has to do with the length and influence of motion pictures.

In Chapter 3, I told you about proper manuscript format. The format is identical for nonfiction books and novels. Your name and address, the length of the manuscript, the placing of the title, and byline stay the same.

Similarly, what I told you about beginning, middle, and end doesn't change. So now that you know the rough word count expected of you, let's discuss some history of storytelling. I've always felt that if you understand where you've been, it's much easier to deal with, and get a grip on, what the future may hold.

If you pay any attention to the fashion industry, you know that history does indeed repeat itself. Styles wane, then return. The music business is similarly cyclical. I've heard all sorts of explanations for this phenomena. In the 1930s, a man named Raymond Wheeler compiled a gigantic database covering all aspects of societies through history. He calculated that cycles of human activity existed and could be monitored to repeat. The Foundation for the Study of Cycles in Wayne, Pennsylvania (see www.pond.com/~cycles/cycles.htm) continued Wheeler's work. Another study that encompasses repeating patterns is the Elliott Wave theory (see www.elliottwave.com) which is mostly used to predict stock market trends. Then of course there's reincarnation. People die in the 1940s. They're fans of big-band music, so when they live another life and become adults, there's a sudden resurgence of big-band music. You get the picture. Theories and ideas abound. What's important to you as a beginning writer, however, is practical knowledge.

So let's take a look at history.

The Story of the Story: American Version

Ernest Hemingway once said that the first real American novel was Mark Twain's *The Adventures of Huckleberry Finn*. I'm sure Twain was pleased by "Papa" Hemingway's comment, but the statement might have troubled Nathaniel Hawthorne. After all, Hawthorne's *The Scarlet Letter*, written in 1850, predated Huck Finn by 34 years. This story of adultery is still relevant today, with Demi Moore starring as Hester Prynne in a 1994 movie of the novel. Hawthorne and his contemporaries, Herman Melville (*Moby-Dick*) and horror master Edgar Allan Poe, helped create a unique American voice in world literature. All three of these writers examined the psychological nature of man and the result of one's actions. Twain did, too, but he was more ebullient in his fiction. His characters were more flippant, even exaggerated. Perhaps this is due to Twain's beginnings on the American frontier, and his time spent in the Western United States, or simply his own nature. Twain brought new vigor to the American voice in literature, and was the first internationally successful humor writer the nation had seen.

At the turn of the twentieth century, technology began to progress quite rapidly. Literature reflected and even inspired these changes. Writers in the Western world began to view humankind as one people, more so than ever before. In a day devoid of radio and television, newspapers were the main conduit of public information. Literature was the most popular form of entertainment. In the early 1900s, public writings reflected a certain mood. That is, the world at large seemed to be relatively tamed. Civilization was being maintained with some ease. In the U.S., the prosperous "Gay '90s" (referring to a happy feeling, not homosexuality) made the oncoming century hold the promise of Paradise. Thus it is no wonder that novelists began to speculate on possibilities. While English author Rudyard Kipling offered amazing tales of the Indian subcontinent, and American novelist Edgar Rice Burroughs produced the wild Tarzan tales, set in Africa, Kipling's British contemporary, H. G. Wells, helped invent a new genre called science fiction. With books like *The Time Machine*, Wells was following on the heels of French author Jules Verne, whose *From the Earth to the Moon* in 1865 was the first popular adventure set in outer space. Wells's and Verne's writings offered potentially dark prospects for the future of humankind, but also spoke to possibilities for overcoming disaster.

This new science fiction also inspired an explosion of American literature in the early part of the twentieth century, but there were other changes in American writing. Beginning in the nineteenth century and continuing up through the 1950s, "pulp fiction" was a mainstay of American literature. Stories of the Wild West and other adventurous settings began in magazines only to later appear in hardcover, novel form. As an example,

Edgar Rice Burroughs's *Tarzan of the Apes* first appeared in serial form in *All Story* magazine in 1912. The science fiction segment of pulp fiction was most important. It not only inspired more writers to try their hand at this form of writing, but prompted generations of scientists to achieve in real life what had only been speculated about in fiction. Rocket ships, space suits, and men on the moon were written about for decades before anyone figured out how to actually achieve such ideas in reality.

During the 1920s and '30s, two other aspects of American writing took on broad significance. One was the modern social commentary novel, as popularized by Ernest Hemingway and his pal F. Scott Fitzgerald, and other prominent writers of the time like Sinclair Lewis and John Steinbeck. In 1926, when Hemingway characters in the novel *The Sun Also Rises* said things like "I feel such a bitch today" and "Oh, to hell with him!" it created a social uproar. Previous to Hemingway, people just didn't talk like that in popular literature. Certainly not the heroes of the work, at least. From that point on in contemporary American literature, authors have continued to challenge the level of acceptability of the outrageous. The rise of Hollywood storytelling has had a similar evolution and impact. These days, just about anything goes, even on network television. Anything imaginable is available in books and on video.

The latest "cutting-edge" fiction is in the field of "cyberpunk," a science fiction, darkly futuristic genre basically invented by William Gibson in his novel *Neuromancer*.

Small wonder that romance novels—which almost never depict explicit sex—and family entertainment is now on the rise. When standards get too loose, or the milieu of cutting-edge fiction too strange, the moral pendulum of history swings back toward the middle.

Your Future as a Novelist

So where does this short history of Western literature leave you as a novelist? It's my belief that this is the greatest time for writers in the history of Humankind. On whole, there are more literate people on Earth than ever before. The computer revolution allows instantaneous translation of text, even the speaking of the translated words. Paralleling this explosion of technology, information, and entertainment-hungry people is the concept of narrowcasting. In the past, a novelist who wanted to write about the life of potters in a small Japanese town might not have received much notice, except in Japan. These days, though, it is possible through the Internet to connect with potters all around the world. The task of marketing such a book to these potters might not have been economically feasible. Large publishers prefer broadcasting, reaching the majority of people and ignoring minority elements of the society. There's simply more money in it. Association magazines (like *Pottery Monthly* or whatever) might help find potters who'd buy a novel like I mentioned, but such periodicals usually operate within geographical limitations. Now, we can easily connect with hundreds of thousands of people whose likes and dislikes fit within a narrow profile. This brings me to a simple conclusion—it is now possible to write whatever you want and find a way to sell it. There are probably plenty of people out there who will appreciate what you've written. This is fantastic news to any writer, and you should do all you can to get on the "Information Superhighway" to take advantage of this increased "traffic."

Let's get back to the development of story subjects. If there's any unifying element to what all the writers previously mentioned were trying to do, it is to explore and understand the human condition.

Do we fully understand romantic love? Do we really know what exists on other planets? Are all the questions of religion fully answered? Obviously for most people, the answer to these questions is no. Thus writers continue to write, and readers to read.

I advise you to remember one constant: Novel means "new." All the writers I've mentioned—and I've mentioned some of the most classic writers of Western literature—strived to expand understanding of life as their society knew it. They concentrated on new ideas.

Maybe you'd be satisfied simply selling a novel—any novel. Maybe you're taken aback by my attempt to push you to think big, to try and write something great. I'd be willing to bet, though, that when I outlined the parameters of a Modern Classic in my chapter on genres, that was the description that widened your eyes. Most writing students I've ever had wanted to write a classic. The writers of classics were able to accomplish the task because: (1) they mastered the basics of writing, so that technique did not get in the way of inspiration; (2) they "pushed the envelope" of societal conventions of their time. They were all willing to risk public ridicule or commercial failure for the sake of writing something that would get people thinking. In Hemingway's case, perhaps, he was simply trying to be controversial to get attention, but I don't think so. That happens a lot more in these "media days" than in his time.

If you would be satisfied writing and selling detective novels the rest of your life, that's fine with me. I'd like to help you reach higher. If I help one writer become great, and thereby improve our culture, then I'll consider I've done a good job as a teacher. I hope to inspire hundreds, if not thousands or more, writers to become great. Whatever you choose to write, whenever you attempt a novel remember the title of this chapter. *Novel* means *new*. Even if you are writing a formulaic romance novel whose pattern has been seen time after time after time, you still need a new story, or a new twist to an old story. You're probably thinking, "But I see the same old thing, every week on TV." You probably do. Just as Polish jokes get converted to "Newfie" (Newfoundlander) jokes in parts of Canada and "Aggie" (students of Texas Agricultural and Mechanical or "A&M") jokes in Texas, tales get told over and over. To break through with any novel, you need to come up with something that rises above the pack, that gets the notice of an editor or publisher, that will make a critic say, "Now that's a new twist on things!"

Remember, when I sold the young adult mystery novels I mentioned earlier, I had previously sold a number of books. At the time I sold my first novel, I had a strong background writing articles in general and for teens in particular. Before I ever sold a thing to a periodical, I put in years composing and writing business letters. Success in writing is a stair-step thing. Even if you write one novel and it turns into a best-seller, you'll have put in some step-by-step hard work to get there. How fast you move up those steps, and how sure your step is, depends entirely on you. Just do us all a favor, and try to write something original!

How It Gets Done

Here's an example of how the Age of Information changed my life. One night I got an e-mail from Jerry B. Jenkins. (This was long before he became a multi-millionaire as an author of the mega-selling Left Behind Christian novel series.) Jerry had read my electronic profile on Compuserve (where we both had accounts) and thought we had very similar backgrounds. He basically just wanted to chat. I was glad he did. Jerry, it turned out,

had written well over 100 books, of all kinds. Sports novels, young adult
mysteries, adult mysteries, biographies, inspirational nonfiction, series
fiction. You name it, Jerry had done it. He'd written books with or about
some of the legends of the day: baseball stars Hank Aaron, Nolan Ryan,
Orel Hershiser, and evangelist Billy Graham, to name a few. I'd written
less than a quarter of the books Jerry had authored, and was anxious to
find out any secrets he might share with me.

He had a big secret all right, but it was one I already knew. Jerry
simply worked hard, and maintained discipline. He rose each morning at
around 7:00 A.M. and wrote until noon. His output was roughly the same
as mine: six to seven pages of fiction per hour, or four to five pages of nonfiction. Like me, he preferred writing fiction because it was more fun and
did not require constant referral to notes, research materials, etc. Unlike
me, he was also disciplined when it came to family time. As long as his kids
were at home and awake, Jerry said, he spent time with them. That way,
he felt a lot better about life and his family didn't feel cheated. That only
changed (but not much) if he was nearing a deadline. Jerry turned out four
to five books per year in this manner, typing about ninety words per minute
(using only two fingers, I might add). When I first spoke to him on the
phone, he had just signed a twenty-seven-book deal with a major publisher.

As you've probably figured out by now, I like to outline. It helps me to
have my destination in mind before I embark on a writing journey. I might
not have all the stops mapped out, but I know roughly where I'm going.
Jerry, on the other hand, did not work from an outline. He also did not
hesitate to contract for more than one book at once, calculating from
experience that he could deliver them all on time. Instead, he worked
from a broad mental story as well as scraps of notes made beforehand
and along the way. He told me about a 460-page novel he had recently
completed in only thirty-two days. Not bad for a "hunt and pecker"!

I asked Jerry if he had a writing philosophy, and he was quick to share
it with me. It was something he tells writers at writing conferences across
the country.

"The only way to write a book," said Jerry B. Jenkins, "is with butt
in chair."

A-ha! So that's it! As simple as that sounds, it's my philosophy, too.
I have a similar feeling toward my kids, although I write more hours per

day. Of course, by the time I reach his level of success, maybe I'll knock off at noon, too.

And that won't be easy, because the Left Behind Christian series (co-written with Tim de la Haye) made such an impact with booksellers they hit the *New York Times* best-seller lists and sold millions of copies. Jerry and Tim were the subject of articles in national publications like *The Wall Street Journal* and the *New York Times* and were interviewed by people like Larry King on CNN.

If you plan to write a novel, you'll have to treat it like a business. You'll have to devote a certain amount of time to it each day, particularly in the beginning. Before you start writing your masterpiece, though, you may need to do some housecleaning. Mario Puzo, the author of *The Godfather*, once wrote a list of "Ten Rules for Writers" for a magazine. One of the rules was, if your wife was giving you trouble and distracting you from your writing, get rid of your wife.

I don't espouse "cement shoes" for your significant other, but there's some truth to Puzo's logic. Writers are born procrastinators. (Jerry B. Jenkins tells writers at his conferences that if they don't naturally procrastinate, they're probably not meant to write.) Too often, I play computer games, watch famous criminal cases on TV, admire the sun coming out from behind the clouds, you name it, before I seriously begin writing. Other than what I've mentioned, I don't procrastinate so much I don't get my job done. I usually meet my daily writing goal, whether it be a chapter or two or finishing up something else. I don't have any serious bad habits that keep me from writing. I don't have "writer's block," whatever that is. (Since I make my living writing, I don't have time for long mental lapses.) If I'm feeling burned out, I'll take a break for a few days, but only after a major project is done. Then I'm right back at it. In short, I bypass any bad habits and keep my life organized.

Even if you have only thirty minutes per day, three days a week, to devote to writing, if you maintain that discipline, you will get your book done. If you cannot maintain a discipline, you should probably give up the idea of writing a major project—until you can be disciplined, that is.

This applies to people in your life as well. If there are people around you complaining about this and that in an unjustified manner, they'll just throw you off course. If you're upholding your familial and social responsibilities and simply trying to carve out some time each day to pursue a dream, what sane person would object? Don't let anyone deter you.

Look at scheduling this way. Let's say you take three months formulating the story for your novel. Maybe you make an outline, maybe you don't. (I suggest you do. Once you've written a number of books, then you can try winging it.) When your story is in order, you make an hour for yourself to write, five days a week, or the equivalent. You are faithful to that schedule. When you are at your writing station, you only write. You get up only to go to the bathroom or make a phone call, and not for long. OK, maybe you allow yourself one refill of coffee, but no donuts. And short phone calls, please. Let's say you turn out five pages per week, or one per day. In fourteen months, you will have a full-size novel (75,000 words). Then you'll need to edit it. Try my method. I edit each chapter as I write it, then do a once-over of the full manuscript when it's complete. With discipline and determination, I'm sure you can finish a novel using this method. One page an hour isn't much, really. You should be able to do two.

If you can't get started, answer a letter. Just write something. You'll get the gears in motion.

Seeing Is Composing

A famous musician I knew once revealed that he always composed with a blank wall in front of him. He would look up and see pictures, inspiring scenes that became music for him. I took that idea to heart. I keep a clean wall behind my computer. Remember the description of the Hopis "sitting in pictures" earlier? If you can see the pictures—that is, watch the scenes of your novel unfolding in front of you in imagination—then the rest is mere description. If you don't already use that method, try it and see if it works.

When I was a kid, I would draw things to entertain my younger brothers. We were too poor to own a TV. Later, as times improved for my family, I quit drawing for my siblings. When I picked up the habit years later, after my own children were born, I wondered why I'd gotten so rusty. Then I realized what I'd done as a kid. I would mentally project the picture onto the blank sheet of paper, and trace around what I was "seeing."

Realizing the method I'd used was a revelation into the mechanics of all art, and I've never forgotten it since.

The Novel's Journey

When you write a novel, you embark on a journey. The reader of your novel goes on that journey with you. Please remember that you are a tour guide. You are doing one of several things as an author, perhaps all of the following:

(a) Taking the reader some place they cannot personally go;

(b) Showing the reader new aspects of some place with which they are already familiar;

(c) Suggesting a place the reader may never have considered or dared dream might exist;

(d) Reflecting upon people, places, or situations in a manner that many may know but few can put into words with your particular expertise or artistic touch.

You may have noticed that I'm big on action. Stories bore me unless they go somewhere. They must *do* something. I want my main character deeply involved in something from the very beginning, and I like "cliffhanger" chapter endings. (My first novel was titled *Cliffhanger*, matter of fact.) I like to make something exciting happen every single chance I get.

All the great stories I've enjoyed over the years have dramatic action. Even if they take place in the same locale, something happens that I want to know about. I must know how it turns out. You should be similarly inclined, particularly if you aspire to write anything that anyone will pay money to acquire. Even your titles and your writing name should be compelling, as far as I'm concerned. Skip Press is my real name. Two verbs, someone pointed out to me once. Maybe that explains it. Action! I can't believe an editor could get a manuscript from Humdrum Haney and think it might be good.

So remember that when you write a novel, you're taking the reader on a journey. Consider this as well: You are actually involved in two journeys at once. That's right, two: an inner journey and an outer journey. While events take place that form the story of your book, the main character or characters should also be transformed. The dramatic people in the theater call it *catharsis*. Story editors at film studios call it *character arc*. In other words, inner changes take place in the character as a result of having lived through the events in the story. Want an example? Look at how Scarlett O'Hara changed from the beginning of *Gone With the Wind* to the end. At first, she's just a spoiled belle, with the tiniest waist in the county and a mind to match. In the middle of the book, she declares to God and the sky that she will never again go hungry a day in her life. By the end, she has done her best to ruin Rhett Butler's life and she's lost him in the bargain. I'm no fan of Scarlett, but Margaret Mitchell told a whale of a tale. When Alexandra Ripley wrote the sequel, *Scarlett*, she reformed the Georgia wench and turned her into a decent human being. It was quite a handy turn of writing to achieve such a major character transformation, but Ripley pulled it off.

Life is a series of changes. Writing is inspired by and reflects upon life. Good writing inspires a better life in others. Whether the changes of life reflected in your writing are positive or negative is your call. After all, you're God, when it comes to your story. (At least until you get an editor, anyway.) Your characters must change, and change dramatically, if you're going to have a novel you can sell.

Red Ink in Your Veins

Now that we've covered history, discipline, and structure, let's get down to what writing is really all about. Namely, editing. Get out your red pen or pencil, and roll up your sleeves. We're going to slice and dice that manuscript of yours! I have an exercise that drives my students crazy. As their first homework assignment, I have them write 1,500 words. It can be an article, a short story, whatever. They usually slave away at that, pulling their hair out, staying up nights, and some of them don't complete the assignment.

Then I drop the bombshell. OK, I say, your next assignment is to cut your 1,500 words down to 1,000. Screams of protest still ring in my ears. After I turn off the fire hoses and get them calmed down (just kidding), I explain how to edit. Basically, it comes down to two things:

(1) Is it essential to the story?

(2) Does it move the story forward?

Let's break that down with some examples. Here's a short paragraph for your consideration:

> Bobby knew he was in trouble. From the time he was a child, he was
> known as someone who had a knack for getting into bad situations.
> There was the time when he'd been caught stealing watermelons from
> Widow Whittle's garden, the Halloween he'd been mistakenly arrested as

a thief, and the time at his father's birthday when he'd been accused of putting vodka in the punch. Now here he was, with a crush on Mary Stevenson, standing on her front porch holding a corsage and feeling like a fool, and her brother Charlie just had to bring up Bobby's troubled past. Mary stood there in front of Bobby, blushing and confused. It looked like their first date was history, before it ever began.

That's not a bad paragraph. It tells you a lot about Bobby and the situation. Unfortunately, it's mostly mental. It's all in Bobby's head. We're told about action, but we don't feel a part of it. The background on Bobby is nice, and shows the compound nature of his current situation. There's a better way to do it:

"Bobby Rivers, you're in trouble!"

Bobby gulped. Mary Stevenson, the crush of his life, stood red-faced before him, angry as an irritated hornet.

Her brother Charlie, the rat fink, stood behind her smirking.

"You'll pay for this, Charlie," Bobby managed to mutter. "I can explain everything, Mary," he added meekly.

Why was this always happening to him? Standing there on Mary's front porch, holding a corsage, Bobby felt like a fool. Their first date was history, before it ever began.

See the difference? The dialogue adds action between people. It's a scene; something happening. It brings the conflict out in the open, rather than making it mental. The story is immediately established, and moved forward. You want to know why Bobby's always getting in trouble, and what will happen between him and Mary. The action happens much more quickly. Granted, it's a young adult scene, but I wanted to give you a simple example.

I suppose I could write a book on how to write a novel, going into a thousand subtle nuances, but the above example is roughly all you need. So where would you bring in examples of other times where Bobby had been in trouble? Do it when he's going somewhere, when he's alone and thinking it over. Call it flashbacks, or back story or whatever you want, just don't confuse your reader by continuously jerking back and forth over a time line to put in the background information.

There's a classic of science fiction that for years most Hollywood types thought might never be made as a movie. It's Isaac Asimov's *I, Robot*, tales often mental in narrative. Brilliant, but movies require action. That's why Hollywood balked for a long time until someone figured out a script that worked for superstar Will Smith in 2004. Most "mental" stories and novels pose translation problems for Hollywood. Perhaps because I sold movie writing before I sold books, my stories tend to be called "very cinematic." Basically, that means I concentrate on action, just as the "moving pictures" of films do. Until you become a skilled novelist, I'd advise you to do the same. When your style is developed, when you're comfortable putting words on the page, then you can more easily belabor back story and the like. The reader will go with you almost anywhere, simply because they feel so comfortable with you as the guide of your story. Don't you feel that way with your favorite author?

Here's another tip: Don't repeat. In editing, I do my best to use different words, even in the same sentence. Here's an example:

> If you have a wish to be a magician, it'll take more than tossing pennies down a wishing well. Years of hard work go into making magic for a living. In fact, it is one of the hardest occupations at which to succeed.

Here's how to say the same thing better:

> Want to make it in magic? Roll up your sleeves. Professional practitioners of prestidigitation commonly struggle for decades before achieving success.

In the first sentence of the first example, the syllable *wish* appeared twice. The word *magician* is in the first sentence, and *magic* in the second. *Work* and *living* are both in the second sentence, with *occupations* in the third. Similarly, *hard* appears in the second sentence, with *hardest* in the third. All these things are repetitive. You may think they don't really matter, but each time a word or meaning is repeated in the short space of a sentence or within a paragraph, it grates a bit on the reader. Just as people don't like eating the same thing for lunch each day, they also want diversity in their entertainment. I remember that every time I write a sentence.

Now study my second example. I substituted words, and I also threw in a bit of alliteration. That is, beginning words with the same sound. "Make it in magic." "Professional practitioners of prestidigitation." Because they are alliterative, those phrases have a rhyme to them. They roll off the tongue. They imply a special expertise, with the latter phrase using an uncommon word that describes making magic. They add some spice, and allude to the thrill you get when watching a magician in action. If you overly use alliteration, of course, you'll be repetitive, and risk turning a reader off. You'll have to judiciously decide.

Previously, I've told you about parameters. Try to keep your novel chapters of uniform length. By doing so, you set up a predictable rhythm, which readers (and editors) enjoy. At the end of each chapter, I suggest a cliffhanger of action. Otherwise, if everything is neatly wrapped up, why would anyone turn the page?

Here's another parameter for you that comes from my screenwriting experience. In a movie script, it's usually a good idea to limit each scene to three pages or less. Why? Because each single-spaced page of a film script usually works out to one minute of on-screen time. After three minutes, viewers usually get a little edgy. They're ready for the story to move to someplace else, geographically, through time, or both. Forty of these three-minute scenes go into a normal, 120-page film script.

I mentioned earlier that my chapters are usually sixteen to twenty pages long. That's 4,000 to 5,000 words per chapter, and my chapters usually break down into approximately three different scenes. Book manuscripts are double-spaced, so a 75,000-word book would have fifteen to eighteen chapters. That would mean, at three scenes a chapter, I'd have forty-five to fifty-two scenes in a book. Since it's much easier to edit down than to fill in, editing fifty-two scenes down to forty is not an impossible task.

I'm not suggesting that you follow my guidelines strictly. This is simply a method that works for me. You should work out your own method, based on what feels right to you. A novel is perhaps the most flexible medium of writing that exists, at least with regard to form and style. In editing your manuscript, however, just make sure that everything you've written is essential to the story, and that each scene moves the story forward in some manner.

Beyond that, you'll simply have to follow Jerry B. Jenkins's advice, and write your book with your butt in a chair. In any event, you should work out a way to write a good deal each week, on a predictable schedule. Whether you're a professional typist, a hunter/pecker, or someone who dictates pages to a secretary, it doesn't matter. You just have to write, and write a lot. You don't even have to sit in a chair, as long as you get the writing done. I didn't have the heart to tell Jerry, you see, that Ernest Hemingway wrote all his books in longhand, standing up.

Given Jerry's success, though, he probably already knew that.

Chapter Seven

Groups, Gatherings, Goodies, and Garbage

Life Is a Group Activity

All the chapters so far have discussed writing activities that are mostly solitary. Articles, stories, books, and novels are the products of a single person, usually. The remaining forms of writing discussed in this book, on the other hand, concern groups of people. Naturally, writers write about people both alone and in groups, but to become a successful playwright it's a very good idea to be involved in an ongoing fashion with a theater group. It's worked that way from the time of William Shakespeare and the Globe Theatre in London. So that's why you find this chapter on groups for writers following chapters on the basics of the most commonly pursued forms of writing.

Once I get you thinking in terms of groups that might be beneficial to your particular writing pursuits, then I'll go into advice on those forms, in later chapters. Here is the world of writers' groups as I have found it.

A Little Help from My Friends

Remember the studio executive in the movie *The Player* who went to Alcoholics Anonymous only because all the Hollywood bigwigs were there? The executive himself was not an alcoholic, but all the others were. "Networking" in any profession is a very important thing to do. I began networking shortly after I began to sell my writing. A friend suggested I join the Science Fiction Writers of America (SFWA). I was admitted as a member because I had sold a script to a science-fiction radio show.

Incidentally, I sold that script to an acquaintance—the producer of the radio show—who had called me, looking for writers. At the time, I was a musician, but my acquaintance knew I "knew a lot of people." I never made a sale because of being a member of SFWA, but I gained insight in dealing with publishers, agents, etc., from reading the publications SFWA sent me as a result of my membership.

The first time I had a play produced, I joined the Dramatists Guild (DG). Similarly, the New York-based DG newsletter, and their Los Angeles meetings, didn't help me sell anything, but I got a lot of good advice from the mailings. DG events in Los Angeles have also been enlightening. How else could I sit in a theater with twenty or thirty other people, having a discussion with legendary playwright Neil Simon? Besides, since very, very few people make a living writing for the theater, I didn't expect much from my DG membership.

Through another friend, I got a job as a managing editor of a brand-new Los Angeles business magazine. The clips from my first three articles helped me get that job. While I was working on that magazine, another friend suggested I join the Independent Writers of Southern California (IWOSC). The group offered monthly meetings, seminars, a newsletter with market tips, and successful new friends who were willing to share their knowledge to help fledgling writers. I got my first regional article sale from an IWOSC market tip, then used that clip (from *Palm Springs Life*) to get a national sale to an airline in-flight magazine. Why did I think of writing for an airline magazine? A friend had edited one—not the one I made the sale to, but the magazine of another airline. Since I did not do much flying in those days, I wouldn't have thought of writing for an in-flight magazine if a friend hadn't suggested it.

Do you see the through-line? You've heard the old saw that "It's who you know." That's not exactly right. What's really true is that when you are starting out, and to an extent even after you are established, the jobs you get through friends and acquaintances often far surpass those you get through letters and phone calls. It's really who you know that can do something for you, and vice versa. But don't think it's all just "friends." The problem with the writing business is that you are selling words on a page. If I had not been able to write well, it wouldn't have mattered what friends suggested, or helped me achieve.

Some beginning writers I know have a confused idea that they will knock out the world's greatest first novel, sell it for millions to New York and Hollywood, and live happily ever after. I always invite them to give me an example of someone who actually did that. No one's ever come forward with such a person.

You must mingle. Unless you want to be Emily Dickinson, stuffing your drawers full of wonderful poems that someone will discover and make millions from after your death, you've got to get out there and meet people to make it as a writer. Those mental pictures and vague impressions you've formed of writers living the life of leisure, staring out blissfully over the Mediterranean from their villa on the Riviera, are—if they're based on real people—of souls who put years of blood, sweat, and bruised fingers into getting there. If you don't believe me, get in touch with your favorite author and ask him or her about it.

When Helping Helped

One of the biggest boosts in my career came when I volunteered to head up a fund-raiser. IWOSC wanted to put on a forty-eight-hour nonstop script-writing marathon to acquire funds for the perennially sparse IWOSC bank account. I got the job since I had script-writing experience, and had produced some plays and a video. Other IWOSC-ans were mostly journalists. I was basically presented with the responsibility of saving the organization from bankruptcy, truth be told.

Giving credit where it is due, I should say that, because of a 2,000-person convention I was producing simultaneous to the last two weeks before the script-writing marathon, the other committee members had to do the bulk of the work just before the marathon. Still, my months of effort paid off; the event came off spectacularly. To our delight, we got extensive newspaper and magazine write-ups and were on the Showtime cable channel and even West German television. The donations we received from the event allowed the finance committee of IWOSC to resume breathing.

I gained something from the event I didn't expect—a teaching career. It was a bit round-about, but it would not have happened if not for a connection I made at the event. Everyone wanted to be there during the day, when TV cameras were rolling and the newspaper reporters were present, but hardly anyone wanted to write all night. Since I had not been able to contribute much during the two weeks prior to the event, I volunteered for the "graveyard shift." I had just lost a big job, had a baby on the way, and wanted to spend some time alone, thinking about the changes in my life and what direction I could take with my career. So I welcomed the solitude. I was manning the computer, in the chilly open air of the Century City, California shopping mall, one morning at three A.M. when fellow IWOSC-an Colleen Todd arrived to take my place. We talked about our careers, then Colleen suddenly asked me to speak to the class she was teaching at UCLA Extension Writers' Program.

I was amazed. I'd shared writing tips and potential markets with others for years—saving the best markets for myself, of course—but I had never considered teaching formally. Did I come across as more successful than I really was? After all, Colleen told me she had published books. Real writing! I had written for television and film, and sold tons of articles, but I hadn't yet published a book. Still, Colleen thought I was worthy. Since I enjoyed speaking in front of groups, I agreed.

It was some time later that I spoke to Colleen's beginning writing students. In the interim, I answered a newspaper ad and sold three young adult books to a Southern California company. They were short books, only 6,000 words, called "hi-los." That is, "high interest level, low reading level," for teens with a third-grade reading level. Still, book sales were book sales, and I was thrilled. When I spoke to Colleen's class, my past success as a writer and my three books made me seem like a legend in the making to the students. Plus, they liked what I had to tell them about vigorously pursuing a career. I was a hit. Colleen told UCLA Extension Writers' Program coordinator Linda Venis about it. I met with Linda, and before long, I was teaching a class at UCLA entitled (you guessed it) "How To Write What You Want & Sell What You Write."

Through Colleen I also met Aram Saroyan, who also taught at UCLA and was Colleen's agent. When Aram found out what I writing for *Boys' Life* and *Disney Adventures* magazines, and had sold the "hi-los," he called me about doing a young adult mystery series. I wrote up a proposal, and to my amazement soon had a three-book deal with Zebra Books for their new young adult line. Real books, 55,000 words long. Not 100,000-word adult mainstream books, but I wasn't complaining.

Except for the newspaper ad I answered, all the work I've mentioned here came through people I met. During that same time, I also wrote almost all of *Boys' Life*'s entertainment articles. My short-story agent of the time, Larry Sternig, got me that job. I met Larry through a friend.

Finding Help

It is amazing how "small" a world we live in. I have my students make a list of everyone they know who might be able to help them directly, or refer them to someone who can help them make their first sale as a writer. The results inevitably astonish them. They discover they have either taken for granted who they know, or learn that friends and relatives have contacts they never suspected. And since I make them complete at least one serious piece of marketable writing before our class is finished, they have a product to show someone. That means the contact will not be embarrassed by referring them, or the contact they already have won't mind reading their work.

If you live in a rural area, or even Antarctica, I firmly believe this networking principle applies. Most people are social by nature. They like meeting new people, and discovering new things. A great new writer is one of the most exciting finds anyone can come across, whether for a reader, an editor, an agent, a publisher, or even a heartless beast like a Hollywood film executive.

What I am telling you is that, once you have a piece of writing that you consider good, you should immediately start cultivating contacts who can help you advance your writing career. Be bold! The worst thing they can do is shoot you (I'm kidding).

Legends Are People, Too

As I mentioned, one of the early highlights of my journalistic career was interviewing Tennessee Williams. I learned about the great playwright living in a friend's building before I went to New York. I immediately proposed to a friend who had a Los Angeles theater magazine that I do a piece on Tennessee. My editor friend leaped at the idea (well, he hopped, anyway), so all I had to do was visit Mr. Williams's apartment and knock on the door. The busy, legendary playwright had not minded taking some time to help me, a fledgling journalist.

Curiously enough, as I was helping brainstorm an event to take place at the Directors Guild of America (DGA) with a friend in early 2005, I discovered that at about the same time I had interviewed Mr. Williams, she had been his assistant on a movie project.

The reality is, it's a small world in the arts and there are friends, friends, friends to be found all over. So pool your resources! If you don't have a writing group to join in your local area, form one. Make it a regular practice to cultivate new contacts who can help you advance your career. Don't be afraid to ask, and don't get hung up if you get a cold shoulder, or even a rude rebuff once in a while.

One of the big Hollywood tricks is "working a room." It's an art and amazing to watch. I've been fortunate in the friends I've had in my life, and I'm continually grateful to them. Through a former roommate of mine from Austin, Texas, I got into a party given by Paul McCartney and his group Wings in 1976. It worked like this:

- My friend was the head "roadie" (equipment handler) on the Wings Over America tour. He offered to get me into the Wings concert when they came to Los Angeles, where I was living.

- Unfortunately, he told me the next day over the phone, he couldn't get me in the concert. There had been a cutback on free tickets for the crew, and the event was sold out. So my dream of meeting at least one of The Beatles was kaput.

- When he called, I happened to be in the room with a public relations professional whose greatest personal desire had always been to meet Paul McCartney. My friend knew a jazz legend named Chick Corea. Thinking quickly, she suggested that Chick wanted to come to the concert. She hadn't checked with Chick first, but that's the way PR people work, sometimes. My friend put me on hold, walked across the stage, and asked Paul and Linda McCartney if Chick could come. The McCartneys said sure, we'd love to meet him!

- My PR friend then called Chick and told him he was invited. To our relief, he thought it was a great idea. On his coattails, we went to the concert, and were then invited to the party.

The party alone cost $250,000, and everyone who was anyone in the music business was there that night. I was a bit dumbstruck by meeting people I had idolized like Rick Nelson, Joni Mitchell, John Mayall, Peter Asher, Keith Moon of The Who, Burton Cummings of the Guess Who, and Paul McCartney. Since I didn't know then how to "work a room," or in this case, the entire Harold Lloyd estate in Beverly Hills, I followed and watched my PR friend as she went around the party with Chick Corea, making small talk and getting to know entertainment legends. I won't go into the details, but this friend greatly boosted her career that night, basically by stating who she was, what she did, and giving the people she met some idea of how she could help them. It was my first big lesson in just how important "working a room" could be, and how, even though I had people on a pedestal in my mind, there was usually some way we could personally interact for mutual benefit.

Unfortunately for me, at that time I had a job writing business letters, and didn't see how that could translate into working with any celebrity. Ironically, this same PR friend of mine later got me a job answering "Elvis mail" for Priscilla Presley, and a few years later made a big business for herself handling fan mail for dozens of well-known Hollywood stars. I could have started the same business that night in Beverly Hills, if I'd thought of it!

Fools on the Hill

The groups I would advise you to studiously avoid are group encounter, psycho-babble "workshops" that have a lot more to do with the hosts making money than actually advancing your writing. I remember all too well an open house for potential students at a university in which one instructor stood up and said, "I believe writing is therapy, and therapy is writing" and proceeded to say that her class would "bring out the inner you." I stood up a short while later and said, "I won't try to analyze you or get you to analyze yourself. I'll simply take you from being a want-to-be to a professional writer who can sell in today's marketplace."

My class filled up that day, and was a smash success. My best student came up to me after our last meeting and thanked me profusely for not having another "thank-you-for-sharing" touchy-feely "inner you" type of class.

Don't get me wrong. I actually think there is some therapeutic benefit from writing, but I lean toward the great advance in self-esteem that comes from a check in the mail. If you want to find the "inner you," I suggest you find a good minister or counselor, not take writing classes. Writing is a craft and can develop into an art. You don't need to add to the confusion by getting lost in a mental or spiritual labyrinth. You can learn craft, and mastering it will nurture your talent. Look no further for a muse than persistent hard work.

The Long and Winding Road to Success

I truly hope you can short-cut your way to the top. I hope you write that first novel you always wanted to write, send it off to a publisher, and make such an impact you get flown to New York on the company Learjet and given a six-figure check.

Just don't count on it. The chances of that happening are perhaps only a little bit better than winning the lottery. You'll probably have to work long and hard, and write a lot more than you ever imagined before you "make it." You can help make your journey more comfortable by getting there with a group. And when you get involved with an organization, don't just sit back and listen to the monthly speakers. Get involved! Help out, make suggestions, work the room. Remember the string of events that were set in motion from one contact I made at three o'clock in the morning? Believe me, the more selflessly you give, the more chances you'll have to get something in return.

The last thing I'll give you in this chapter is a list of major writers' groups that I feel might be of interest to beginning writers, throughout the United States. It's impossible to list them all, and perhaps some of them will have ceased to exist, have moved, or reformed into other entities by the time you read this book. They may have a Web site, they may not. That's life. Remember, if you don't find a group located near you, you can still join one which will send you helpful mailings. You may be able to subscribe to the publications you want without actually joining the organization. Or—and I think this is ultimately better in any case—you can start your own group. All of the organizations listed below offer worthwhile publications; most offer much more. As one example, I was able to pay the rent one month only because of a last-second, interest-free loan from the Authors Guild.

Please check with the organization(s) that appeal(s) to you for full details on how you might mutually benefit from an association. Usually, their Web site provides all the information you need. I suggest you be involved in as many groups as possible, since it multiplies your chances. That approach continues to work well for with each passing year.

Brett Harvey
Executive Director
American Society of Journalists & Authors (ASJA)
1501 Broadway, Suite 302
New York, NY 10036
(212) 997-0947 phone
(212) 768-7414 fax
execdir@asja.org
www.asja.org

From the Web site: "Founded in 1948, the American Society of Journalists and Authors is the nation's leading organization of independent nonfiction writers. Our membership consists of more than 1,100 outstanding freelance writers of magazine articles, trade books, and many other forms of nonfiction writing, each of whom has met ASJA's exacting standards of professional achievement."

ASJA offers many "benefits and services focusing on professional development" including Writers Emergency Assistance Fund for writers over 60 and the ASJA Contracts Watch free electronic newsletter. The organization is a strong voice for writers' rights, including in new media. Headquartered in New York City, ASJA also has active regional chapters in Northern and Southern California, the Rocky Mountain area, and Washington, DC. Membership qualifications are described on the Web site. Roughly, you need to have published "a minimum of six full-length, by-lined articles written on a freelance basis (typically 1000 or more words in length). If you submit shorter articles, you should send a greater number." These articles should be from major publications (a sample list appears under "How To Join" on the site). Two or more nonfiction books, nonfiction freelanced TV, film and radio scripts (e.g., The History Channel, NPR), and articles for major Internet magazines (e.g., Slate, Salon) also count toward ASJA membership qualifications. Dues are $195 per year, with a one-time application fee of $25. You can download an application from the Web site.

The Association of Writers and Writing Programs
Mail Stop 1E3
George Mason University
Fairfax, VA 22030-4444
(703) 993-4301 phone
(703) 993-4302 fax
www.awpwriter.org
Membership Services: services@awpwriter.org

AWP UPS/FedEx Address (For Deliveries Only)

The Association of Writers and Writing Programs
10808 Kelley Drive
Fairfax, VA 22030-4415

AWP is a national nonprofit service organization founded in 1967 "to support the growing presence of writers in higher education & thereby foster new generations of writers & new audiences for literature." Important writers who have attended university writing programs and worked as professors of writing and literature include Terry McMillan, John Barth, and Pam Houston. AWP provides services to over 25,000 writers, 400 member colleges and universities, and eighty-six writers' conferences and centers. Individual membership is open to all. An individual membership in AWP for one year costs $59 or $99 for two years. Currently enrolled students in the United States pay only $37 when they enclose a photocopy of their valid student ID. E-mail services@awpwriter.org for international rates. With membership you get six issues of their *Writers' Chronicle* magazine and seven issues of their jobs list, but there is such a cornucopia of resources available from AWP that I highly urge you to read all about it on the Web site.

The Authors Guild
31 E 28th St, 10th Floor
New York, NY 10016-7923
(212) 563-5904 phone
(212) 564-5363 fax
staff@authorsguild.org
www.authorsguild.org

From the Web site: "Book authors and freelance writers may qualify for full membership. Literary estates, agents and attorneys may qualify as at-large members...

Freelance writers qualify for membership if they have published three works, fiction or nonfiction, in periodicals of general circulation (those readily available on newsstands nationwide) within the last 18 months. Freelancers with a substantial publishing history prior to the last 18 months will be considered on a case-by-case basis. Regarding online journalism: Online works for which a freelancer is paid may qualify a writer for membership.

Members-at-large may be established literary agents, heirs or executors of the estates of deceased authors, or attorneys and accountants representing authors."

Enrollment is contingent upon receipt of full payment of first-year dues of $90. You can see if you qualify for membership by filling out an electronic form on the Web site. One thing I like personally about Authors Guild is that I get a discount on registering Internet domain names, have privacy protection on same, and was able to build a workable site of my own with minimal effort via the Guild's easy-to-use Web Tools.

The Dramatists Guild of America
1501 Broadway, Suite 701
New York, NY 10036
(212) 398-9366 phone
(213) 944-0420 fax
membership@dramatistsguild.com
www.dramaguild.com

(Note the difference between the Web site and the domain name to which membership inquiries are directed.)

All theater writers are eligible to apply to the Guild. According to the Web site:

> *Active Members* must submit a copy of a program or review from a First Class/Broadway, Professional Off-Broadway, or main-stage LORT production.
>
> *Associate Members* must submit either a completed work for the stage, or a program or a review from any production or reading of their work.
>
> *Student Members* must submit proof of current enrollment."

International Association of Business Communicators
1 Hallidie Plaza
Suite 600
San Francisco, CA 94102
(415) 544-4700 phone
(800) 776-4222 toll free
(415) 544-4747
service_centre@iabc.com
www.iabc.com

(Note the underline in the e-mail address.)

This is a massive all-encompassing organization for business writers with extensive resources offered via worldwide chapters. From the Web site: "Founded in 1970, IABC provides a professional network of more than 13,000 business communication professionals in over sixty countries." IABC members hold positions in community relations, corporate communications, government relations, investor relations, marketing communications, media relations, public affairs, public relations, and other forms of writing. Yearly dues vary by region. See www.iabc.com/join/ for a membership application and description of fees and dues. If you want to commune with professional business writers around the world, this is the group for you.

International Women's Writing Guild
PO Box 810, Gracie Station
New York, NY 10028
(212) 737-7536 phone
(212) 737-9469 fax
dirhahn@aol.com
www.iwwg.com

Founded in 1976 and headed by Hannelore Hahn, the IWWG offers members "a network for the personal and professional empowerment of women through writing." No portfolio is necessary to join. According to the Web site: "The Guild nurtures and supports holistic thinking by recognizing the logic of the heart—the ability to perceive the subtle interconnections between people, events and emotions—alongside conventional logic." One caution: You might find the music that loads when you access the site to be more than a bit annoying.

Mystery Writers of America
17 E. 47th Street, 6th Floor
New York, NY 10017
(212) 888-8171 phone
(212) 888-8107 fax
mwa@mysterwriters.org
www.mysterywriters.org

Being a member of MWA can be highly illuminating. When I joined after having several young adult mysteries published, the President answered the phone and I told her which company published my novel. "Oh, they're the worst!" she said. "I know," I replied, happy to know that I wasn't alone in my feelings about that publisher. I still hope to win an Edgar award from WMA someday. Here's what it takes to join, from the Web site:

"Active Membership is open to professional writers in the crime/mystery/suspense field whose work has been published or produced in the U.S., who reside in the U.S., and who meet specific criteria set by the Board for this category. Currently, some of those criteria are

1. The applicant is a professional creative writer of fiction, nonfiction, or drama (including TV, screenplays, radio, and staged drama).
2. The writer has received a cumulative minimum of $100 for his or her work. Proof of payment is required.
3. The work is neither self-published nor cooperatively published; no monies were required of the writer by the publisher.
4. The publisher is on MWA's list of approved publishers or eligible to be added to that list; similar criteria are set for dramas, films, and video productions.

Only Active members may vote, hold office, and serve on Edgar® committees in MWA.

Associate membership is open to professionals residing in the U.S. who work in certain allied fields.

Affiliate members are writers of crime/mystery/suspense fiction who are not yet professionally published, and others with an interest in the genre, including unpaid reviewers.

Corresponding members are those who might be in any of the above categories, but who live outside the United States."

Sandy Whelchel, Executive Director
National Writers Association
10940 S. Parker Road #508
Parker, CO 80134-7440
(303) 841-0246 phone
(303) 841-2607 fax
anitaedits@aol.com
www.nationalwriters.com

General membership is open to all; regular dues are $65 per year. Professional membership is $85 per year; for a full-time student dues are only $35 per year. There is an additional fee of $20 for anyone living outside the U.S. One qualifies for Professional status by three sales to national or regional magazines, a book sold to a royalty publisher, a play produced, or employment as a writer, journalist, or editor. A free critique of forty lines of poetry or a 1500-word manuscript is a bonus for joining. The national conference the second weekend of June is host to professional movie producers, authors, agents, and editors so that writers have a chance for face-to-face meetings with the pros.

Gerard Colby, President
National Writers Union
113 University Place, 6th Floor
New York, NY 10003
(212) 254-0279 phone
(212) 254-0673 fax
nwu@nwu.org
www.nwu.org

The NWU is affiliated with United Auto Workers and AFL-CIO and works continuously to improve conditions for writers. The NWU grievance committees are a great resource for members, as is the NWU jobs hotline. It has chapters around the U.S. See the Web site for contact information. According to the site, qualifications for membership are as follows:

Dues are based on your annual writing income. Membership in the National Writers Union is open to all qualified writers, and no one shall be barred or prejudiced within the union on account of age, disability, ideology, literary genre, nationality, race, religion, or sexual orientation. You are eligible for membership if you have published a book, a play, three articles, five poems, a short story, or an equal amount of newsletter, publicity, technical, commercial, government, or institutional copy. You are also eligible for membership if you have written an equal amount of unpublished material and are actively writing and attempting to publish your work. You do not have to live in the United States or be a U.S. citizen to join the NWU. If you write for U.S. publishers, publications, employers, or clients, the NWU welcomes you.

Stefania Heim
Director, Development & Membership
Poetry Society of America
15 Gramercy Park
New York, NY 10003
(212) 254-9628
stefania@poetrysociety.org
www.poetrysociety.org

Membership open to anyone who writes, reads, and appreciates poetry.

From the Web site: "Whether you write poetry, read poetry, or simply want to widen your literary horizons, the Poetry Society of America has readings, seminars, and competitions intended to challenge and inspire. W. H. Auden, Robert Frost, Langston Hughes, Edna St. Vincent Millay, Marianne Moore and Wallace Stevens were among the original members who envisioned a society that would not only be a local meeting place for poets, but a center from which a national poetry renaissance would emerge. Current members, such as John Ashbery, Rita Dove, Kimiko Hahn, Brenda Hillman, Yusef Komunyakaa, Stanley Kunitz, Sharon Olds, Robert Pinsky and Adrienne Rich carry on their great tradition—and so can you."

Online signup is available on the Web site. If you do not live in the United States, please add $10.00 to your Membership Level in order to cover postage. Being on the mailing list is free, while regular membership is $45 per year. Students may join for $25 with a valid student ID. With membership you receive a subscription to *Crossroads: The Journal of the Poetry Society of America*, discounted admission to PSA events and the option of reserving tickets in advance, as well as free entry to PSA Annual Awards competitions. There are several other levels of supporting membership including the Lyric Circle, which you can read about on the site.

Poets, Playwrights, Editors, Essayists & Novelists (PEN)
PEN American Center
568 Broadway, Suite 303
New York, NY 10012-3225
(212) 334-1660 phone
(212) 334-2181 fax
www.pen.org

For general information, call Joy Chen at extension 103 or e-mail pen@pen.org.

PEN American Center is the largest of 141 Centers worldwide that compose International PEN, the world's oldest human rights organization and the oldest international literary organization. The organization was founded in 1921 to dispel national, ethnic, and racial hatreds and to promote understanding among all countries. PEN American Center, founded a year later, works to advance literature, to defend free expression, and to foster international literary fellowship. The Center has a membership of 2,900 distinguished writers, editors, and translators. In addition to defending writers in prison or in danger of imprisonment for their work,

PEN American Center sponsors public literary programs and forums on current issues, sends prominent authors to inner-city schools to encourage reading and writing, administers literary prizes, promotes international literature that might otherwise go unread in the United States, and offers grants and loans to writers facing financial or medical emergencies. In carrying out this work, PEN American Center builds upon the achievements of such dedicated past members as W. H. Auden, James Baldwin, Willa Cather, Robert Frost, Langston Hughes, Thomas Mann, Arthur Miller, Marianne Moore, Susan Sontag, and John Steinbeck.

Members are elected by the Membership Committee. Standard qualification is the publication of two or more books of a literary character, or one book generally acclaimed to be of exceptional distinction. Also eligible for membership are editors who have demonstrated commitment to excellence in their profession (usually construed as five years' service in book editing); translators who have published at least two book-length literary translations; playwrights whose works have been produced professionally; literary essayists whose publications are extensive even if they may have not been issued as a book. Candidates for membership should be nominated by two current members of PEN, or may nominate themselves with the support of a current member. Membership dues are paid annually, and all PEN members in good standing are welcome to participate in the work of PEN committees and programs.

All PEN members receive a subscription to the PEN Journal, the PEN Annual Report and qualify for medical insurance at group rates. Members living in the tri-state area or near the Branches are invited to PEN events throughout the year. Membership in American PEN includes reciprocal privileges in foreign PEN Centers for those travelling abroad. Membership in American PEN includes reciprocal privileges in foreign PEN Centers for those traveling abroad. The PEN Cafe, an on-line conversation and discussion group, is available to PEN members.

Friends of PEN is open to everyone who has an abiding interest in literature and human rights, and to writers who may not yet qualify for PEN membership. Annual affiliation ranges from the Supporter level ($50) to the Benefactor level ($1,000). Friends of PEN are invited to PEN events and receive the PEN Annual Report. At higher levels of participation, Friends receive copies of books honored recently with PEN awards.

Elliot Figman, Executive Director
Poets & Writers, Inc.
72 Spring Street, Suite 301
New York, NY 10012
(212) 226-3586 phone
(212) 226-3693 fax
www.pw.org

California Office
2035 Westwood Blvd., Suite 211
Los Angeles, CA 90025
(310) 481-7195 phone
(310) 481-7193 fax

The nation's largest non-profit literary organization describes itself as "the primary source of information, support, and guidance for creative writers." Their *Poets & Writers* magazine is the cornerstone of their publishing program and they also offer a free electronic newsletter (see site for details). If you would like to be listed in its annual publication, *A Directory of American Poets and Fiction Writers*, contact directory@pw.org. The organization offers funding for readings and workshops and a lot more. See the Web site for details on this and its other benefits. The "Links to Other Resources" Web page alone is worth a visit to its site.

Public Relations Society of America (PRSA)
33 Maiden Lane, 11th Floor
New York, NY 10038-5150
(212) 460-1400 phone
(212) 995-0757 fax
membership@prsa.org
www.prsa.org

The Public Relations Society of America, based in New York City, is the world's largest organization for public relations professionals. The Society has more than 28,000 professional and student members. PRSA is organized into 114 Chapters nationwide, 19 Professional Interest Sections, along with Affinity Groups, which represent business and industry, counseling firms, independent practitioners, military, government, associations, hospitals, schools, professional services firms, and nonprofit organizations. The Public Relations Student Society of America (PRSSA) has 255 Chapters at colleges and universities throughout the United States. There is a huge amount of contact information for all the professional members and chapters, so please see the Web site to access someone in your area or e-mail chapters@prsa.org. For PR professionals with two or more years of experience, there is a one-time $65 processing fee. Dues are $225 year. You may also join as an associate member. If you have less than one year's experience in public relations, it is $115 for the first year, over one year's experience but less than two is $155 per year. There is also a category for PRSA graduate members, who get started in PRSA student society chapters on college campuses. Check with PRSA for a list of campuses, as they are not listed on the Web site; get in touch with Brent.Hendrix@prsa.org.

Romance Writers of America, Inc. (RWA)
16000 Stubner Airline, Suite 140
Spring, TX 77379
(832) 717-5200 phone
(832) 717-5201 fax
info@rwanational.org
www.rwanational.org

A national non-profit corporation dedicated to promoting excellence in the romance writing field, RWA has over 150 chapters around North America, with online chapters available for those not physically located near an existing chapter. In case you didn't know, the romance novel industry generates almost half the sales of fiction, and generates more than $1 billion in sales each year. So why not write a romance; couldn't the world use a little more of it? General Membership is open to established romance authors and writers interested in pursuing a career in romance writing. Associate Membership is open to booksellers, editors, agents, and other industry professionals. Annual dues are $75, with a processing fee of $25 for new members and a $25 reaffiliation fee for lapsed members. RWA offers the "Romance Writer's Report," a monthly magazine, and other benefits. RWA sponsors two contests each year. The RITA contest is for authors published by an RWA-recognized publisher (a list of these publishers is available on the site), and the Golden Heart contest is for the unpublished manuscripts of writers who have not yet sold to an RWA-recognized publisher. See the site for details on the contest and the annual convention where the awards are presented.

Jane Jewell
Executive Director
Science Fiction and Fantasy Writers of America, Inc.
PO Box 877
Chestertown, MD 21620
execdir@sfwa.org
www.sfwa.org

SFWA Bulletin
PO Box 10126
Rochester, NY 14610
www.sfwa.org/bulletin/subscriptions.htm

There is no established national office. You don't have to be a member to subscribe to the *SFWA Bulletin*. The address changes as the officers of SFWA change, so check the Web site for the most current information. Membership requirements as listed on the Web site:

"To become an Active member of SFWA, applicants must demonstrate either:

1. Three Paid Sales of prose fiction (such as short stories) to Qualifying Professional Markets, with each paid at the rate of 5c/word or higher (3c/word before 1/1/2004), for a cumulative total of $250, minimum $50 apiece; or
2. One Paid Sale of a prose fiction book to a Qualifying Professional Market, for which the author has been paid $2000 or more; or
3. One professionally produced full-length dramatic script, with credits acceptable to the Membership Committee.

"Paid Sale" and "Qualifying Professional Market" are as defined below.

To become an Associate member of SFWA, applicants must demonstrate:
One Paid Sale of prose fiction (such as short stories) to a Qualifying Professional Market, paid at the rate of 5c/word or higher (3c/word before 1/1/2004), minimum $75.

To become an Affiliate member of SFWA, applicants must be an allied professional (such as an agent/editor/reviewer/artist/publisher who works with Qualifying Professional Markets) with credentials acceptable to the Membership Committee and must be able to provide the names of three Active members as references. No agent, editor, or publisher who charges authors an upfront fee in exchange for representation or publication is eligible for affiliate membership.

To become an Institutional member, applicants must be organizations with legitimate interest in science fiction and fantasy (such as high schools, colleges, universities, libraries, and similar institutions, as well as broadcasting organizations, film producers, futurology groups and similar organizations) or individuals associated with these groups. Applicants must present credentials acceptable to the Membership Committee and must be able to provide the names of three Active members as references.

To become an Estate member, applicants must be the legal representative for the estate of an Active member.

While every attempt is made here to detail the membership requirements, ultimately the SFWA Membership Committee's decision on criteria and qualifying for membership is final."

Do yourself a big favor if you are an aspiring writer and read through the "Writer Beware" page of the site at www.sfwa.org/Beware. You might save yourself a lot of heartache from being taken in by unscrupulous people.

Society of Children's Book Writers and Illustrators (SCBWI)

8271 Beverly Blvd.
Los Angeles, CA 90048
(323) 782-1010 phone
(323) 782-1892 fax
General Questions: scbwi@scbwi.org
Membership Questions: membership@scbwi.org
www.scbwi.org

From the Website: "Membership in the SCBWI is open to anyone with an active interest in children's literature or media. We welcome aspiring and published writers and illustrators, librarians, educators, artists, students, dramatists, musicians, filmmakers, and others. A passion for children's literature is our #1 criterion. Dues are US $75 for the first year and US $60 each renewing year."

Full Membership is "Open to those whose books, articles, poems, stories, illustrations, photographs, films, television or electronic media for children have been commercially published or produced. Professional editors, agents, and publishers are also included in this category."

Associate Membership is "Open to unpublished writers and illustrators of children's literature or media, and those with a general enthusiasm for the field. Writers or illustrators who have been published in markets other than children's literature (but not in children's literature) would be considered Associate Members."

There are currently more than 19,000 SCBWI members worldwide, in over 70 regions, making it the largest children's writing organization in the world.

Writers Guild of America, east
555 West 57th Street, Suite 1230
New York, NY 10019
(212) 767-7800 phone
(212) 582-1909 fax
www.wgaeast.org

Writers Guild of America, west
7000 West Third Street
Los Angeles, CA 90048
(310) 550-1000
wga@wga.org
www.wga.org

Screenwriters living west of the Mississippi River should join the WGAW, while those east of it should join the WGAE. The organizations are different in orientation and often bicker with each other, so you'll need to navigate their respective Web sites to determine what each is about at the current moment. The Writers Guild has a system of 24 units of credit that must be accumulated to make one eligible for membership. Contact either office for a brochure explaining details, or read the Web site for membership requirements. What most people do not know is that you can gain a great number of benefits from either organization as an Associate Member. For example, "The WGAE Associate Program is open to anyone with an interest in writing for screen and television." Each organization offers a lot of free information online, various publications, and other resources including online script registration. If you have Hollywood aspirations, do a lot of reading on these sites.

Writers' organizations change all the time, so if you find something here that is inaccurate, please let me know. I'm at skip@skippress.com.

I've tried to provide information in this book in a step-by-step fashion. By the time you read about these organizations, I hope that you have mapped out a writing career for yourself, or this book has helped boost a career you have already started. If you have any questions or comments of any kind, get in touch. Otherwise, go make friends, learn some things, and write on!

Chapter Eight

Plotting Your Career, With or Without an Agent

Getting Your Bearings

In selling articles, stories, even novels and nonfiction books, you can usually do fairly well without an agent up to a certain level. Joining a writing group or just communicating with professional writers can help you find markets, and more writers make sales by networking than via agents. Long-term, you might be able to build a successful, full-time writing career without the services of an agent, but to break into the big leagues you'll probably need one. That's why, before I get into chapters on areas of writing that require collaboration to see your writing realized—stage, film, and theater most particularly—I wanted you to have a diverse amount of information on not only finding a good agent, but building a career.

Now that I've gotten you orientated toward groups, I hope, I can give you a road map to negotiating the often-murky waters toward mainstream, big-time success.

Agents can be very helpful, even if getting a good one may seem an elusive quest. Where do you start? Well, before the advent of the technological age, the best agents for screenwriters were in Hollywood, while the best agents for authors were in New York. Now, with jet planes, picture phones, fax machines, e-mail, and the Internet, a good agent can live practically anywhere on Earth and still do a good business. That's good for you, because contrary to modern media perceptions, most of the world does not live in L.A. or New York. If you're like me, and write lots of different kinds of things, save yourself some trouble and quit looking for a "general" agent. If you only write one type of thing, all the better in finding an agent. Agents specialize; they don't generalize. Since they make only ten to fifteen percent of a writer's income, good agents have a number of clients. Accordingly, they don't have time to sell short stories, articles, and such. Agents want writers who will provide them a steady income, and fifteen percent of $450 for an article isn't much. It might be worth a phone call, a letter, and a stamp, but why bother when you can sell a screenplay for $50,000 or more and collect fifteen percent of that with only a bit more effort? (Although I should add that by California law an agent can only charge ten percent; managers generally charge fifteen percent in Hollywood.)

Try to think like an agent and your chances of finding a truly good one will be multiplied. Here's a little exercise along that line. You're an agent, a really good agent with a fine income and the respect of your peers. What is the source of that income? Other than your own expertise, it's your writers. If a new writer comes your way, you want someone who has long-term financial rewards written all over them.

The best way to find truly fine agents is normally through truly fine writers. Hardly any writer who has had a book published, a screenplay sold, or done any amount of work is without an agent, a manager, a lawyer or all of the above. Other writers are where you start looking for an agent. Rather than finding lists of agents that you know nothing about and sending them your manuscript(s) without contacting them first, try meeting some success-ful writers and getting referred to an agent. Granted, the writer(s) you meet will probably want to read your work before recommending you, but all the better. They might teach you something. Since you've read my chapter on the benefits of writers' organizations (I hope), you know how to go about meeting other writers and might have already begun to do so.

Negotiating the Territory

Now, here's the big surprise. Even if a successful writer refers you, even if you get signed with an agent, don't think it will all be gravy from there. Chances are, your agent won't do a lot for you until you generate some sales on your own. Even then, you'll probably do a lot of the selling your-self. I once wrote highly successful science-fiction writer Poul Anderson to ask about his agent, H. N. "Swanee" Swanson. An agent at the Swanson Agency wanted to sign me, and I just happened to know that Swanson represented Anderson because of our mutual membership in the Science Fiction Writers of America (as it was known then). I admired Anderson's writing and had read about him in the SFWA Directory. Swanee Swanson was a legendary agent in Hollywood, having represented writers like Raymond Chandler (*The Big Sleep* and other Philip Marlowe novels). Normally, I would have gleefully accepted getting signed by an agent at Swanson, but since I knew about Anderson's relationship with Swanson, my curiosity was aroused. Anderson wrote back and said that he couldn't recall Swanson really selling anything for him—Anderson had done it all himself! But, he added, having Swanson as his agent was worthwhile. Swanson, whose reputation was well, legendary, had negotiated some good contracts for Anderson. In other words, Anderson had found the deal, but Swanson had made the deal a lot sweeter than it might have been.

I was amazed, but I subsequently learned that this arrangement was more usual than unusual. Writers who get out and mingle make contacts, out of which come sales. This book, for example, was sold to its publisher after both my agent at the time (David Andrew) and I pitched it to different people from the same company at the American Booksellers Association convention in Los Angeles. We both generated interest; David closed the sale and handled the negotiations. When I sold my You-Solve-It Mystery novels to E. K. Gaylord II Productions, I made the initial contact and sale. My then agent Sasha Goodman (David's part- ner) negotiated the terms of the sale (increasing my money substantially), but I made the sale myself. When it came time to hash out the terms of the contract, Sasha did the initial work (with my input), then my lawyer, Bruce Grakal, added some important points and supervised the final contract. The books were originally sold to the publisher by another agent, who made a very bad deal for me with regard to the publisher's cut of film rights (a publisher shouldn't get any). That agent subsequently stopped being an agent and got a job with the federal government, if that tells you anything. That's how it usually works—the writer garners the interest and the agent closes the deal. When a writer is hot enough, though, the agent often "fields offers" like the Sydney Pollack agent character described in the movie *Tootsie*.

The important point is that agents and lawyers know about contracts and the implications of certain contract items. Unless you have a legal background, you probably won't. That's why you need a representative.

Other than what I've mentioned, all the other sales I've made I negotiated on my own. My screenplays, my videos, my magazine articles, everything else, were all negotiated without the benefit of an agent or lawyer. There are a couple of exceptions. Larry Sternig, whom I described in an earlier chapter as the most successful short-story agent of all time, put me in touch with two important magazine accounts: *Reader's Digest* and *Boys' Life*. Through Larry, my writing was introduced to Senior Editor Elena Serocki at *Reader's Digest*. I became the entertainment reporter at *Boys' Life* for over a year thanks to Larry's relationship with the editor-in-chief, William McMorris. Granted, my writing had to measure up to Larry's recommendation, but without him those high-profile magazines would have been much tougher to crack.

Unfortunately, I paid dearly for flying solo. One how-to video I put together went gold, meaning it sold over 100,000 copies. I trusted the producers I got involved with on a handshake deal. In the words of a popular country song, they got the gold mine and I got the shaft. I ended up getting bought out of the project for a small sum—and then only because I got a lawyer.

So that's what good agents do: They provide useful introductions; secondly, they negotiate terms, and sometimes they make sales that you have little to do with (other than the quality of your writing). Agents become the source, when they represent you well, of good "word of mouth" on your writing. Word of mouth, in case you hadn't noticed, is by far the most important means of convincing anyone of the worth of anything. Later in your career, when you are well enough known, you might not need an agent, just a lawyer to handle the contracts that people offer you.

Why is life made this way? Maybe it's because everyone wants a piece of a successful pie and no one wants a pie in the face. People are generally fearful. We do not live in a brave world. "So what did you think?" we ask after watching a movie with someone. "What's he like?" a girl asks when someone tries to set her up on a date. "Do you think I should buy an American car?" we ask our mechanic. This is where agents come in. They develop relationships with publishers, production companies, film studios, and producers. These writing consumers either find that the agent provides them with quality material on a regular basis, or they don't. Agents are the natural screening process of the entertainment business. They are part hype artists and part good friend. They may embellish the worth of something they sell, but they can't elaborate too much for too long and stay in business. They must supply quality product, time and time again.

Occasionally, writers refer other writers directly to producers, publishers, etc. Then writers get work without the "middle man." This "sans agent" practice used to be much more prevalent than it is today. Remember the story about F. Scott Fitzgerald referring Ernest Hemingway to his editor, Maxwell Perkins? Ah, the simple days of yore. Today, Fitzgerald would likely refer Hemingway to someone at Creative Artists Agency (CAA), which is the most influential agency in the entertainment business. The CAA agent would have a subordinate read Hemingway's novel, synopsize and critique it. Then the agent would read the "coverage" on it and comment. If all were favorable, the agent would call up one of his friends who owns a publishing company and/or a studio and talk about his hot new "find," Ernest Hemingway. Hemingway's book would be sold to a publisher, with the film rights negotiated at the same time. Possibly, an auction would be held, with the publisher and film company making the highest bid getting the whole pie. Beyond that, a screenwriter from CAA would get attached to "the project," along with a CAA star client like Tom Cruise, a director signed with CAA, and other top clients of the agency. What started out as a novel manuscript would become a "package." CAA would make a percentage from each of their clients, then another percentage from the movie studio for "putting the package together." Roughly, that's what might happen if "Papa" Hemingway came around with a hot new novel these days.

And guess what? The Los Angeles and New York offices of big agencies are often badly coordinated between each other, so you the writer might still have a lot of work to do.

Yes, you say sadly, but you don't live in a major metropolitan area. You don't know a CAA agent. You don't know any successful writers, or even a writer who has an agent. Where does that leave you?

Well, there's the fine book I mentioned earlier, the *Writer's Guide to Book Editors, Publishers, and Literary Agents* by Jeff Herman. Jeff, who has his own agency in New York, put the book together to give writers "fair access to the powers that be." With articles by himself and others, the book not only provides a directory of book publishers, editors, and literary agents in the U.S. and Canada with lengthy and helpful descriptions, it also offers advice on contracts and other aspects of the writing business.

Unfortunately, it doesn't say much about the movie business, but I do, in my *Ultimate Writer's Guide to Hollywood*. The Internet has made selling scripts and books to Hollywood from a remote location much easier than ever before, but sooner or later you might have to spend some time in a place where films are made. Meanwhile, you can also contact the Writers Guild of America (see the chapter on writers' organizations) for their agent list; maybe you can read that list online. If you display any talent at all, you'll probably find an agent who will pay attention. Believe me, though, if you join a writers' organization and mingle a little, the agent you need won't be far away.

Reaching Your Destination

The greatest thing a good agent does for a writer is to listen. John Grisham told *Writer's Digest* magazine that he comes up with fourteen or so plots for books, then flies to New York to visit with his agents. They discuss the various ideas, and the one that the agents and Grisham agree is the best is the one Grisham writes.

As a writer, you need to pay attention to what the market is doing, what people are looking for, but you can't spend the majority of your time doing that. Otherwise, you'd never get any writing done. For an agent, knowing the market is a full-time job. That's one reason you need an agent. Another is to have someone to bounce ideas off of who knows what will likely sell. Sure, I know, you've heard stories, like how Richard Bach was turned down by publisher after publisher before an editor put her job on the line to get *Jonathan Livingston Seagull* published. I tell writing students the story of Jeremy Joe Kronigsberg, who had over fifty producers turn down his script "Every Which Way But Loose" before Clint Eastwood bought it. Jeremy and I were in a film class together; I learned that his wife was in line at the airport one day and struck up a conversation with the lady in front of her. The lady turned out to be Eastwood's secretary. Eastwood was scared to death of filming "Every Which Way," but he took a chance, even though he'd never done a comedy before. Guess what? The film made more money than all Eastwood's earlier films combined.

Stories like that, however, are exceptions. The gods were on Bach and Kronigsberg's side, it seems. They were destined (or just plain determined) to make it.

In the Joseph Campbell "myth structure," the hero of the story always finds a mentor early in his journey to guide him. Obi Wan Kenobi or Yoda in the *Star Wars* movies, for example. You may find a more experienced writer as a mentor for your writing. You will also, if you're smart, find a mentor in the marketing department. That's a good agent. If the relationship lasts, you'll become chums; it's like a marriage, with ups and downs, thrills and spills, and children of a literary sort.

Making Your Way

While you're seeking and finding the right agent, here are some other steps to take, to plot out a successful writing career:

(1) Get your life out of the way while you're writing. Don't let anyone bother you as you write the same time each day, with no distractions.

(2) Find someone who will listen and respond intelligently. This could be a "significant other," an agent, an editor, or all of these. You need someone to bounce things off of.

(3) Until you're very successful, pick a genre and write in that genre. You'll succeed more quickly.

(4) Don't be picky about where you get published, or where you sell, within your own moral limits. Use any success you have to tout your next creation.

(5) Work hard to develop lasting personal contacts and industry information. Join writers' organizations. Take college classes from working writers. Read appropriate publications regularly.

(6) Find common ground. Learn what the public is buying, and why. Try to adjust your own writing to something the public wants while maintaining your own integrity about writing things that you love, too.

(7) Remember that other people have opinions, even if they're wrong. Editors might chop up your work. Movie people might tell you you'll never sell a thing. Take a hint from the rhinoceros, with

regard to your career. Let it all bounce off your thick skin. (I keep a ceramic rhino on my computer to remind me.) Meanwhile, keep adjusting your writing when it makes sense to you. One day, people will stop trying to stick their two cents in. A greatly diminished number of people, anyway. At that point, you'll be "over the hump." You'll be an accomplished writer. But don't fail to stand up for yourself, if someone offers a critique that you don't understand. Get them to explain it. If they can't, or won't, what do they know?

(8) Write your butt (or another part of your body) off. In the end, it will be your body of work that will be admired. The race in writing goes mostly to the prolific.

(9) Promote, promote, promote! Great writers do not live in ivory towers, or seek to. Get whatever equipment, resources, and knowledge necessary to allow you to write a lot more and send out a lot more. Many writers get the job over other writers simply because they are the most persistent, if not the most competent.

(10) If it's working, don't fix it. If you're selling an article a week to your local paper, don't drop that to pursue the Hollywood dream or the American blockbuster novel. Approach your career gradiently. Let each success build on the previous one, as if you're building a stairway of easily negotiated steps.

(11) If you make a big sale, don't get too "rich" overnight. A big paycheck may go a long way, but chances are you put a lot of days and a lot more sweat into creating the product that got you that check. If you get a million-dollar bill for your first screenplay, don't think you'll be getting a payday like that every other month. Your next script might not sell. It might be a decade before you sell another screenplay. Be extravagant and prolific with your writing, but be very conservative with your rewards. It's hard to write when all the money is gone.

(12) Remember the people who got you there, or helped. Which includes me. If my advice helps you, all I ask is that you pass it on to others. Tell them about this book, or what I advised you to do. There is an old Hollywood maxim that you see the same people on the way up as you do on the way down. If you reach the top, you'll discover how rarefied the air is up there. Don't forget "the

little people," those lucky leprechauns of life who helped you when you needed it. Start helping other writers make it, once you've succeeded. Competition? I never worry about it. There's plenty to go around for everyone in the writing business. I've never heard a single person complain, "There's just too damn many great writers!" I have heard them repeatedly ask, "Why aren't there any good writers?!"

If you follow the above dozen hints, by the time you do find an agent who is just right for you, he or she will probably think you are the greatest client they've ever had. Most agents are used to writers with egos the size of Mount Olympus. If you have your outlook on the writing life (and life in general) in order, you'll seem like a gift from Heaven. It's also my opinion that if you are actively pursuing your career in a thoughtful, persistent, and ethical manner you will seemingly stumble across the right personnel to assist your career as if the Angel of Serendipity is your personal guardian.

Speaking of guardian angels, I would have difficulty listing all the fortunate events that aided my literary career. Maybe that's why my first stage play was about a writer who screwed up, only to be rescued by his guardian angel, who was a frustrated apprentice. Viewing my top lucky breaks in retrospect, my being "in the right place at the right time" was mostly due to my dogged, relentless pursuit of my goals. I did not sit back and wait for someone to do it for me, unlike other writers I've known. The most successful writers I've met had a similar approach.

A Career Map

I get my students laughing every time I draw them a graph of what a successful career looks like:

It looks like a side view of a wave, doesn't it? I tell my students that plotting a career is like… OK, go ahead and laugh, but it's like surfing. You have to venture into deep water, way over your head to ride that wave. It's tough, learning to keep your footing, to master your vehicle (your writing, your surfboard) and catch that elusive wave of success. This might seem to be a ridiculous analogy, but allow me the luxury of explanation. When I started out, it seemed my career grew excruciatingly slowly—like that line with the long, slow rise I drew above. Then, when my career began to take off, it seemed to have an almost vertical climb until I reached a crest, a plateau of sorts at a whole new level. That's the top of the wave above. In my case, beginning of the crest of the wave was where I went from scratching by selling magazines articles to when I began selling books, with the crest of the wave being the sale of my You-Solve-It Mystery books for film and television.

Of course, there have been other waves of success in my career. I've ridden them all, with some "wipe-outs" and some happy rides. My point to my students is that they realize that life comes in waves. Unless they create something that provides them the "endless wave" that surfers travel the world trying to find, they'll simply have to start over every time they have a big success. How long each wave lasts depends on how well they do at riding the crest.

Note that my graphic has a curl at the top, like a real wave. There's a chance you might drop off the edge into the trough of the wave, and be tumbled end over end, get caught in the undertow of ego, or even "drowned" by a sudden big success. That's the "don't get too rich" type of thing I discussed earlier.

Some successful writers tend to ride only one wave for their entire career. J. D. Salinger had such a tremendous success with *Catcher in the Rye* at an early age that he seemed to never recover. He wrote *Franny & Zoey* and other works, but none like the international sensation that *Catcher* became. He retired to a New England town and was rarely heard from again. Harper Lee was of a similar mind after *To Kill a Mockingbird*. It's too bad. I feel great writers should write as much as possible, and not let success get to them. Maybe they'll have a great ride next time, maybe they'll wipe out. That's just the ocean of life.

When I taught the class at UCLA Extension Writers' Program on which this book was based, I didn't know about something called the

Elliot Wave then (see www.elliottwave.com if you don't know about it). Sometimes you get a sense of your life and where you're going before you get into the full richness of it. I have since studied this theory extensively and written about how it aligns with not only the structure of great stories, but life itself. If you visit my Web site, www.skippress.com, you'll find a free article there about how it applies to a writing career. I also write more thoroughly about it in the second edition of my *Complete Idiot's Guide to Screenwriting*. In that book, I show the alignment of the five-wave "bear market" of the Elliott Wave with the story structure of successful movies, encompassing Aristotle's *Poetics* principles, Shakespeare's five-act structure, Syd "Screenplay" Field's script paradigm, Joseph Campbell's hero's journey, and some elements that I teach in my screenwriting course.

There is a lot to learn about the waves of life and a writing career, and once you understand some basic principles, it's a much easier ride.

Five Steps to Success

One of the early exercises I give my students—after I tell them all about the value of networking and how to go about it—is a one-year plan to achieve a goal. In a writing career, one year isn't a very long time. Here's what you do:

(a) Define a goal for your writing that you feel can be achieved in one year. We've already talked about writing two pages a day and having a screenplay in two months. Figure out something you can reasonably achieve in a year.

(b) Outline a seven-step plan to reach your goal. Why seven? Because it's a lucky number, or because most people feel comfortable with that number, which isn't as daunting as ten. Seven steps just seems to work, so that's what I use.

(c) Write down a list of ten people who might help further your writing career and your one-year goal, now that you have it clearly defined. Contact them, explain what you're doing, and see what they can do to help. They'll probably be glad to be of assistance, and refer you to other people who can do the same. Learn to prospect. If someone gives you some help but doesn't mention other contacts, or if they can't help you personally, ask for someone they know who might be able to help you. You'll be surprised who your friends know.

(d) When you've completed step (c), take another look at your plan for the next year, and reevaluate where necessary. For example, you might find that someone you know will hire you as a writer. If your seven-step goal was to get hired as a writer, you've already achieved it. Don't just pat yourself on the back; redo your one-year goal so that you keep moving up.

(e) Lastly, write out a short statement of what you want to achieve at a specific point in the future and try to read it out loud to yourself at the same time each day. This is called an "affirmation" and was codified in the works of Orison Swett Marden, the founder of *Success* magazine and the originator of the American self-help movement. I have found that reciting a daily affirmation can have transformative results. For example: "By December 31st (insert year here) I will be a successful author with readers around the globe and regular contracts with publishers who love my writing." It might seem silly at first, but after a while you begin to believe it, and when you believe it, you begin to act it. Then you become it, and you'll find it's as if the world begins to believe you, and it comes about. This is old, old wisdom. After all, the Roman Marcus Aurelius said, "Our life is what our thoughts make it."

Now here's another Hollywood story, and an illustration of why you need to plot out your career. It took me roughly fifteen years to "make it." I didn't always draw up a written plan for myself and actively pursue it. I feel I would have succeeded much faster if I had. I heard Burt Reynolds tell a story once about how he and Clint Eastwood had their contracts terminated at Universal Studios the same day. Supposedly, it took both of them fifteen years to reach the top. Whether that's accurate or not, I've known scores of successful writers and other people in the entertainment business who took well over a decade to reach the success they envisioned. There may be "overnight successes," but most of them lived through a very long night to get where they were going. When I was thirty, someone told me I might not really make it until I was forty. That was a common age for writing success, I was told. I was aghast. I vowed I'd get there quicker, but that person was right. So if you're planning to make it big, get ready to put some years into getting there, and don't worry about it. The rewards will be worth the struggle!

This started off as a chapter about finding an agent, segued to a discussion of surfing, then finished with an overall assessment of how to plan the first year of your career. If you don't think I'm crazy by now, you probably learned something. I know I did. See you on that golden shore.

Chapter Nine

The
Passionate Stage

"**T**HE PLAY'S THE THING!" SHAKESPEARE EXCLAIMED.
"Is the theater really dead?" Paul Simon wondered in a song. He probably felt like it was, after his musical *Capeman* started getting bad reviews after opening on Broadway.

Sorry, I couldn't resist starting a chapter about play writing without quoting the dialogue of the Bard of Avon. And how could I deny the fact that Broadway may not be what it used to be? Personally, I don't think theater will ever die. Why? Look at how coffeehouses proliferated all over the U.S. in the mid-1990s. People love intimate gatherings and shared experiences. Theater provides that. You might own a fifty-inch TV, but do you want to watch the Superbowl or the Academy Awards alone? Not likely. It's my personal belief that, as our electronic society and all-encompassing media grows larger in reach and more available to all, people will feel an increasing need for real, human connection. The kind they get in a theater.

Obviously, the basic writing form for theater is a stage play. Most anyone knows that, but do you know the proper format in which to present your play? I had plays professionally produced and had qualified to become an active member of the Dramatists Guild before I found out about and began using the accepted standard format for stage plays. I learned the proper format from a small booklet published by the Dramatists Guild. It cleverly explained basic information on play writing presented in the standard format of a stage play. There's another example of the benefit of belonging to groups, you see. Since the time I bought that booklet, I've come across numerous references that lay out play format, but the Dramatists Guild reference was the first I ever found. That said, here's how your title page should look:

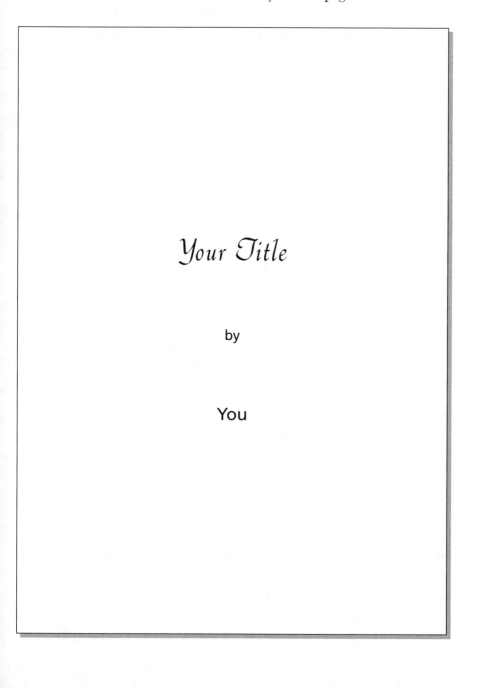

Your Title

by

You

(Note: The title line should be twenty to twenty-four lines from the top, but no one will yell at you or reject your manuscript if it isn't. Basically, it should simply look nice on the page. Most purists specify not using any special type style or font, but I disagree. Something that attracts attention might make your play stand out. Also, there are four lines between each of the lines above, but it won't hurt if you only use two, and don't capitalize the "by" or your name, like so:

Your Title

by

Your Name

At about the fiftieth line or so (again, so long as it looks good):

Your Name

Your Address

Your City, State, Zip

Your Phone

Your Agent's Name,

Address

Phone

Copyright (year) by Your Name
(spell out the word and use
the symbol as well)

Naturally, you'd add your e-mail address if you have one. Remember what I said about an agent pasting his or her label over your address? Most agents don't want anyone directly contacting the people they represent until a deal is made. Your name and information might not even be listed on the title page. More on agents later.

The first page of any script is the most important, because it will often determine whether or not anyone reads any further, or goes on to the next play on the stack. Since many theaters have limited resources with regard to sets, available number of actors, etc., the first page often tells a dramaturge (the person who determines what plays to consider doing) whether your work is feasible to produce. If your setting is "The Follies Bergere, turn-of-the-century France," chances are you'll be out of luck. That's why you see so many plays set in motel rooms, dilapidated lobbies, living rooms, etc. Sets that don't cost much money to put together are highly desirable for most small theater companies. Similarly, a desirable cast list on the front page should not be too lengthy.

SETTING: A MOTEL ROOM IN ANY CITY IN THE MIDWEST.

UPSTAGE WALL, STAGE RIGHT, IS A WOODEN BED WITH A WORN CHENILLE BEDSPREAD THAT SHOULD PROBABLY BE THROWN AWAY. ON EACH SIDE OF THE BED ARE BEATEN-UP NIGHTSTANDS WHICH DON'T MATCH.

ON THE NIGHTSTANDS ARE DILAPIDATED LAMPS WITH RAGGED LAMPSHADES HALF HANGING OFF THEIR BRACKETS.

OVER THE BED IS A FADED POSTER OF MARILYN MONROE, STUCK TO THE PAINTED WALL WITH MISMATCHED PUSHPINS.

UPSTAGE WALL CENTER IS THE MOTEL ROOM DOOR, WHERE A RUSTY HORSESHOE HAS BEEN TACKED IN PLACE OVER THE DOORFRAME.

UPSTAGE LEFT AGAINST THE WALL IS AN OLD TELEVISION ON AN OLD TV STAND. IT LOOKS LIKE IT PROBABLY DOESN'T WORK. THERE IS A CHAIR BY THE TELEVISION. THIS PLACE HAS SEEN BETTER DAYS, AND EVEN THOSE WEREN'T VERY GOOD.

CAST:
CASSIE MILLER .AGE 35, A RARE BEAUTY
JAKE JACKSON . . . . .SOMEWHERE IN HIS 30s
MADGE MILLER . . . . .CASSIE'S MOM, 60s

BOB DOBSON, MOTEL CLERK, IN HIS 20s

DEPUTY JACKSON, JAKE'S COUSIN, IN HIS 20s

TIME:

THE PRESENT

In case you don't know, "upstage" is the rear part of the stage, away from the audience. Downstage is the front half of the stage, near the audience. Stage directions are written from the point of the view of the actor, who normally enters the stage from the rear, or "backstage." If you mean for an actor to move toward what the audience would consider its left and front of the stage, you would write "downstage right."

So that is the first page, which should tell you quite clearly where this play takes place and who is involved. Note that Bob Dobson and Deputy Jackson are not listed in the same manner as the top three characters. That's because they are minor characters. The major characters are listed in their order of importance. The minor characters are listed in their order of appearance. You don't need to make any comments about the characters (like "a rare beauty"), but I do. Again, it's just something to catch the attention of the reader and pique their interest in reading the play. "In his 30s and not sure why" is a humorous commentary, and I've rarely seen humor hurt. You'll have to determine what you want to say. If unsure, leave out any commentary except age.

If the play takes place over different time periods, those times would be listed. For example: MID-60s, LATE 80s, PRESENT.

Note the single-spacing of the script. Play scripts, like film scripts (screenplays) are always written single-spaced. Here's how the body of the play should look

ACT I: LIGHTS UP. JAKE IS STAGE LEFT, LOOKING UP AT THE
          POSTER. MADGE ENTERS, FOLLOWED BY CASSIE, WHO
          QUIETLY SHUTS THE DOOR BEHIND HER. MADGE LIGHTS
          INTO JAKE IMMEDIATELY:

          MADGE
          There he is, daughter of mine! Your dream prince, ensconced
          in his castle!

> JAKE
> (SITTING ON THE BED)
> What was that old song?
> (SINGING)
> "The devil must have sent you here, mother-in-law, mother-in-law…"
> (IMPROVISING LYRICS)
> I think I need a beer, mother-in-law, mother-in…
>
> CASSIE
> Jake, that's really enough! We came here to try and work things out.
>
> MADGE
> Out. What a good word. What a useful word. What an apropos term!
>
> (MADGE GOES OUT THE DOOR, SLAMMING IT BEHIND HER.)
>
> JAKE
> What a relief!
> (PAUSE)
> Cassie, Lassie. Look, I… uh…
>
> DEPUTY JACKSON ENTERS, HAT IN HAND.
>
> DEPUTY
> Howdy, you lovebirds.

And there you have it. It's not a real play, just something I wrote on the spot while composing this chapter, but it does put you right into the conflict that is obviously going on. If you decide to further explore the lives of Cassie, Jake, and Madge, feel free. Might be fun.

A comment on the above. Some of the stage direction (THE PART IN CAPS, LIKE THIS) was enclosed by parentheses. That was the direction for the individual actors. When Jake is SINGING, it's from a real song, which means as a playwright you might have to get an OK from the song's publisher, if you have your character sing more than a certain number of bars. You'll have to investigate the copyright restrictions. When I have Jake

IMPROVISING, he's making up lyrics, but he's still (we assume) singing the same tune. For this reason, if you want to make your life simpler I advise you to use songs that are in the public domain. That means no one owns the copyright on them. "Greensleeves," for example, or any other song you normally see denoted "traditional" when published. Again, make sure you know the legalities of using any song you haven't personally written. The same goes for a poem or a quote from another author.

The stage direction not enclosed in parentheses bears reference to the stage as a whole, such as Deputy Jackson entering the room. Some playwrights, such as David Mamet, don't like to use stage direction. They feel that's the job of the director and/or the actors. I somewhat agree, but it's your call. Some direction is usually essential, particularly if you think your play might be a success, get published as a play, and be sold for years to come. If Madge needs to leave the room, have her leave the room. Other directions, such as Jake sitting on the bed, could be left out. That's the kind of stage direction the director and actors will "play with," anyway. In the plays I've written, three of which I also directed, I used minimal stage direction. There's enough to tell a reader what the characters are doing, but not so much as to intrude upon the creative choices of the other people who will be involved (hopefully) in putting on your play.

Unless it is one-act in structure (usually not much longer than an hour in running time), your play will be divided into two or three acts. The norm these days is a two-act play. At the end of each act, use the following format:

END OF ACT I

At the end of the play (let's say you have a two-act play), use the following format:

END OF ACT II

<u>THE END</u>

That's basically all you need to know about the proper format of a play. I suggest you contact the Dramatists Guild for their booklet on play format. It's a fun read, and you'll probably learn a lot more than I've given you with my simple examples.

For much more detailed information about playwriting format and the medium in general, I recommend www.playwriting101.com, which was created by playwright and screenwriter Jon Dorf. Jon Dorf's plays have been produced in more than twenty-five states and on three continents. He received his B.A. Magna Cum Laude in dramatic writing and literature from Harvard College and his MFA in playwriting from UCLA, where he won the Hal Kanter Comedy Writing Award and the Marty Klein Comedy Writing Award.

The Playwright's Passion

Despite a good bit of experience over a number of years, I don't claim to be an expert on the stage. That's why I've consulted a number of true experts for this chapter. When you write an article, a story, a book, or even a play, you're usually alone. When it comes to the stage and other entertainment mediums, however, if you want to succeed as a writer you'll have to learn about collaboration. That's why, before I got into stage, television, film, and the other writing disciplines in the remainder of this book, I told you first about writing groups. If you're serious about being a playwright, join the Dramatists Guild as an associate member. Start reading their publications. If you live in one of the major metropolitan areas where the Guild holds workshops and meetings (most often in Los Angeles, Chicago, and New York), all the better.

So now that you know the proper format to use for your play, how about the proper content?

That's easy. There is no "proper" content. That's the wonder of the stage. Writing for the stage may not be my best contribution to the culture, but in many ways it is my favorite thing to write. Why? The people. To put words on paper, to feel and express strong emotions and deep philosophies, and then see someone else feel and express them, using your words in perhaps an even more artful manner than you originally envisioned, is a thing of rare beauty. Like Cassie Miller. You'll have to experience this personally to see what I mean. When you write any other form of script, it could be years before you see your work performed. If you do what it takes to get your play staged, though, you'll see your words come to life with a vigor and immediacy that will amaze you and perhaps frighten you tremendously. (The latter, of course, when you see that it doesn't always sound the same in real life as it did in your mind.)

We'll get into working with actors later. Right now, let's discuss how some successful modern playwrights go about their craft, followed by some excerpts from an interview I did with American playwright Tennessee Williams. If I leave out one of your favorite playwrights, sorry. My thanks to all the playwrights I do mention, for sharing their bountiful wisdom, and their words.

Great playwrights fall in love with the stage at an early age. For Peter Shaffer, winner of the 1992 William Inge award for lifetime achievement in the theater, the moment came at age eight, when he "became an addict of the theater and the worshiper of William Shakespeare." In a Liverpool classroom, Shaffer and nineteen other students were transfixed as a teacher told them the details of a "ghost story" which Shaffer later learned was Shakespeare's *Hamlet*. The teacher broke off at three o'clock without finishing the story, and Shaffer was hooked. He was completely enchanted. Years later, after authoring a successful play, he traveled to Morocco and watched raptly as a marketplace storyteller held a crowd transfixed with an enchanted story. These incidents, Shaffer told an audience when he accepted the Inge award, convinced him that narrative is the bedrock of drama. The playwright is, to Shaffer, an enchanter.

In the same issue of the *Dramatists Guild Quarterly* where I read Shaffer's astute comments, Murray Schisgal said that play writing is a "programmed outpouring of [one's] total self." I've found both men's comments to hold true. Remember what I mentioned earlier about "why is this tale special?" With a play, you allow an audience an intimate view of a unique world. You want them to be enchanted enough to at least sit through the performance. More likely, you want them to be charged with enthusiasm after seeing the play, so much so that they spread the word about your ideas like an unstoppable prairie fire.

To engender that type of emotion, wouldn't it seem likely that you would need to be as honest as possible, to hold nothing back in your writing, to outpour your total self as Schisgal suggests?

David Mamet reported in a *Playboy* magazine interview that audiences who first saw his play *Oleanna*, which is about sexual harassment, had very highly charged emotional responses. Some stood up and said, "Bullshit!" Others applauded vigorously, but most all left the theater talking incessantly about what they had just seen. This says one thing: When you write a play, it had better be about something that means a great deal to you. Even if it's a "light comedy," if you are compelled by what you are writing, the chances of an audience doing likewise are much greater. Just as you try to keep them turning the pages when writing a book, in a play you try to keep them in their seats, with their emotions and intellect constantly stimulated by the events on stage.

In the time of Shakespeare, the demands of the audience were high. The best seats were in the balconies of the Globe Theatre, not on the floor level. There was no front row, only a bare space where the "groundlings" watched the stage. These were the "cheap seats," only there were no seats. The groundlings sat on the ground; think of those who frequent TV wrestling matches and supermarket checkout line tabloids and you'll get an idea of the groundlings. They were hard-working people who wanted rigorous entertainment, and the stout ale they drank loosened their emotional responses to the action. Thus, Shakespeare literally wrote to audiences on several levels with his plays. He offers sword fights and bloodletting galore, as well as tricks of language for the intellectuals.

The Bard of Avon obviously wrote from deep emotion and strong philosophical exploration. He was trying to entertain, certainly, but he was also urging people to examine life, to consider how life might be bettered. In addition, he was faced with a unique problem. He wanted to comment on the structure of society as a whole, starting at the top. In a day when beheadings were still common, it wasn't sensible to write too intimately about then-current English royalty. After all, Shakespeare started out as an actor with the Lord Chamberlain's Men, and had access to the court. So, he did something very clever. He studied the history of royals, and created characters based on them, with themes that had bearing on his own times. The groundlings were fascinated to see "how the royals lived," while the royals were fascinated by their own "history."

Of course, Shakespeare had many influences other than English kings, but you get the idea. His work aroused great commentary in his time, because it dealt with deeply felt (and argued) passions.

In our day, work for the stage is divided, roughly at least, into three categories: (1) entertainment; (2) important work; (3) experimental. Any given piece might be all three, like Tony Kushner's *Angels in America*. It's open to individual interpretation. Will Neil Simon's *Broadway Bound* one

day be viewed with the same reverence as Shakespeare's *As You Like It?*
It's possible, even if it seems unlikely from our current perspective. At this
juncture, I would generally classify Simon's body of work as entertainment
first and important second. It is certainly not experimental—a category in
which you would find "performance art" and other such public offerings.
Who cares? It's funny as hell, and a fine comment on the human condition.

So what is "important work"? By that I mean any play that gets people
thinking, and perhaps doing something, about an important public issue.
Marsha Norman's award-winning *'night, Mother* was about suicide. Did
the number of suicides decrease after the success of Norman's play? No,
but it got people thinking about why anyone would commit suicide. Did
Kushner's *Angels in America* inspire a cure for AIDS? Not as of this writing,
but it painted a more sympathetic face on the plight of people dying from
the deadly disease.

To me, the stage is a place where we come to try and better understand
community—that is, ourselves and our relations with each other. From the
days of the Greeks who influenced Shakespeare up to the present day, this
has always been so. David Mamet, author of *Glengarry Glen Ross* and other
noted works, disagrees somewhat. He says that the "purpose of literature
is not to do good, but to delight us." Mamet also believes, however, that a
good play creates in the viewer a "new, happy understanding of the world."
He likes to quote Stanislavsky, who said that the theater brings to the stage
the life of the human soul.

Like Peter Shaffer, Mamet became fascinated with the theater at an
early age. He was a child actor, but it wasn't until he was fourteen, when
he discovered the works of Samuel Beckett and Harold Pinter, that he
got his "wake up call" and became enamored with writing. By the time
he was twenty-seven, his *American Buffalo* was on Broadway. Still, the gap
between fourteen and twenty-seven is a long time, which might explain
why Mamet feels that persistence is the only sure route to success.

The same holds true for Wendy Wasserstein, author of *The Sisters
Rosenzweig* and other fine plays. Once she saw her first Broadway play, at
age eight, she was forever hooked. Persistence must be her middle name,
because she never gives up on a project. *The Heidi Chronicles* took eight
years to finish, and she doesn't even show her work to anyone (and then
only to her husband) until she's done "eight or nine drafts." Edward Albee,

author of *The Zoo Story* and numerous fine works, admits to a similar amount of drafts, but most of them are "in his head." He basically uses the first draft he commits to paper.

The Actor's Passion

So what goes in your drafts? Well, Horton Foote says each character has to want something. David Mamet goes further, saying no one ever speaks unless they want something. Actors call this "motivation." Actors and even directors will, in fact, drive you crazy at times trying to get you to explain character motivation. John Guare, author of *Six Degrees of Separation* and other famous plays, turns the tables a bit. When auditioning a director for a new play, he asks the director to tell him the story of the play. The director who can do that with an understanding most like Guare's own gets the job.

The great thing about play writing—and hopefully it will never change—is that in the theater the writer is given the ultimate power of decision. Playwrights are respected. If they say a line stays, it stays. The director is never—as opposed to film—seen as the "author" of a stage production. When the audience cries "Author!" it is the playwright who comes out and takes a bow. Remember that. When you write a play and it gets to the point where it's being read aloud in your presence by real, live people, you maintain the ultimate authority. If it doesn't sound right, you can change it. Just remember the rule Stephen King uses: If ten people make the same comment, maybe it needs to be changed; if ten people all make dissimilar comments, leave it alone.

Similarly, your influences as a playwright may differ from other writers you encounter. You may enjoy Sam Shepard's *Buried Child*, while others will think it's the sickest thing they ever saw put on a stage. Horton Foote advises that you learn from all sources, then "find what best serves you in your material."

There is a term in the theater called "chewing the scenery." That refers to an actor given free rein to emote wildly, even out of control. Too often, acting to many thespians means loudly expressing anger or rage. That is not acting, but chewing the scenery. Even when Marlon Brando yelled "Stella!" in *A Streetcar Named Desire*, there was still something held in reserve, something on his mind. Otherwise, everything that was on his mind would have come pouring out of his mouth.

Which, of course, brings us around to Tennessee Williams. I've already told you how I met Mr. Williams. Now let me share with you some comments he had on writing for the stage, as featured in my article for *Black Mountain Review*. Williams revealed to me that he thought any beginning writer should write about material that was "most organic, most emotional" to that individual. He said he wrote "just about what I am emotionally concerned with." He was also glad for his Southern upbringing, because of the "rich and protean" background of life in the region of the Southern United States.

"I have more sensibility than intellectual power," Williams told me. "I don't like cerebrating over things, you know, thinking them out. I like to function from intuition and inspiration."

Williams once remarked that he tried very hard to "not only attract observers but participants" in the performance of his plays. To effect this, he had to be himself deeply emotionally involved in his characters and situations. How deep? Here's the best example I found—when I asked him if his most famous character, Blanche DuBois in *A Streetcar Named Desire* was based on a girl he'd been fond of in his teen years, he laughed. No, he told me, the lady who utters the line about always depending on the kindness of strangers was actually "closest to a self-portrait."

"It's like Flaubert's *Madame Bovary*, you know? He was a funny little fat man, and somebody said 'M'sieur Flaubert, who was Madame Bovary?' He said Madame Bovary! C'est moi! [It's me!]"

So let your emotions run deep. It's worked since the time of the Greeks, and will work on the stage into infinity. If you don't believe that, read *Oedipus Rex* by Sophocles. You know, that little tale about a boy separated from his family who grows up to become a great warrior who kills his father and marries his mother, then blinds himself when he finds out what he's done. That should stir your emotions, whether you like the brew or not. If comedy is your ticket, then study *Lysistrata* by Aristophanes. It's a fine plot, about a sex strike by the women of Greece, designed to get their husbands to make peace, not war.

Like I said, strong emotions have always been the stuff of the stage.

The Group Passion

Another common denominator that you will find among many successful playwrights—other than their early passion for theater—is that at some point in their careers they become heavily involved on an ongoing basis with a theater group. David Mamet began as an actor and director before turning to writing plays, and even then it was mainly because his company couldn't afford to pay the licensing fee to use plays from other authors. For Horton Foote, the formative group was the American Actors Theatre. John Guare's first big break came when he got the job as assistant to the manager of the National Theatre, a post which actor Warren Beatty had just abandoned. Wendy Wasserstein held readings of her plays with the Seattle Repertory Company. For Eugene O'Neill, the first American playwright to win the Nobel Prize for literature (1936), his early group was the Provincetown Players. French playwright Molière (real name Jean-Baptiste Poquelin) worked with the Illustre Theatre in much the same way Shakespeare worked with the actors at the Globe in London.

If you can become involved with a group of actors on an ongoing basis, learning all the aspects of the theater and participating in the group effort, you'll stand a much better chance of having great success as a playwright. If there's no group near where you live, and you are passionate about play-writing success, either move to a major metropolitan center or start a group of your own. Regional theater has enjoyed a renaissance in recent decades, and New York's Broadway is not the ultimate end-goal it once was.

To further illustrate the importance of how a group can impact the theater, consider the Group Theater in New York. At one time, actors training under Lee Strasberg—people like Marilyn Monroe, Marlon Brando, Geraldine Page, Rip Torn, Paul Newman, Rod Steiger—could listen to Arthur Miller, Clifford Odets, and Tennessee Williams discuss the play process on a weekly basis. My late actor friend Manu Topou, whom I considered to be the finest acting coach in America, was there during those days. He was personally trained by Strasberg, in fact, to pass on the knowledge of the acting profession the master had acquired. Knowing that Manu has often starred on Broadway (Black Elk in the original *Black Elk Speaks*, for example), I was always fascinated listening to him discuss the Group Theater days.

"There was always an irony to the work," Manu told me once, "and a built-in internal combustion taking place, a dramatic explosion from within. Everything, everyone there, was concerned with social issues, and the impact of our work. We talked about issues of repairing damage in society, the worth of labor based on sex. It was wonderful, all-around training for writers and actors, and we were consumed with the new drama of a changing world."

Ah, passion. Such people, such passion. I hope you find such passion and such people, and put emotions as deep as the people mentioned here have put into their work. Just don't forget that the word *drama* is derived from the Greek verb *dran*, meaning "to act" or "to do." In writing your plays, keep in mind the need to make things *happen* onstage. A good play does not consist of some people standing around merely talking. A great play is a true wonder, filled with happenings, and it's not easy to bring a great play about.

Composer Stephen Sondheim, who has had no small success on Broadway, thinks playwriting is the most difficult creative discipline. Sondheim, like most great geniuses of the stage, is inspired by the natural music that comes from the rhythm of the speech of the common people, in all languages. Whether you write for the groundlings or the people in the balcony (or hopefully, them all), I implore you to listen long to the music of life, and write passionately of the melodies, harmonies, and even discord of your world.

Hope I see you—or your words—on a major stage soon.

Chapter Ten

Screenplay
Savoir-Faire

SAVOIR-FAIRE IS A FRENCH WORD WHICH LITERALLY MEANS "knowing what to do." Hollywood is a place where anything is possible, when it comes to writing, but not many people truly know what to do. Chances are good that no ten so-called script experts would be able to agree on what scripts should be made and what scripts should not be made. This isn't merely my opinion. In the 1970s, screenwriter William Goldman was viewed as the dean of all screenwriters, thanks to his script "Chinatown," which many thought to be the perfect screenplay. In his book *Adventures in the Screen Trade*, Goldman offered one maxim of advice for dealing with Hollywood. "Nobody knows anything," he said.

This brings to mind my favorite Hollywood script story, which is probably a myth. In 1941, director and screenwriter John Huston made a film out of the Dashiell Hammett novel *The Maltese Falcon* with actor Humphrey Bogart in the lead role. The story goes that Huston was going on vacation and didn't have time to write the script for the film. So he handed the book to his secretary and told her to "turn it into a script." Supposedly, she did and that's what they filmed. Since the movie is word-for-word and scene-for-scene virtually the same as the original novel, it has a chance of being true. One caveat is that the Shakespeare reference that is Bogart's last line in the film—"That's the stuff that dreams are made of."— was suggested by Bogart. Since Huston thoroughly storyboarded the film (drew the scenes out like cartoons) before shooting, however, he might have not been as capricious as the rumor suggests. Still, stranger things have happened and will continue to happen in Tinseltown.

I began making money in the film industry shortly after I forayed into it. After winning a substantial amount of money on a game show in 1977, I was able to "retire" for a short time to pursue my writing dreams. I wrote the novel I always wanted to write (which I still haven't rewritten to my satisfaction). I also learned the rudiments of writing for the screen. The first story I wrote for film was "optioned," which is to say I received a small amount of money, with the full price to be paid if the budget to make the film was raised by the people who "optioned" my story. You've probably heard the term *option* before. It merely means someone buys, or talks you into giving them for free, an option to purchase a script within a given time period. These days, that option period is at least a year and more often, eighteen months, with an option to renew for a similar period of time for the same financial terms. In the film business, the usual option is ten percent of the final purchase price, which is generally paid to the writer on the first day of filming. That's when they're paying you, however. When they don't want to pay you, or claim they can't, they want the option for free. In most "free" cases, you should tell them to take a hike and hope they find money on the trail; if they do, they should come back to you and get serious. I never saw the rest of the riches I envisioned because the film budget never got raised. This is probably good, because Hollywood success at an early age might have gone to my head, and I could have ended up burned-out at thirty. In any event, I continued making money for film stories and scripts for over a decade before receiving the full price for a screenplay. And guess what? My first story sale still hasn't been made into a film, or even a script. This isn't very unusual at all. The screenwriting duo of Cash & Epps ("Top Gun" and other blockbusters) made a large living for a long time writing scripts for studios before one of their scripts finally got made. So why does this kind of thing happen so often in Hollywood? Because nobody knows anything.

What does that mean? Basically, no one has ever devised a surefire formula for gauging public taste in films. An added burden is the fact that the majority of film studio executives these days do not come from creative backgrounds. They are lawyers, accountants, and agents who worked their way up. Or wormed their way in, however you choose to look at it. Many of them are creative only in figuring out ways to get as much money as possible into their own off-shore bank accounts. Scripts that film executives think are terrible one month might be the hottest things in town the next month. These execs commune with each other, trying to guess what the other is doing. They "copycat" each other's moves. They jockey for the best table at the best restaurants. Their underlings want their jobs, and make a practice of saying *yes* to the bosses and *no* to creative types. Hollywood is a corporate atmosphere that is to a large degree death on creativity. When you're a film executive getting a nice six-figure salary, it's much safer to say *no* and not take a chance. Saying *yes* might mean you authorize spending $100 million to make a box-office flop. You might bankrupt your studio. Accordingly, film executives tend to hedge their bets and play it safe. They try to "package" film with scripts from writers who have written other hits, directors who have won awards, and stars the public is likely to come see in any film at all. This makes agents at large agencies—which champion various talents from all areas of filmmaking—some of the most powerful people in town.

To understand all this, and write to sell in this kind of atmosphere, you have to try to understand Hollywood. Lord knows I've tried. It is very important that you try to understand how Hollywood works, if you have any desire whatsoever to succeed as a screenwriter. It took me a long time to figure this out, even though I literally lived in Hollywood for years. Of course, I was in love with the image of the town, not the reality of it. When I fell out of love with the image and faced the reality, I finally began to actively get somewhere.

Books Are Where the Real Money Is

I tell my writing students to forget about writing screenplays, unless they're just eaten up with the desire to make films. Not be screenwriters—make films. If a student has a good story, I advise them to write a book first, get it published, and sell it to Hollywood, and then get a job writing the screenplay. Why? Two reasons: (1) they'll make money three times with a book; and (2) Hollywood filmmakers, though they might vociferously disagree with me, still consider films to be a secondary medium, after "serious" writing like books and plays. Let me give you an example.

In 1983, I wrote a screenplay with Michael Sean Conley called "Fair Game." It was a great story (if I must say so, and I must) about modern piracy in the Caribbean. The first producer team we showed it to immediately optioned the script. They didn't get it made on their first attempt, but they kept at it. When one "option" ran out (we gave them exclusive rights to the script for a year), they picked up another option. In all, Ron Hamady and George Braunstein had three options on "Fair Game." Mike and I made the full price of the script, but still owned it. In 1994, we sold the script to another production company, who had the money in the bank to make the movie.

After that sale, we ended up making—considering all the options and the sale—twice as much as the Writers Guild basic screenplay rate. Not bad, but not as good as a book. In contrast, my You-Solve-It Mystery novels brought me a small advance for each of the first three books, but a nice chunk of change nonetheless. When I later sold the books for film and television, I got money for the book rights, and was hired to write scripts. Which means I made money on those stories three times: (a) book sale; (b) book rights sale; (c) scripts.

See why you should write a book if you have a good story? And let's say you have a story that is good for the video game market. You might make additional money for "electronic rights" which encompasses video games and electronic books and other such computer age items. You can't do that as easily with a mere screenplay.

On the other hand, if you write a great screenplay, you could be set financially for the rest of your life. You could enter a world of amazing money and amazing frustration to match. You might be able to direct the filming of your next screenplay. If you're one of those people convinced that writing scripts is the way to go, let's take a trip to Hollywood.

From Script to Screen

Let's say you get lucky. Let's say you write your first screenplay, find someone who will buy it, and it's so brilliant someone puts up several million dollars to bring it to the silver screen. Here's what will most likely happen then:

(1) You sign a contract that, hopefully, gives you the chance to write any revisions that are made to the script;

(2) Your first rewrite is not very much enjoyed;

(3) Another writer comes on board;

(4) After the producer, director, and studio executives are satisfied they have a script that they can live with;

(5) The director creates his or her "shooting script";

(6) Actors are cast, locations are found, a detailed production and shooting schedule is drawn up—in short, "pre-production" is done;

(7) The film is shot, hopefully on schedule;

(8) The film is edited, special effects are added, sound is "mixed" and the score (music) is added;

(9) A "rough cut" is shown to all who have an interest in making money from the film;

(10) The film is exhibited in theaters, then on television, then goes out on video. It might go "straight to video." Got the idea? A large number of people are involved in getting your story from script to screen. Film is the most heavily collaborative medium that exists. That's why selling a script is akin to creating the blue-print for a multimillion dollar skyscraper, which is also built within a corporate atmosphere.

Naturally, there are low-budget and very low-budget films that are made for what seems like little or no money by Hollywood standards. 1994's *El Mariachi* for $35,000, for example. These exceptions are made by skilled filmmakers, however. Unless you are willing to make the commitment to not only write a script, but do whatever is necessary to get that script on film, forget those examples. Besides, if you're that kind of person, chances are good you won't be reading this book, anyway.

From Story to Synopsis

There is a very basic difference in a screenplay and a novel. Almost all screenplays are written in the present tense, while most books are written in the past tense. Why? Perhaps it comes from the natural transition of the stage directions for stage plays to plays written for the screen. The first screenwriters, by the way, were called "scenarists." Some were playwrights, but most were not. They wrote action sequences, since films were silent and there was no dialogue to be heard at the movies. They simply had to write coherently.

On the other hand, using the present tense makes a kind of sense because movies primarily deal with the immediate culture. Filmmakers strive to disseminate to the broad world the happenings of smaller portions of the world. A dance form might have been around for years in a region, but when it is popularized in a hit film it can become the hottest thing in the world for a time. Books can do the same thing, but not with the same sense of immediacy that belongs to film. I was first truly convinced of the world impact of films when an acquaintance of mine, a filmmaker from Tunisia, told me a story. He was in the heart of Africa, in tribal country with only rudimentary structures for hundreds of miles around, when he stepped into a mud hut and saw the famous *Saturday Night Fever* movie poster of John Travolta in a disco pose. He was dumbfounded. I can think of no better example of the enormous reach of films; it's no wonder that the annual Academy Awards ceremony is one of the most-watched (and longest) television events of the year.

You don't have to be able to read to watch a movie. You don't even have to speak the language used in the film to understand it. You usually watch a movie straight through. You don't set it aside to be continued later as you do with a book on a nightstand. A movie is immediate, a "witness this now" type of event. That's why it seems appropriate that scripts are written in the present tense. The most notable exception I ever saw to this rule was the script for "The Wind and the Lion" by John Milius, which remains my favorite screenplay. It was written in past tense, with the description reading like a novel. The subject of the film was a turn-of-the-century story, however, so past tense seemed right.

Before you try to get too clever with a script, however, I suggest you get competent. Milius is a very skilled screenwriter and was able to make the example I give work. When you write your first script, unless you have a very good reason for doing something different, use the present tense in your description of the action.

Here's the next thing you need to remember about films. They are "moving pictures." Although you might remember and repeat great bits of film dialogue for years, films are primarily an action medium. As a playwright, it took me a long time to really get this point. I was in love with dialogue. As a result, my early screenplays were filled with pages of people talking to each other. "Talking heads," it's called in the business. The person who got me out of this was Edward Hunt, a writer/director who had done ten feature films by the time we met. Ed and I collaborated on three feature film scripts, and by the time we finished the first one I was convinced of the need to keep things moving and cut down on the dialogue. All my writing improved as a result.

When Harry Cohn ran Columbia Studios during its heyday, he was famous for the "butt twitch" method of determining whether or not he liked a film. If he shifted in his seat too many times—if his butt twitched too much—he felt that audiences would do the same, and the film was boring, no good, or needed more work. If you think Cohn was a yesteryear version of grumpy music judge Simon Cowell on TV's *American Idol*, try Cohn's method yourself. When you write a script, think of what it would look like if you were sitting in a theater watching it. As a good index of what I mean, you should know that most screenplay scenes are no longer than three pages. Since one single-spaced screenplay page averages out to one minute of onscreen time, that means few film scenes are longer than three minutes. Some scenes are much shorter, and as more filmmakers graduate from the ranks of music video makers, very short scenes become more normal.

So try and keep your characters doing something, not just talking, and have them do it in three minutes or less whenever possible.

Wesley Strick, the writer of several hit films including *The Glass House*, uses a simple method of constructing a film story line. He writes a short description of each scene on a Post-It. The Post-Its are then placed on a blank wall in sequence. If he wants to move the order of a scene, he merely pulls it off the wall and sticks it in another place, adjusting the other Post-Its. Other writers use a similar method, shuffling index cards, but I like Strick's method. Forty Post-Its at three minutes each equals 120 minutes of screen time. You can "see" the entire film in front of you, in sequence. Remember, 120 minutes is just an index. Some films are only ninety minutes long. The more action you have in a film, the shorter your script will likely be.

So let's say you have a story you want to turn into a script. You know you should keep your scenes down to three minutes or less, and you have a supply of forty Post-Its. Now what? The next step is figuring out the beginning, middle, and end. Film scripts roughly follow a three-act structure. Syd Field, whose show business career began as a reader of scripts, was for many years the resident "authority" on scripts, thanks to his book *Screenplay*. Was Field an expert due to hit scripts he'd written? No, he had simply read a lot of screenplays and noticed a pattern. He wrote that pattern down in book form. He proposed that the turning points of a 120-page script were at the thirty-minute, sixty-minute and ninety-minute marks. The thirty-minute mark was the end of the first act. The ninety-minute mark was the end of the second act, and the sixty-minute mark was the crucial turning point of the story. He noted that Steven Spielberg, the most financially successful filmmaker of the last two decades, had an extended third act in his films. Field called his outline of structure a "paradigm," using the definition of an example serving as a pattern.

Of course, these days most scripts average 110 to 115 pages, and Aristotle's *Poetics* was the model from which Field drew his theory, but the point is that Hollywood formulas exist.

Before Field penned his observations, Lajos Egri had been the resident "guru" for Hollywood writers. In Egri's *The Art of Dramatic Writing* he stated that a play should deal with premise, character, and conflict. He emphasized characters in constant change working out their own destinies. Then came the influence of the works of Joseph Campbell, who wrote *The Hero with a Thousand Faces*. John Truby, another screenwriting teacher, breaks Campbell's findings down into almost thirty steps that should go into a script. The most well-known screenwriting seminar-meister, Robert McKee, draws from Campbell. And if you want to get a great dissection of Campbell's story matrix by someone who has worked in Hollywood, read Christopher Vogler's *The Writer's Journey*.

I do not intend to break down the works of any of these men for you any further than I already have. There are a myriad number of books available on screenwriting, and screenwriting teachers who tour all the major cities of the country. There are correspondence courses available, and most likely courses at your local college. It could be my own course, which has innovations none of the teachers above figured out. See www.screenwritingcourse.com to see if one of the almost 1,000 schools that offer my course is near you.

No one's theories or observations change this fact: A good story is a good story. Syd Field studied successful scripts and noticed a pattern. Lajos Egri studied great writing and wrote down his observations. Joseph Campbell studied the great stories, myths, and religions of Earth and noticed a pattern. Scores of people have studied Campbell and made a nice living out of passing on their findings. None of the people mentioned, however, ever made a living writing screenplays. I have, but certainly not always. All you should worry about is whether or not you can write a great story. If you can, you can learn to write a great screenplay of that story.

Where does your screen story begin? With an event. By that I mean an action, a turning point that impels the main character or characters toward a great change from which there is no return. The protagonist will be forced to leave their "normal world" and struggle in a "new world" that is unfamiliar and difficult, even if the action takes place in the same geographical area where the movie started.

In the middle of the first act, and there will be foreshadowing prior to this event, something arrives that I call the "Shaping Force." This can be an object like *The Maltese Falcon* that everyone wants. It can be a villain who must be dealt with conclusively like Darth Vader in the original *Star Wars*. It can be a natural object like a meteor that might destroy Earth as in *Deep Impact*. It can be a concept like Time in the movie *Cast Away*. Look in successful major movies and you will find this, and you will not be constrained by form like the Campbell matrix. I discovered this when developing my course entitled "Your Screenwriting Career."

Next, what is the middle of the story? The sequence of events that puts the main character(s) in some sort of peril or conflict that must be resolved. As they struggle to find their way and figure out how to win the battle in their "new world" they will reach a crisis point that might involve a "leap of faith" or death-defying act that will transform them and/or their efforts. The clearest example I know of this is when Tom Hanks knocks out his abscessed tooth in the middle of *Cast Away*. If he does not do this, he will die from infection on his deserted island. When he recovers, he transforms himself and becomes master of his fate—but only on the island.

So then we come to the end of the second act and what I call the "deepest dilemma." It's a "how's she going to get herself out of this one" type of situation. This is done in the third act, generally by the protagonist solving his or her own basic inner conflict presented in the movie *first*, and then being able to focus enough to win the outer conflict, such as getting over the reef in *Cast Away* and back to the open sea and civilization.

What was Tom Hanks's inner conflict in that movie? We learn about it when he needs more rope for his raft and gets it from the top of the island's tall peak, where he was going to hang himself at one point. (It's a shocking and very realistic scene when we see him retrieve that rope and realize what he's been through.)

This brings us to the end, the emotionally stirring resolution of the conflict. And at the tail end, often something called a denouement (or in television, a "tag") that is often comedic and allows us to more easily mentally separate ourselves from this story in which we have been absorbed. It's basically that simple, and I discuss it in detail in my *Complete Idiot's Guide to Screenwriting*, now in its second edition.

Why do you go to the movies? To be entertained, primarily. One Hollywood studio boss was reported to observe that "If you want to send a message, use Western Union." Whether it's a horror film that scares you to death, a love story that makes you cry, a comedy that makes you laugh, or an action film that leaves you breathless, most people go to the movies with the primary purpose of having their emotions roused.

So, when crafting your movie story, ask this question: "Will anyone really care about this but me?"

If the answer is probably not, maybe you'd better pick another story. On the other hand, if you are so compelled by the story that you will do anything to put that story on film whether anyone else cares or not, you probably should pursue it. You might find there are a lot more people out there than you think who will care about your story. Given all the hurdles necessary to write a script, sell it, and get it filmed, only those passionate about a script ever get it made. I advise you to be completely passionate about any screenplay you write. Director Richard Donner (the *Lethal Weapon* films and other hits) told me that the main determining factor of whether he wants to make a movie is if he reads a script and wants to see the film. With a story you're passionate about, it shouldn't be too difficult figuring out a beginning, middle, and end. In figuring out the beginning of the story, remember what I told you earlier about Steve Allen's comment on "where does this story really begin?" The middle is where the great transformation takes place—hence Syd Field's observation that it is twice as long as the other turning points, and the fact that the middle portion had its own midway turning point.

With the primary portions of your story determined, get out your supply of thirty to forty Post-Its (or index cards) and figure out the sequences. Remember, each scene should lead to the other. There should be no sudden jumps that go unexplained. Think of what it would look like to you, sitting in a theater. Write down a paragraph that describes what happens in each scene. Once that is done, you'll have what is called a "step outline," which can then become a polished story.

Producer Joel Silver, known for his ability to turn out action hits, believes there should be a big explosion and/or breathtaking action sequence every ten minutes of a film. It's also a commonly held belief in Hollywood that at least five times during the film there should be some major piece of action. Naturally, they should be spaced evenly through the script. If you want to write action, study action films.

Once you've figured out your story, you may want to go on to a treatment. You may have heard this term. Don't get it confused with a synopsis. A synopsis can be one page, three, or five. A step outline shows, scene by scene, the entire action sequence of a film story. A true film treatment is a step outline expanded. It could be upwards of half the length of a script, with bits of important dialogue added in various places to flesh out the scenes for the reader. A synopsis describes a film. A step outline provides the sequences, while a treatment allows the reader to basically see the film mentally, minus most of the dialogue.

In trying to get someone to read your script, you might be asked to tell him or her the "high concept" or "logline." They both roughly mean, "What's it about, in twenty-five words or less?" (A "high concept" is a bit more focused and commercial, such as "Prince Charming is discovered to be wooing Sleeping Beauty, Cinderella, and Snow White all at the same time." That was a pitch sold by Hollywood pitch king Robert Kosberg.) You might combine two hit films to describe your story. For example, you might describe a script about a frontier widower coming to a city to meet a mail-order bride who turns out to be a Native American as *Sleepless in Seattle* meets *Dances With Wolves.*

From Step Outline to Script

You'll probably need to do a good deal of studying to learn to write a great screenplay. With some scripts selling for a million dollars or more, the stakes are high, and the competition is voluminous if not fierce. Given that admonishment, here's your next rule: Make your script as perfect as possible and you'll greatly increase your chances of success. When I first met producer Ron Hamady, he told me of some successful writers he knew who spent a year and a half perfecting the first script they ever wrote, before they showed it to anyone. In my youthful vigor to make it big as quickly as possible, eighteen months seemed like a lifetime. I couldn't imagine spending that much time on one script. After all, hadn't Mike Conley and I written "Fair Game" (the script Ron and his partner optioned) in only three months? I should have listened; it took me years to learn the wisdom of Ron's advice. Ron told me that, although the writers he mentioned had never had their first script actually made into a film, the script got them one writing job after another. It was one of the finest "spec" scripts he had ever written.

You'll hear that term a lot in Hollywood. A "spec" script is one written speculatively. You write it without commission or pay, hoping someone will buy it, or merely to show what you can do as a screenwriter. Your first screenplay, unless you're very lucky or your Uncle Joe runs a studio or plans to finance the making of your movie, will most likely be a spec script.

What elements go into a script? The same elements of any good story. Read the screenwriting books I mentioned earlier. I've given you some other basics, but that's all I have room for in this book. Meanwhile, here's the basic screenplay format:

FADE IN:

EXT. YOUR HOUSE - NIGHT

A small bland house in suburbia, distinguished only by a light in a corner window. We hear the sounds of a late night radio talk show.

TALK SHOW HOST (ON RADIO)

And that's my opinion whether you like it or not!

INT. SMALL HOME OFFICE - NIGHT

Your office. Sitting at a desk cluttered with papers and bills is YOU, red-faced, on the phone, talking to the talk show host. A computer sits in front of you. Near it is the radio, the volume turned down.

> YOU
> You opinionated jerk! You can't treat me this way!

> TALK SHOW HOST (ON RADIO)
> Oh, yeah!? Watch me!

We hear a DIAL TONE. The talk show isn't off the air, but you are. You slam the phone down in disgust and turn up the radio. The host DRONES ON, congratulating himself on the air.

> YOU
> I could do better than that. I really could.

(Note: This is feature film script format, not a script for any form of television show. It is also a "master scene" script, which is to say it only describes the scene and dialogue, and not things like camera angles and special effects, which are the domain of the director and other specialists.)

Let's examine the various components. "FADE IN" merely means that you gradually focus in on the scene. Not every script has FADE IN at the beginning, but it is generally the accepted form to use, so I'd advise using it. "EXT." means "exterior." The first shot in a screenplay is the "establishing shot," but you don't need to say that. Just know that the first shot should orientate the reader and give an idea of where we are. Each time you move to a new location, you should try to help the reader in that way. Some screenwriters use "CUT TO" to separate scenes. This means that we switch from one scene to another quickly, as if the film has been cut with scissors. Most screenwriters don't use CUT TO at all, but simply begin the next scene.

Speaking of which, the next scene above begins with an "INT." which naturally means "interior." It could be EXT. if it was another outdoor scene, but I chose an indoor one that moved in closer on the location of my first shot. After we know whether we're outdoors or indoors, we tell the reader IN CAPS where the action is taking place: "YOUR HOUSE" and "SMALL HOME OFFICE." Then after a dash (-) we say whether it's DAY or NIGHT.

The first time we see a character onscreen, his or her name is CAPITALIZED. After that, it is not capitalized. BOB becomes Bob (as long as he's the only Bob) thereafter.

When we hear someone talking but don't see them onscreen, that is noted to the side of their name such as (ON RADIO) above. You might also use (O.S.), which means "off-screen" and means the character is in the location where the scene takes place but not seen by the camera. V.O. for "voice-over" is used when the character speaking is *not* present in the location or within hearing distance of the other characters in the scene. If you have some direction for the actor, such as "whispering" that would be given this way:

> YOU
> (WHISPERING)
> You jerk, I'm losing my voice arguing with you!

Remember what I told you in the stage play chapter about leaving off stage directions? In screenplays, less is more. Try not to use voice inflections like (whispering) unless absolutely necessary. In Hollywood slang they are called "wrylies" because amateurs often write (wryly) under some statement by a character.

Unless it is imperative for the scene, leave off directions for actors. Similarly, don't get fuzzy and cute by adding "WIDE SHOT" or similar camera directions in your script. That is the director's job, and many of them take offense if you attempt to tell them where the camera should be. Unless it's imperative that you do so to illustrate a point, leave off camera directions.

Back to FADE IN. Let's say the director might not want to fade in. He might want the action to begin immediately. Bam! There's the scene. Similarly, at the last scene of a script many writers add the following:

FADE OUT.

Should you? Might as well, since it's generally accepted. But if you're ever in doubt about what to put in or leave out of a script, remember the K.I.S.S. rule: "Keep It Simple, Stupid." You'll be better off.

Lastly, you should use CAPS when you describe a sound, special effect (like an explosion), or a computer-generated item (CGI) in a script. There are people who will comb through a script and find this type of thing when figuring out a budget for shooting the film. These effects cost money, you see. It's not absolutely necessary that you put such directions in CAPS, but you'll make the budget-maker's job much easier by CAPITALIZING. Why not help them out a little?

And that's it. Seriously. Everything else about a script is extra. Instead of "CUT TO" you want to say "DISSOLVE TO" (signifying passage of time between scenes) or "FADE THROUGH TO" (similar)? Ok, go ahead, even though it's a director type of decision. Unless it truly emphasizes a point, a simple CUT TO: (don't leave out the colon, please) will be sufficient, but most mainstream writers these days don't even use that.

I hope you noticed that there is no space between the character name and the dialogue. Dialogue is roughly two tabs in, with a similar margin on the right. One-inch margins should be used on all four sides. There's only one other basic thing you need to know about format. What if someone's dialogue gets cut off at the end of the page? Here you go:

> YOU
> (hoarse)
> You jerk, I'm losing my voice arguing with you! And furthermore, if you don't let me tell you why I called and what I have to say, and by golly I mean absolutely everything I have to say, buster boy,
>
> (MORE)

On the next page:

> YOU (CONT'D)
> (yelling)
> I'm going to come down to that radio station and cut your little power line!

Like other writing examples I've given you, the one above was made up on the spot, but it gets right into the action of the story. The script for

How Rush Limbaugh Got Started or whatever. (No offense, Rush!) With one character in a simple, nondescript room, you have conflict and action, and get a good idea of where this story will go.

Once again, though, forms change. Many writers these days would tell you not to use (**MORE**) and (**CONT'D**), that they are old form. All I know is, most major screenplay formatting software programs allow you to turn an automatic placement of them on or off.

That brings us to an easy shortcut to getting the format for a screenplay right. If you have a computer and a commonly used word processing program like WordPerfect or Microsoft Word, there are free software templates available for them on the Internet. Full standalone programs that are in wide use include Screenwriter, Final Draft, Sophocles, and others. I always tell people to simply find what works for them that they can afford, and use it.

As you know, this is a "basics" book. There are dozens of books and hundreds of classes on screenwriting, so don't expect me to give you more than fundamentals in this chapter. I suggest you read the books I've mentioned above and make your own inquiries into further study. Do a lot of study before you write your script, but start your story right away. With just the basic idea that a two-hour script should be ninety to120 pages long, with scenes usually no longer than three minutes each, you know the basics. As I mentioned, the more action description there is on a page, the more likely the page will be more than one minute screen-time. That's why some action scripts are no longer than ninety pages. Comedies are generally shorter, too. But that is all "extra." Start with the basics, then learn the variables and exceptions.

Here's another piece of Hollywood wisdom (is that a contradiction in terms?). Alfred Hitchcock, a pretty fair filmmaker who made amazing films like *Vertigo* and *Psycho*, said that suspenseful movie plots should revolve around something called "The MacGuffin." In other people's lexicons, it's called "the cookie." Whatever you call it, it's a real object, such as *The Maltese Falcon* or *The Treasure of the Sierra Madre* or the Ark of the Covenant in the first *Indiana Jones* film. In action and suspense movies, the MacGuffin is most always something tangible, real, and concrete. In other films, the MacGuffin is a person, a place, or a status. In the case of Scarlett O'Hara in *Gone With the Wind*, the "MacGuffin" she wanted was to never go hungry again. The MacGuffin in *The Wizard of Oz* is the magical ruby red slippers, at least as far as the Wicked Witch of the West is concerned. Judy Garland's Dorothy has the slippers, but that's not what she wants. She wants to go home to Kansas. In *It's a Wonderful Life*, George Bailey wants to be a success in life. That's his MacGuffin. When it looks like the MacGuffin has slipped through his hands due to the apparent failure of his family's savings and loan, George thinks his life should be ended. Clarence the Angel shows him what life would be like without him, and George does a drastic rethinking of his MacGuffin. Life, he realizes, has to do with friends and family and loved ones, not the more temporary ups and downs of material things.

When you're plotting out that first script, ask yourself this question: What is the MacGuffin? What is the main thing in this story that everyone wants? Answering that question can greatly help you clarify your story, if you don't have it focused already.

As previously mentioned, the last element of a good script is the "tag." In fancy French terms, it's the denouement. Basically, it's the wrap-up of any loose ends of the story, usually with a laugh or a cheery note but not always. Think of Rick and Louie, now even better friends, walking into the fog at the end of *Casablanca*. Simba and Nala showing off the new lion prince at the end of *The Lion King*. The bell tinkling at the end of *It's a Wonderful Life*, showing that the angel Clarence got his wings. The feather floating away in the wind at the end of *Forrest Gump*. Or the family of superheroes now able to freely use their powers to fight bad guys at the end of *The Incredibles*. Audiences love tags.

So let's say you get your script finished. Then you spend as much time as you think necessary to make it as perfect as you can get it. Now what? How do you sell your script?

From Script to Sale

Your best bet in selling a script, as I mentioned before, is to write a wonderful script with an original story that gets Hollywood types salivating at the commercial potential. What sort of script is that? First of all, it's a great story. It's a story that will appeal to audiences forever. A classic. To learn what that is, you should study scripts. Get your hands on the scripts for films that won Academy Awards for writing and for best picture. Study the works of highly successful screenwriters. Read screenplays of current box-office hits if you can find them at Web sites like Drew's Script-o-Rama (www.script-o-rama.com). Tony Bill, who produced *Hearts of the West* (one of my all-time personal favorite films), once told me that a great script is so hard to find it is worth its weight in platinum. That is darn near literally true, given the prices some scripts sell for these days.

The problem is, people can get focused on the money and forget about the deal. Actor/producer Michael Douglas once offered to pay me $50,000 to write a script from a story of mine—$5,000 up front and the balance upon completion—but the intermediary on the deal turned it down! After I stopped complaining, I was advised that I should write the script "on spec" then go back to Douglas with it, and get twice the price. Meanwhile, Douglas bought a little script called "Romancing the Stone" from Diane Thomas, and I was history. People all over town had bid for the script, but Douglas got it.

A great script gets a lot of attention. A friend of mine was working with Mel Gibson once on a rush basis to complete the video about the making of Gibson's *Hamlet*. Gibson and his producer dropped everything to read a hot script in the parking lot, one that top people all over town were supposed to bid on that day. This is the kind of attention a truly great script will get. Everyone who is anyone in Hollywood will drop everything they are doing to read the script by bidding time.

So let's say you've written your script, rewritten your script, perfected your script, and now it's time to try and sell it. What next? You could contact the Writers Guild and ask for their list of agents who will look at scripts from unknown writers (also available at www.wga.org). You might get lucky, but by and large the top agents in Hollywood aren't on that list. I suggest you do what I advised you to do in the chapter on writing organizations—network. That's how most projects (and writers) get discovered in Hollywood. Someone knows someone, or knows someone who knows someone, a script comes to their attention, someone falls in love with it, and it eventually gets bought. I have a free discussion group called "Skip's Hollywood Hangout" at Yahoo.com in the groups area—surf on over and apply for membership.

You can get lucky while networking. Dale Launier sold producer David Permut on *Blind Date* by telling him a true story at a party. Permut was floored by the story, and brought Launier in to the studio to "pitch" it for a film. Which brings up a very important point.

SOMEONE MUST FALL IN LOVE WITH YOUR STORY/SCRIPT FOR IT TO EVER BE MADE. Want an example? *Forrest Gump* received six Academy Awards at the 1995 Oscar ceremony, including those for best picture and best adapted screenplay (it came from a novel by Winston Groom). As one of the producers, Wendy Finerman, who accepted her Oscar for best picture explained, it had taken a decade to get *Gump* from book to screen. This sort of thing is not unusual. It took Sir Richard Attenborough decades to get his epic film *Gandhi* to the screen, even though Mahatma Gandhi was one of the major political figures of the twentieth century. If Attenborough had not been in love with the project, it would have never made it, or won the accolades it did.

Even if you write a truly great script, you'll have to find someone who not only realizes its greatness, but falls in love with it. Even though people all over Hollywood drop what they are doing to bid on your script, someone will still need to fall in love with it to outbid the others and turn it into a film. It's merely the nature of the business—usually, you need a champion.

If you ever compare the number of books submitted to publishers versus those accepted for publication, then in turn compare the number of scripts submitted to movie studios and production companies versus those actually made into films, you'll be aghast at the odds of selling an original script. You have a much better chance of selling a book. That's another reason I advise writing a book if you have a great story. It's harder work, but the rewards and percentages are better. If you're a convinced aspiring screenwriter, however, here's how to get it sold:

(1) Study everything you can get your hands on about screenplays;
(2) Write a great script.
(3) Move to Los Angeles, even if only for six months. It's possible you can sell your script without ever coming to Southern California, but your chances are greatly diminished. New York City, or the film studios in Florida, North Carolina, or even Vancouver, British Columbia are also possibilities, but L.A. is still "the place" for the movie industry, and should remain so for the foreseeable future.
(4) Make sure you have a means of support. This could be a job, an inheritance, or a significant other who supports you while you try to make it, as Sylvester Stallone's first wife did until he sold "Rocky."

(5) Subscribe to the Writers Guild of America west's publications and read the material on their Web site www.wga.org. Do the same with the Writers Guild of America east (www.wgae.org).

(6) Find a screenwriting course that appeals to you. There are many fine ones available online. Sign up and go to class.

(7) Find out where directors and producers hang out. For example, Morton's restaurant on Monday nights was "the place" for years. Of course, socializing will cost you some serious money. You don't have serious money? Get some. Other writers are nice to meet and can introduce you to their agent, but it is only directors and producers who will get your script made into a film. These folks hang out at certain distinct places.

(8) If you haven't met an agent you like by this time, start looking for one. Have your storyline ("high concept") ready to pitch to them.

(9) Read the industry "trade papers" daily, and pay close attention to their thicker issues. For example, when the American Film Market (a gathering of independent filmmakers to sell to overseas film distributors) is held each year, the *Hollywood Reporter* and *Daily Variety* do special issues. All the films being shown at the market are described, along with the principal owners of the production companies, their addresses, and phone numbers. It's a simple matter to contact everyone in that issue telling them about your script. Study "the trades" on a daily basis, developing more contacts and learning what's going on in "the business." There's nothing worse than being industry ignorant if you are at a party or watering hole where movies are being discussed. You can also read the *Reporter* on the Internet every day at www.hollywoodreporter.com and *Daily Variety* at www.variety.com.

(10) Keep a log of everyone who reads your script: who, where, when, and the result. You'll not only learn from this but have a written record, should you ever need it for legal purposes. You'd be surprised how good records can help you.

(11) When you find an agent who will work with you not only on your first script but developing an overall career plan, sign with that agent and get your script sold. If the agent doesn't seem to have time for you at any point, find out why or find another agent.

(12) Write some more scripts. Your career will depend upon your body of work, not a single screenplay. Your writing will improve the more you write, period, so keep on writing, keep perfecting, and keep learning.

Last but not least, buy my book on selling to Hollywood, the *Ultimate Writers Guide to Hollywood*. I cover in great detail all the things mentioned above, as well as offering detailed listings about people who will buy your property or sell it for you.

Remember the story I told you about the script Mike Conley and I sold? That was over a ten-year period of time. I could have cut that much shorter by going to the right Hollywood parties, joining more writers' organizations, and meeting people. Since I was also editing magazines, writing and producing videos, teaching writing, and generally making a living during that time, I did not "make it" as quickly as I could have. My friend Bob Bonney, on the other hand, spent his first two years in Los Angeles completely studying the business and taking classes. He read all the top books on screenwriting and outlined them to further understand their points. His script "The Texas Boys" got him a lot of recognition, a good deal of money, and still has not been made, but he began working as soon as he wrote that first script. In fact, he networked so well that he found five people who put up money for him to write "The Texas Boys"! Which means Bob never wrote a "spec script"! He was paid to write one script after another including "The Night the Lights Went Out in Georgia" and a "Godzilla" script. His single-minded pursuit of screenwriting success followed the basic write a great script/get busy networking pattern outlined above. Since Bob came from a highly successful background in advertising, it's not surprising to me that he took the approach he did.

The View from the Top

Speaking of approaches, would you like to know what the most financially successful filmmaker of all-time has to say about screenwriting? I was hoping you would, because I just happened to have interviewed Steven Spielberg. What many people don't know is that Spielberg's first success was as a writer, and the frustration he had with the studio who bought his script is one of the big reasons he decided to direct. The 1973 script was

"Ace Eli and Rodger of the Skies," co-written with a friend. Spielberg sold it to 20th Century Fox while still in college, and after all was said and done they received credit for the story alone. Given that the director is generally seen as the author of a film, Spielberg advised me that in the film business one should aspire to be a filmmaker, not merely a writer.

"You have to be a self-starter these days," he said. "Get interested the way I did. Make a movie, and then make two, and then make five, and then make ten. By the time I got to college, I had made over eighteen amateur short films in eight- and sixteen-millimeter. So I was ready when the studio came to me, finally, and said 'We want to offer you a contract to be a TV director.' I had had years of teenage and preteen-age experience making movies."

What inspires his films, and the stories he chooses? Much of it has to do with childhood memories. It's no wonder that his films appeal not only to children but to the child in all of us. *E.T., the Extra-Terrestrial* was based on an alien from space that Spielberg imagined lived in a tree behind his home in Arizona. His interest in UFOs came from a description of an encounter by some fellow Boy Scouts.

"For the first time," he told me, "I was listening to eyewitnesses describe how they saw this great bright light in the midnight sky taking some screwy turns and disappearing behind a mountain. Hearing it from friends made it that much more realistic. My whole interest in UFOs was the reason I made *Close Encounters [of the Third Kind]*." The last time I checked, Spielberg's films alone had made billions of dollars, with no end in sight, and his company DreamWorks wasn't doing bad with film franchises like *Shrek*.

The Last Scene

So learn about writing great scripts, then work at it until you get a great one. Do what Spielberg advises, and write scripts that really inspire you. The kind you'd just love to see as a movie, like Richard Donner says. After you've studied the books I've mentioned, found others on your own, taken classes, broken down scripts to see their structure, written a few scripts, and perfected that sample script of yours, it's all marketing, and with the stakes so high you'll need intense marketing. If you can't or won't move to Los Angeles, you can probably still sell your script—if it's a great one. I'm sure you can find an agent who will work on selling it for you. Excellent good scripts tend to rise to the top. If, however, you ever want to stand on the podium and say, "I'd like to thank the members of the Academy..." for that little gold Oscar they just gave you, I suggest you work on getting to know some of the members of the Academy by immersing yourself in the community where most of them live.

Somewhere up the road, I hope it's your special screenwriting touch that thrills me in a darkened theater. I'd love to see your name twenty feet high on the silver screen, and I'll bet you would, too.

Chapter Eleven

Television Is Terrific

It Began on Broadway

Early television, broadcast out of New York, was heavily influenced by events on the Broadway stage. Early hits like *Peter Pan* with Mary Martin and the variety program *Your Show of Shows* starring Sid Caesar were the kind of entertainment theater patrons of "The Great White Way" (Broadway) knew well. There was a clear division, however, between TV and film people. Generally, film stars wouldn't be caught dead on television, and film studios saw television networks as potentially putting filmmakers out of business. That "opposite poles" sentiment lasted a long time, but the eventual studio involvement in television is obvious. What you may also have noticed is that only in the last decade have film stars done original television shows without being seen in the entertainment business as a fallen star no longer quite so popular with the filmgoing public.

I cite this example merely to point out how television has grown in popularity over the last five decades. As an aspiring writer, you should realize that television might offer you the most lucrative potential of all mediums, particularly if you also learn to produce programs. In television, the greatest success story of recent years is Anthony E. Zuiker, the creator and executive producer of *CSI: Crime Scene Investigation*. Zuiker, a Las Vegas native with an English degree from the University of Nevada Las Vegas, was holding down a blue-collar job when an audition monologue written for a friend led to representation by the William Morris Agency and the sale of a screenplay to TriStar for almost a million dollars. Zuiker's wife loved forensic specials on cable TV. This inspired the show, fueled by the fact that Las Vegas is #2 in forensic police work only to FBI headquarters in Quantico, Virginia. Zuiker talked his way into a ride-along with the local police on an investigation, and used his knowledge of the area to create the show. As of this writing, there were three versions of the show on CBS, one set in Miami and another in New York City.

Outsiders have been breaking into the Hollywood television industry in a big way for decades. The richest man in Hollywood may well be Aaron Spelling, the producer of *Beverly Hills 90210* and dozens of other hit shows. Spelling was as an award-winning playwright before coming to Hollywood from his native Texas.

Although television shows produced by Spelling and other TV mainstays regularly get trashed by intellectuals and cultural critics, the medium remains the most influential cultural force in the world. Newton Minnow, the former head of the Federal Communications Commission, called television "a vast wasteland." Marshall McLuhan predicted that after three generations of television watchers we would have a society of savages. Maybe they were both right, or maybe they were way off base, but the fact remains that television eats up writing and spits it out on a regular, daily basis. Writing for television may be hard to break into, but it also offers great rewards for writers, often far beyond their wildest dreams. Just ask Aaron Spelling, in his castle overlooking Beverly Hills, or former tram driver Anthony Zuiker, who is now a multi-millionaire.

It Ended Up "Due South"

Back to film versus television. I started out in Hollywood at the same time as Paul Haggis, a friend who went on to write and produce a number of hit TV shows, including *Due South* on CBS. (He was also one of the creators of the long-running Chuck Norris hit *Walker, Texas Ranger*.) I was determined to remain "true" to film, while Paul actively pursued TV, hoping to break into films later. His first break came when Peter Devaney, a strawberry grower from Canada who wanted to get into the film business, came to a meeting of a writers group Paul and I put together. The man invested $10,000 in Paul's fledgling career, which gave him the freedom to write some sample scripts for animated shows, Saturday morning cartoons.

Once Paul started working in animation, he wrote "spec" sitcom scripts, which eventually lead to sales to a number of situation comedy shows. That in turn led to writing and producing *Facts of Life*, which in turn led to writing and producing for the popular drama *thirtysomething*. Paul won an Emmy for a script he co-wrote on that show, which established him firmly as a writer who could do it all, drama and comedy, sitcom, and one-hour episodic drama.

His next venture was co-writing and directing a feature film. But, as you know from reading my descriptions of the film business, fickle fate fingered the feature, and Paul ended up in a legal battle with the producers, although he finished the film and did a fine job.

Back to television he went, ending up creating *Due South* for CBS and having a hit show that was all his own. How long did all this take? About fifteen years.

In the first version of this book I wrote: "Of course, there's every reason to believe that Paul will return to his main dream, which is writing and directing feature films. Meanwhile, he has the respect of his peers, and the public loves his work. He might have done as well if he had stuck to writing films, but I venture to guess he would not have been as constantly financially successful or had the training ground of being a staff writer, had he not gone into television from the start."

Well, Paul has done pretty well since that time. In 2005 he was sitting in the audience at the Oscars as Clint Eastwood and others involved with the 2004 film of Paul's script "Million Dollar Baby" went to the stage to accept their golden statuettes, including the one for Best Motion Picture of the Year. (Paul's screenplay was nominated but did not win.) As of this writing, he's perhaps the hottest screenwriter in Hollywood.

If you do some research, you'll find that a number of top writers and filmmakers got their start in television. The normal route is to get a staff job and work your way up, as Paul Haggis did, but occasionally you can come in after selling a feature film, like Anthony Zuiker. However you manage to do it, you can make a lot of money and perfect your screen craft in TV.

All Over the Compass

Like Paul Haggis, Emmy award-winning writer David Axelrod also started out writing for a young audience. David's Emmy came for 1979's *Hot Hero Sandwich*, a show for adolescents on NBC. He also wrote for two other Emmy-winning shows, the old Dick Cavett late-night variety show on ABC, and "Irving Berlin Celebrates His Ninetieth Birthday" on NBC. His TV experience is filled with amazing anecdotes, like the night health expert J. I. Rodale, the editor of *Prevention* magazine, died while guesting on the Cavett show. David got started in TV in 1962, writing for *Captain Kangaroo*. Television was much less structured in those days. He discovered that, even though the medium was over a decade old at that time, there was no established format for scripts.

"Each show did it a bit differently," he told me. "If I came into an existing show, I just looked at copies of older scripts to see how they did it. If it was a show we were starting, we just made up our own logical construction for the script format, based on whatever scripts we were familiar with, and how they were structured. There was no 'right' or 'wrong' way to do it." Now, he says, "I struggle with WGA-approved formats. I keep hearing horror stories about how someone's script was rejected because even though it was good, it was in the improper format."

If he were starting out now with the knowledge he accumulated over the years, David says he would write more and "learn how to pitch better. It's so different now from when I started, I don't know as I would have started!" he exclaims. "There were no schools for TV writing, or sitcom courses or anything much to learn from. TV was still newish (and black and white) in those days."

Directions You Need

My, how things have changed. To keep you from becoming one of those horror stories David has heard about, I offer you some basic TV script formats to help get your scripts taken seriously. Remember, if you think the stakes are high in film, think of what they are in television. The chances of your creating a new TV show and selling it, and remaining on board the production of same are about as remote as an astronaut landing on Mars in this century, but that's not to say it couldn't happen. It worked for Susan Harris when she created *Soap*, but that was a fluke. Just try to approach breaking into television realistically, and you won't have your hopes so easily crushed.

A TV movie script, called a teleplay, is normally shorter than a feature film script (screenplay). Some sources say 105 pages is correct, others say scripts can run 120 or so. The length of the script and the act breakdown relates directly to commercial breaks, in case you didn't guess. You'll be safer with the shorter length—if a network has to choose between cutting minutes out of your script and selling advertising time, guess which will win? Contrary to the three-act structure of feature film scripts, a teleplay is usually seven acts. Naturally, this varies with different TV movies, but you can get a good index of where the breaks are by watching a few and timing the breaks. Since tastes change at networks, rather than advise you on where to put the act breaks in this book I simply advise you to time it out yourself. That way, you'll get a better idea of currently accepted structure.

A basic index, however, is roughly along these guidelines:

> Act 1 - first twenty minutes
>
> Act 2 - shorter, about fifteen minutes
>
> Act 3 - longer, about twenty-five minutes

Note that the first three acts comprise an hour.

> Acts 4, 5, 6, and 7 are all about fifteen minutes long.
>
> At the end of each act, insert the following:

> END OF ACT [NUMBER OF ACT]

For example: END OF ACT ONE

Other than that, teleplay scripts look the same on the page as the format I gave you for screenplays. Note that I said "about" a few times above. The actually running time will be less, since there will have to be room for commercials to air. Also, each act should end on something that arouses your attention. A cliffhanger perhaps, a dramatic revelation, or a turning point in the story. The house catches on fire, for example. Just as long as it's something that impels the viewer to hurry back from the fridge with that sandwich!

Michael McGreevey, a successful TV writer who has also produced hit shows (*Fame*, among others), has another bit of advice for the aspiring TV writer—visit an editing room.

"That's where you see the little nuances that advance the story," says McGreevey. "You get to see all the different shots that were filmed, which ones go in and which ones stay out. It enhances your ability to tell a story to watch this process."

It also gives you an idea of writing within financial boundaries, McGreevey adds. The average "license" (price to broadcast it a specific number of times) is currently an average of $2.9 million. A film for the USA Network is less, about $2.4 million. A film McGreevey wrote, *Bonanza: The Return*, was a little more, done for NBC for $3.2 million.

"You need to know that kind of thing," McGreevey adds. "Otherwise you could write something beautiful that will never be filmed. In TV, you also need to know network tastes."

What do TV development execs look for? McGreevey laughs. "Something unique, but derivative," he says, shaking his head.

Another tip this TV veteran offers is that you must know how to "pitch" to make it in television. That is, once you've done something to prove you can write, then you have to go in and explain your show to a development executive. That's where some fine writers fall short, because they are not adept at speaking, or telling a verbal story.

"You're dealing with a generation that grew up on TV, in these executives," McGreevey confides. "They're smart, and many of them have Harvard MBAs, but they are verbal and visual, not literary. If you have visual aids to add to the story you tell, all the better. I've had writers get completely tongue-tied when pitching to me as a story editor and producer. In one case, I told the man to go home, write it up, and mail it in to me. I knew he was a fine writer who just couldn't pitch to save his life. We bought a script from him, but usually you don't get that chance."

Some writers these days, McGreevey adds, take acting lessons to get over fear of pitching. There is even one acting coach in Hollywood who makes most of her living off coaching writers about to pitch.

There's another reason you should live in Southern California, if you have any aspirations of making it in television. It's one of the few places where you can find acting (and pitching) coaches in the Yellow Pages.

Your Map to Success

The next thing you need to know about writing for television, particularly in trying to write TV movies, is that there are lists of "approved writers" at networks. That is, people who have proven themselves to be competent at writing for TV, meaning that things they wrote received high ratings and/or awards. Also, if you are not a member of the Writers Guild of America, your chances are greatly diminished in selling a TV movie. The Guild gets quite upset when non-Guild members write for television. Since producers for major networks are all "signatory" with the Guild, meaning they agree to abide by Guild rules when hiring writers, almost everything you see on network television (other than feature films which are being shown on TV) is written by members of the Writers Guild. The Guild also supposedly gets upset about lists of approved writers, which are not legally supposed to exist, but it's a well-known truth that they are used. Similarly, there are lists at networks of actors who have "TV Q." This is a public popularity index—a quotient—that is also not legally supposed to exist, but does. How do you figure out who has "Q"? Well, just look to people who have hit TV shows. Just about any of the principal stars of a hit TV show could get a TV movie made in a heartbeat. Of course, the script would have to make ratings sense to the network in question

Many proven TV stars (if they are smart) start their own production company, and acquire "pay or play" deals from networks. This means that the networks want these stars to be in TV movies and thereby hopefully draw correspondingly high ratings. So they pay them to do a certain number of TV movies. If no movies are made (due to inadequate material or whatever), the star still gets to cash the checks. If you think you have a great TV movie possibility going, you should contact a TV star who could be in your story and solicit their interest. Find out if they have a production company and who the Director of Development is at that company. Forget calling or writing the network. It's very simple to contact any star. Just call the Screen Actors Guild in Los Angeles at their "Agency Department," which fields calls about who represents whom. All TV stars are members of the Guild—they have to be, due to collective bargaining agreements. What if the SAG Agency Department doesn't have a representative listed for a star? Try reaching them through the network. Get the network's main phone number from your local affiliate. But before you do that, watch the star's TV show (if they have one currently running) and find out what production company produces the show. You can then call the network and ask for the phone number of the production company and the address. Chances are the production company is "on the lot" of the network, meaning they are housed at the network studio where the show is filmed. Other times, they are located at a major studio such as Paramount Studios in Hollywood (the only major studio actually in Hollywood).

If you don't have success in calling the network (although you shouldn't have a problem), call Los Angeles information. This might require some work, because there are a number of area codes in Southern California, and the production company could be at an 818, 213, 310, 619, 805 or other area code. Still, since it's going to require a lot of work to break into writing TV movies, if you have to make dozens of phone calls it's a good way of getting used to what you're up against. Once you locate the production company's phone number and reach someone there who will take your call, explain what you have to sell them. They will ask if you are represented, which means, "Do you have an agent (or lawyer)?" Say yes, whether you do or not. They won't give you a name or address unless you do. Why lie? Because everyone does! In the Hollywood jungle, this is not morally reprehensible but mere survival. Actors lie on their resumes, agents lie about the worth of their clients, etc. The white lie is a big, everyday cloud covering Tinseltown.

Normally, I wouldn't advise anyone to lie about anything, but in Hollywood nothing is normal.

The most reliable source of contact information in Hollywood is the Hollywood Creative Directory, online version. The information is updated at least weekly. See www.hcdonline.com and test out their trial version to see if you agree with me about its reliability.

Once you know who to send your script to and where, call an agent. If there aren't any agents where you are located, call a lawyer. In a later chapter, I go into where to find a representative. Once you've found someone who you feel might do a good job as your legal representative, tell him or her, "So and So at [Star's Name] production company wants to see my script. Will you represent me and send it to them?"

If you're speaking with a reputable person, they'll probably say "Sure!" They will at least say, "Let me read it." This is how you get around the "Catch 22" in Hollywood of "Can't get my script read unless I have an agent, can't get an agent unless someone wants my script." The worst an agent (or lawyer) could say is, "Sorry, I'm too busy." With someone at a production company "asking" to see your script, the agent or lawyer probably won't turn you down.

Could you send a script you intended for a feature film to a TV star with hopes it could be a TV movie? Sure you could, but movies for major networks usually have to do with things in the news, domestic horrors like stolen children or the like. If you watch many TV movies, I'm sure you know what I mean. Always popular are true stories, but if the story has received any national publicity at all, chances are very good that a TV producer has already contacted the personnel involved in that true story long before you have. If you can secure the rights to someone's true story, however, or if you have a personal story that you feel would make a good TV movie, then you're in the driver's seat. A good agent or lawyer can advise you on the steps to take in "tying up the rights." That's the question a production company person will ask if you're trying to sell a true story: "Do you have the rights?" Never lie about this, hoping you'll tie up the rights later. It will all get entirely too complicated. This is the voice of experience speaking, so pay attention.

Other than the major networks, TV movies take on different characteristics. The Lifetime cable network advertises itself as "the women's network." All their films have strong women characters who are usually in jeopardy. The Turner Network (TNT), owned by CNN magnate Ted Turner, loves political and historical themes and does well with Westerns. The Sci-Fi Channel loves great stories that can be filmed cheaply. A movie made for HBO or Showtime is little different than a feature film. Do your homework, and figure out which network is best for your story. Then try to determine if the star you have in mind would appear on that network. If the star has an existing deal, which is to say a signed contract with a network, you might be able to get something done. You might be able to find this out by calling the star's production company, maybe not. More likely, you'll need a TV producer to work with.

There are hundreds of people who keep up with who has network deals and who doesn't. If you call and are ignorant of such contracts it could make you look like an amateur. If you find a good agent, they'll be "up" on all this sort of information.

How much can you earn for a TV movie script? Call the Writers Guild and you can find out, or search on their Web site at www.wga.org for "Schedule of Minimums." They have a standard "Writers Guild minimum" for every conceivable form of script written for features or television, and that is what all Hollywood script prices are based on, when a production company is a signatory of the Writers Guild. See what I mean about the corporate nature of Hollywood?

Where the Jokes Are

There are Hollywood writers who spend an entire career writing only situation comedy scripts. Let's define what that is: a thirty-minute TV program in which the comedy springs from an ongoing situation. Roseanne's sarcastic but oddly normal family, for example, or the fact that John Ritter had beautiful teenage daughters that he was overly protecting from dates in 8 *Simple Rules* (which came from a hit book).

The next situation is with each particular episode. Lucy goes to work in the pie factory in *I Love Lucy* is one example. So is the *That '70s Show* kids sneaking around their parents to do any number of unacceptable things.

Beyond that, the structure of a "sitcom" is pretty easy. It's a running string of dialogue jokes as the plot moves along. The jokes are like this: (1) setup, followed by (2) payoff. Let's use one of the oldest jokes in show business as the example:

> *"Who was that lady I saw you with last night?"*
> *"That was no lady, that was my wife!"*

My personal all-time favorite is when 1950s and '60s TV star Jack Benny was approached by a robber. "Your money or your life!" the criminal demands. Benny, whose onscreen persona was that of the biggest tightwad in show business, hesitates and doesn't answer. "Your money or your life!" repeats the thief, waving his gun. "I'm thinking about it!" Benny barks.

If you can't write jokes, forget about writing sitcoms. One writer told me of selling his first sitcom script (a "Barney Miller"), then sitting with the story editor, going over the script page by page. The TV veteran would mark a "J" at various points on the script without comment. When my friend finally asked what he was doing, the wizened old writer smiled wryly and said, "Jokes. You need two jokes a page. That's the rule." Since sitcom scripts are double-spaced, meaning two pages make up a minute, two jokes a page equals one every fifteen seconds.

Sitcoms began to change with the advent of a program called *All in the Family*. Prior to the appearance on TV of the household dominated by Carroll O'Connor's wonderful bigot "Archie Bunker," little political or social commentary took place in sitcoms. Currently, sitcoms are often a proving ground for testing societal issues. Roseanne being kissed on the mouth by Mariel Hemingway's lesbian character caused an uproar for more than a week before the episode aired. Ellen DeGeneres "outing" herself on her show was life defining for her.

When you are starting out, social and political "cutting edge" commentary is best left to the successful writer/producers. You might be the exception to this advice, so don't let me stop you from writing your heart. Just know that the chances are not good of your writing an episode of a sitcom and selling it to that sitcom. This kind of "over-the-transom sale" is very rare in television, although one new writer sold three "spec" scripts to "Cheers" in one season, years before that hit series ended. He subsequently became a staff writer for the show.

(A transom is that small window above office doors in older buildings, made so it could be propped open, secured by a chain, in hot weather, allowing better air circulation. Writers encountering locked doors in old Hollywood would literally hurl their scripts over the transom in an attempt to get them into the office and read. Actors would do the same with their pictures and resumes.)

If you are serious about writing sitcoms, you must get your hands on some sample scripts. Check your local bookstores. If they don't have scripts available, call the Los Angeles Yellow Pages and ask the operator what they have under scripts. You can also call the Academy of Television Arts & Sciences in North Hollywood for information on where to purchase sample scripts. (See www.emmys.org for info.)

You should understand that the common practice in breaking into writing sitcoms is that you write a "spec" script which is good enough to get you an agent who deals mostly with TV writers. Pick a long-running TV series *which is still on the air* for which to write your spec script.

Since people in Hollywood know hit series well, which is to say what the characters are like, how they would normally behave and speak, your "take" on the characters and the situation(s) you put them in will tell the person reviewing your script if you: (1) have done your homework; (2) can write authentically; and (3) can write exceptionally well.

It used to be that writers weren't advised to write a spec script of a show you wanted to write for, because the staff writers knew it too well and would pick your script apart. That has changed. These days just about any kind of good script writing will serve as an example, even an original screenplay.

I mentioned earlier that, when you are breaking in as a writer in the big time of Hollywood or mainstream adult New York publishing, your first works need to be spectacular to get attention. I emphasize that even further in breaking into writing for television, and particularly in writing for sitcoms. I know, I know, you've seen so many TV shows that were so bad. How can I say such a thing? Well, those shows that were so bad were probably shows which were not doing so well in the ratings, which meant they didn't last long. With thousands of proven writers available in Hollywood at any given time (the Writers Guild could give you some idea of the numbers), the competition necessitates that you do something that gets you noticed. Think of that spec script of yours as a first job interview where first impressions not only count, but may be your only chance.

So what if you just can't wait to get started? It's a mistake to write a sitcom without reading at least one script from an established show as a reference, but here's what a sitcom script is all about.

On the title page, the show goes first, spaced down at the same place the script title would go on a feature. This is followed the name of the episode, the byline, and the scene and page indicators, then the representation in the usual place. Scene and page indicators aid the reader in finding various scenes. Scripts which are filmed or videotaped often go through scads of rewrites, with the number of the rewrite designated by pages of different colored paper. Don't worry about that for now—if you sell a script, they'll explain it. Meanwhile, here's what your script should look like:

CHEERS
"The Last Shot"
Written by
Your Name

SCENE - PAGE NO.

A - 1

B - 10

C - 19

Representation:

The Great Agency (Your Agent)

Address

Phone

To explain the scene numbers, a sitcom runs about twenty-four minutes onscreen. The rest of the thirty minutes is taken up by commercials. The page numbers given are where the acts in "The Last Shot" begin.

In the actual script, many things are different than a feature film screenplay or TV movie. The dialogue is double-spaced, for example, and the stage directions (most sitcoms are shot on a studio set, so it's like a stage) are IN CAPS and single-spaced. The beginning of a new act has only about half a page's worth of typing. Don't ask me why—this simply developed over time. The double-spaced dialogue has to do with the fact that TV actors and directors like to tinker with things. With dialogue double-spaced they can more easily jot in their changes.

The best way to assure that you will get formats right, and a way to get a large number of sample TV show scripts to study and use as a template, is to buy a script formatting software like Screenwriter (see www.write-bros.com for a trial download and more info). You'll save yourself a lot of worry that way. But if you're anxious to get going, here's a sample to use as a rough guide that came from the Screenwriter program.

ACT ONE

SCENE ONE

INT. HELMER'S STUDY - NIGHT

HELMER AND NORA STAND IN THE CENTER OF THE STUDY.

> NORA
>
> Oh, Torvald, it hurts me terribly to have to say it, because you've always been so kind to me. But I can't help it. I don't love you any longer.

> HELMER
>
> And you feel quite sure about this too?

> NORA
>
> Yes, absolutely sure. That's why I can't go on living here any longer.

HELMER TURNS FROM NORA BARELY ABLE TO CONTROL HIS EMOTIONS.

> HELMER
>
> Can you explain why I have lost your love?

CUT TO:

CLOSE SHOT OF NORA

> NORA
> (evenly)
> Yes, I can. It happened this evening, when the miracle failed to happen. It was then that I realized you weren't the man I thought you to be.

I hope this helps you get the idea of how a show begins and the format. When you start another act or any new scene, you use the same structure of the blank top half of the page. Again, I have no idea why this structure evolved, but that's what is currently in use. An act ends thusly:

END OF ACT ONE

Please don't depend on this short example, however. If you can't afford a script formatting program with built-in examples, at least get your hands on the current show scripts and study how they are laid out. You might also do some study at www.tvwriter.com.

One last note on sitcoms: Since there are twenty-four minutes of onscreen time available for a sitcom, and since the dialogue (which makes up the majority of the script) is double-spaced, most sitcom scripts are in the forty-eight-page range. Don't take my word for it; get some sitcom scripts and study them thoroughly. I can't emphasize that enough.

Where It Will Seem No One Has Ever Gone Before

I could give you examples here of other types of TV shows (like soap operas), but I'd be wasting my time and yours. Those one-hour shows you've enjoyed, like *C.S.I.* are written by highly paid, experienced TV writers who mostly all live in the Los Angeles area, or at least in the area where the show is filmed. The format is roughly the same as that for a screenplay or teleplay (TV movie). Obviously, in a one-hour show you would not have the seven-act structure of the TV movie, but you'd have almost as many commercials! Just kidding—it would only seem like you had just as many commercials. If you are interested in writing one-hour TV episodes, you should get your hands on some scripts as mentioned above. Write your spec script and shop it around as I've described.

To give you an idea of how tough it is selling one-hour scripts or selling yourself as a green writer for one-hour shows, here's a personal story. The only spec TV script I ever wrote in my life was for *Star Trek: The Next Generation*. I wrote a controversial script about a civilization that had outlawed sex because of nuclear contamination and mutation. To literally keep life pure, sperm and eggs were combined scientifically; it was a post-nuclear all "test-tube baby" society that had devolved into one where few knew how the science worked. Science had become religion; if they followed established procedures they could have children. If not, the race ended. The catch was that the daughter of the leader wanted to mate (that is, have a baby normally) with someone from the Star Trek crew. The penalty was death, and this caused some problems.

My script floated around at the Star Trek offices at Paramount for a full year before it was finally turned down. The reason, I suspected then, was that the sexual aspects were simply too controversial. Later, after I got to know Mike McGreevey, I realized that my script also combined the two big "don'ts" of network television—politics and religion!

And I didn't have this book as a guide before I wrote the script!

Actually, I never wrote the "Star Trek" script to try and sell it to the show; I just wanted to get an invitation to come in a pitch show ideas. I knew someone who worked on the show, who gave the script to the executive producer directly. The script was good enough that it was considered for a long time before it was finally turned down, and it came in handy as an example of my TV writing abilities when it came time to sell my You-Solve-It Mystery novels and get myself attached as a writer and producer when we tried to turn the books into a TV series. So I didn't waste my time. The point of the story is to give you some example of how tough it is to break in to writing "one-hour episodic" shows for TV, even when you have an inside track, and a fine track record. If you don't know the unspoken rules of the territory, even great writing won't help you.

The Way to Toontown

The animation field is similarly dominated by established writers, but it's one of the places where it is much easier to make your first sale. Since the prices for animated series scripts is half or less that for "prime time" sitcom or other TV scripts, the competition is not as fierce. That's a big reason your chances of breaking into the medium are slightly better. Several of the successful TV writers I know (remember the Paul Haggis story?) got their first break in writing Saturday morning cartoons for companies like Hanna-Barbera, who produced *The Flintstones* and other cartoon hits.

Cartoons are created by far fewer people than work on a film or TV show. Likewise, the scripts are somewhat different. In some cases, every single detail must be written out, so that the artist knows what you want drawn. An animation script is akin to a novel, where everything is fully described. Unlike a novel, you normally wouldn't attempt to depict a thought in an animation script, because the only way to show it effectively is by a character looking upward into a "cartoon balloon."

Michael Maurer is one of the prime animation writers in Hollywood. He has the added distinction of being the grandson of legendary funny man Moe Howard, the leader of "The Three Stooges." Ninety percent of everything Michael writes gets produced, which ain't bad. He was the story editor for the animated versions of *Karate Kid* and *Police Academy*, and for the long running hit *Scooby-Doo*. He sold hundreds of animated scripts and he wrote the series "bible" and pilot for a number of shows. (A TV show "bible" is a full description of the characters, world, and basic plot lines of a show.)

Michael helped a number of writers get started in animation. First, he advises them to study the different genres of animation. Some are akin to live action shows. Others, such as *The Simpsons*, are basically a sitcom. He told me you have to learn to break scripts down. First, isolate the genre. If it's a "like live action" show, then the script can be roughly like a feature film script, although the sound effects should be written in. For these, Michael uses the following description: <ROAR OF ENGINES> (or whatever the sound may be). If it's more a cartoon-like show, that means the visual gags must be described fully. Something like this:

EXT. BIG HOUSE - DAY
<WHIRRING OF WHEELS> as BOBBY speeds along the sidewalk away from CAMERA toward the front door of the house. The door opens wide as Bobby BOUNCES across the front step and pedals inside.

INT. BIG HOUSE - DAY
JEEVES the butler stands behind the door, trembling, as Bobby whirs by him. WIDEN to reveal a house full of newly constructed wooden tracks which resemble a makeshift roller-coaster throughout the expansive rooms of the mansion.

BOBBY (VO)

Wow, is this the life or what?!

ON JEEVES, looking petrified by this display of childish danger.

JEEVES

Bob-by! Young man, your uncle won't like this!

WIDER TO INCLUDE BOBBY as he catapults off a track through the air.

Get the idea? Note the spacing (with the beginning action line jammed up against the location line), and how the character line and dialogue are closer to the left margin than in a screenplay? Also, you're writing in camera angles and the like because you are in essence the director of the script—you're providing the "what to draw" direction to the animators, at least. (There are directors of animated shows who oversee the animators and voiceover talent, in case you wondered.) Once again, you need to get your hands on an animation script (or several) and do some study.

A boom in animation began in 1985, when Disney came out with the first season of *The Gummi Bears*. The quality of that show inspired all animators, and the popularity help boost a surge of animation activity that shows no signs of decreasing. Animation (including CGI animated shows like *Jimmy Neutron*) is still an area of Hollywood where you can call a story editor and get in to pitch a show. With scripts going for several thousand dollars, the money isn't bad. How long do the scripts run? About half a minute a page.

A group you can contact to get tips on getting started in animation writing is the Animation Caucus at the Writers Guild of America, West (see the chapter on groups for the address and phone). Caucus members will tell you which agencies represent animation writers, and offer personal advice to beginning writers. In addition, they offer the following tips to those who want to write animation:

(1) You have to really want to do this kind of writing; it's lots of hard work.

(2) Duplication is the key word. You should tape shows you admire, then outline them scene to scene. Read scripts and get to know the show before you try to write for it.

(3) You need a great sample script, one that stands out.

(4) Find a mentor in the business. Pay attention to the notes you get, and be prepared to do a lot of rewriting to get it right.

(5) Persist. Be willing to throw away everything you've done on a script if it just isn't going right.

Another person who offers fine advice on animation, and won the first Writers Guild award for Animation, is my friend Christy Marx. See www.christymarx.com for a wealth of information from her about all sorts of writing, including video games. The last time I checked, she was writing a book about animation and games; I set her up with the guy who sold it for her.

Are you an aspiring animator as well as writer? Contact the Cartoonists Guild, located in Los Angeles. A combination writer/animator (or vice versa) is a very rare breed, however. There hasn't been one of those who really made it big since"…oh, Walt Disney or that team called Hanna-Barbera (*Tom & Jerry, The Flintstones, The Jetsons, Yogi Bear* and a dozen others).

See you in Toontown!

Where the News Is

On television you'll see a lot of other programs than what I've mentioned in this chapter. How-to videos, "infomercials," and commercials fall under a different heading, as far as I'm concerned. They are made for business, and/or advertising purposes, and usually follow the audio-visual script two-column format. Educational films may or may not be written in that format—that will probably depend on what the producer prefers, or has grown used to. I'll discuss all these in a later chapter.

The last big area of writing for television is news, which ranges from your local news report to tabloid shows like *Access Hollywood* to prime-time hits like *60 Minutes*. To keep things simple, let's discuss how you might be able to break in, which is most likely at your local news station. That's what Steven Weakley did at WSMV-TV in Nashville, Tennessee. Based on the strength of a short story he wrote, he got a job as a writer and eventually became producer for a program that in 1984 won the Edward R. Murrow Award as the best newscast in the United States and Canada. Steven went on to be the producer for the KTLA-TV *Morning News*, then Senior Producer for *Good Day L.A.* on Fox Television's KTTV in Los Angeles. *Good Day L.A.* won an Emmy Award in 1993 as "Best Morning News Program." Continuing to move up on the cutting edge, Steven moved on to software giant Microsoft and the world of multimedia.

At the time I first interviewed him, Steven was the Senior Producer for the Fox affiliate in Dallas, Texas.

Formats for writing television news, Steven says, are fairly standardized in structure. "As in all journalism," he related to me, "you need to tell the audience the four W's. When, What, Where, and Why. The key is to write simple but descriptive declarative sentences. Write simply but clearly as if you were verbally describing the story to a friend. The more your words sound like speech instead of prose the more natural they will seem on the air. Active verbs are preferable to passive ones. The lead should summarize what's new or exciting about the story and intrigue the viewer to listen to the rest of it. Since video is crucial to television the aspiring news writer needs to learn to write to pictures. This is a delicate art; one needs to learn to time the pictures and write to the action so that the words and pictures augment each other on screen. Video directions for the show director and tape editor are generally typed in all capital letters on the left side of the script page. While each producer and station have their own idiosyncratic lexicon for these instructions their basic function is to tell the director when to roll the tape for a voice-over (newscaster reading over pictures), a package (reporter voiced piece prerecorded on tape) or a voice-over with a sound bite (a prerecorded piece of sound on tape, like a witness description of a murder). The most common abbreviations are, in order, TAKE VO (voice over) and TAKE SOT (for reporter voiced piece or sound bite)."

The news industry mostly works on PC-based word processors but don't be surprised if as a news writer you have to learn something different. Steven advised me that the pace of news is so frenetic one is often thrown into the frying pan after an hour or so of cursory instruction on the station's facilities. Even if you read books on news writing for television, things can vary widely from market to market.

If you think the competition is fierce, you might not be correct. "Surprisingly," Steven said, "many news writers even in large markets are poor writers." After sharing his thoughts about the news business with me, Steven also showed me "an abbreviated but illustrative" sample script, which I offer you below.

ANCHOR VOICE-OVER SCRIPT

SIMPSON ESCAPE (This is the slugline assigned to story by producer)

06/17/94

(ANCHOR'S NAME)

O. J. SIMPSON FLED FROM A FRIEND'S HOUSE TODAY AND LED POLICE ON A WILD FREEWAY CHASE ACROSS SOUTHERN CALIFORNIA.

TAKE VO   (ANCHOR VOICE OVER)

SIMPSON JUMPED INTO A BRONCO WITH HIS EX-TEAMMATE AL COWLINGS AND ESCAPED SHORTLY BEFORE HE WAS SUPPOSED TO SURRENDER HIMSELF TO POLICE ON MURDER CHARGES. THE DAY-LONG CHASE RIVETED THE NATION ON TELEVISION AND PARALYZED L.A. FREEWAYS.

COMMUTERS CHEERED FROM OVERPASSES AND MILLIONS OF OFFICE WORKERS STOPPED THEIR WORK TO WATCH.

SIMPSON REPORTEDLY POINTED A GUN AT HIS HEAD AND THREATENED TO KILL HIMSELF, WHILE PURSUING COPS PAVED A CLEAR PATH FOR THE LOW SPEED CHASE THAT ENDED AT O. J.'S HOME.

SIMPSON FINALLY GAVE HIMSELF UP TO POLICE OUTSIDE HIS ROCKINGHAM HOME IN BRENTWOOD AFTER HOURS OF TENSE NEGOTIATION WITH SWAT TEAMS.

THE FORMER HEISMAN TROPHY WINNER FINALLY GAVE UP PEACEFULLY AFTER BEING ALLOWED TO SPEAK BRIEFLY WITH HIS FAMILY.

THE MAN MILLIONS ONCE WATCHED FROM THE SIDELINES AS A RUNNING BACK AND A SPORTSCASTER WAS LED AWAY IN HANDCUFFS.

HE IS ACCUSED OF KILLING HIS EX-WIFE NICOLE BROWN SIMPSON AND HER FRIEND RON GOLDMAN AT HER BRENTWOOD CONDO THREE DAYS AGO.

TRT:30

("TRT" stands for total running time of the tape)

The script as you see it is exactly as Steve presented it to me. Again, be warned that script formats might vary from station to station, but if you write a sample script with the above guidelines, your chances of getting a shot as a news writer are greatly enhanced.

I also asked Steven where writing for the news could lead, and this is what he told me:

"Breaking into television news writing is most easily done in smaller television markets where the standards and the pay are lower. Take journalism courses in college extension programs or major in Mass Communications if you are a student. Many television stations offer paid or unpaid internships and this is the golden path to employment. Hang around as long as you can as an intern, do the dirty work no one else wants to do, be ambitious but not overly pushy, and when you have made yourself indispensable ask for a job.

"Other courses of action involve more chutzpah and chicanery. Write some sample scripts and send a resume to the News Director of the television station in your town. Emphasize your experience, enthusiasm, and experiences as a writer. Beg, crawl, and cajole until he or she agrees to grant you an interview. You can then graduate from writing to actually producing the show, and even become an executive producer, news director, or reporter yourself, given your talents and the size and upward mobility of the market. Salaries in small markets typically pay as little as fifteen thousand dollars a year, while a news writer in Los Angeles or New York can earn as much as fifty- to seventy-five-thousand dollars annually."

Note: These salaries have risen since I did that interview. For ongoing news all about television, try *Television Week* magazine; its Web site is www.tvweek.com.

If you have a nose for the news and a desire to offer "breaking stories" to the public...or if you have aspirations to be the next Dan Rather, Bill Moyers, or Barbara Walters? Well, I hope you interview me some day!

Across the "Vast Wasteland"

So is television awful, terrible, and mind-numbing? Surely it can be, but so can anything, taken to excess. I prefer to think that although I grew up with a "TV babysitter" for a number of hours after school each day, I still managed to come out all right. So did my younger brothers, and I don't feel that my young children's minds have been unalterably ruined by hours and hours of watching Disney videos over and over again (their choice). It seems to me that, for all the bad effects of television, people have enough of a self-correcting mechanism to know when to turn it off.

It used to be that you had to take what you were given. Namely, broadcast "free" network TV. Now, with the explosion of satellite, cable, and computers, people have so many choices it's hard to know where to begin, even if it often seems like Robin Williams was right when he said, "What do you know? Fifty-two channels and nothing on!"

In the 1990s, coffee houses proliferated across the United States. People get together, go out, watch live performances, drink coffee, and talk. The characters on the long-running sitcom *Friends* spent tons of time in a coffee shop. Why did places like Starbucks get so popular? I think it's because no one can be coerced into watching a "boob tube" (television) for too long. When so many people look at a computer screen all day, the last thing they want to do after work is sit in front of another small screen. It's my prediction that the more people use computers, the less people will watch the old standard network television formats. There are only so many computer and video games you can play, and only for so long, before you go into mental meltdown. People nowadays selectively watch only that which specifically appeals to them, and they can use devices like Tivo to determine when they watch. This is "narrowcasting" as opposed to the old "broadcasting."

Maybe I'm wrong about this, but you'd better hope I'm not. The more choices there are, the more writers will be needed to write that programming. Which makes me think that, all things considered, television is indeed terrific. Used correctly, it connects societies, informs, and entertains, in a way the world has never seen before. If you write for any form of television—and that would include anything seen on a small screen such as video games—I just ask that you try and keep the welfare of the world in mind. As you've no doubt seen on television, ours is an increasingly smaller world.

Chapter Twelve

Right on Radio

Theater of the Mind

"The main difference between radio and television," Susan Steinberg told me, "is that with television the picture can augment the words. In radio, all you have is words. With radio you're painting a picture on the canvas of the mind."

As simple and obvious as that might seem, no truer words could describe what you need to know when writing for radio, and Sue should know. A radio veteran now working in television, as music director for KMET in Los Angeles she created the *Breakfast with the Beatles* show that ran every Sunday morning for years and made its host, Deirdre O'Donahue, famous. Radio is special, Sue told me. No matter how far you get away from it, there is an affinity to working in radio that remains. "Radio people" can spot each other across a crowded room, she claims. "There's just something about it."

Why? The immediacy of radio, and the intimacy. Sue cited an example to me. When musician John Lennon was killed, TV news crews scrambled to find file footage of Lennon and snippets of music. With radio, all anyone at a station had to do was reach up on a shelf and pull down a Lennon or Beatles record. A few bars of music and the awful, fateful news of Lennon's assassination, and the point was made. Bloody pictures and wailing fans weren't necessary.

"Think about it," Sue said, "when there's an emergency what's the first thing you do? You turn on the radio."

A Good Place to Get Started

Curiously enough, the first script I ever sold was a radio script, to a nationally syndicated science fiction drama series called *Alien Worlds*. It was my mother's generation that grew up huddled around the radio listening to dramas like *The Shadow* and comedies like *Fibber McGee and Molly*, but I knew enough of the shows to feel fondly toward them, so the idea of a real live radio show that I had written was thrilling. When I sold the show, the episodes were recorded onto vinyl discs and shipped to stations around the country. When I played the record of the show at home and heard the announcer stay "…by Skip Press" it was a stunning moment.

Similarly, hearing comedy disk jockey "Dr. Demento" play a spoof tune I'd done on the air was a huge thrill, just as it was the first time I heard a rock tune of mine played on Los Angeles station KLOS. If you ever interview a music star and ask about their most memorable moments, you'll likely hear something along the lines of "The first time I ever heard something of mine on the radio."

I came to Los Angeles to pursue an entertainment dream. What I didn't know was that I could have started right where I came from, in North Texas, had I started in radio. I learned that from Susan Steinberg. What do I mean? Well, let me explain by capsulizing her story. It's as good an example of successfully climbing the show business ladder as any I've ever come across. Sue was a student at San Francisco State, majoring in broadcasting. She'd grown up listening to station KSAN, a major outlet owned by Metromedia Broadcasting. It occurred to her that the station might have an internship program, so she inquired, telling them she was willing to work for nothing, just to learn. They didn't have an intern program, but she persisted, telling them she could get college credit if they'd let her come aboard. So they considered it.

Meanwhile, she went back to the college and told them that KSAN might take her on as an intern. Could she get credit for the work?

OK, so there was a white lie involved. You've heard this before, haven't you?

Well, the college wasn't sure. It had never been done. So they turned her down, good academics that they were. But KSAN took her on after getting an OK from the national office in New Jersey, and Sue was in heaven. She worked for nothing, but the "perks" (perquisites) were tremendous.

Like the time she helped rocker Tom Petty pick out music to play on a show, or "all the vinyl [free record albums] you could eat."

She wrote a thesis about her experience, and got extra college credit after all. And the next year, interning at KSAN became a course at San Francisco State. Ten years later, after working at KMEL in San Francisco and the RKO Radio Network, Sue moved on to KMET in Los Angeles, a station that was also owned by Metromedia. She had to laugh when KMET asked her to do something special—start an intern program. Could she do it? Maybe, she told them. After all, she'd been the very first intern Metromedia had ever hired.

Her secret was simple. "No job was too small," she confided to me. "And there was plenty to do, because radio stations were relatively cheap. You could buy them cheap, sell them cheap, and staffs were not as large as they are these days."

Will It Play in Cleveland?

Sue Steinberg first began to look for other horizons when the program director at KMET wouldn't let her program David Lee Roth's version of "California Girls" on the playlist. Sue was music director, so she felt challenged.

"It didn't test well in Cleveland," she was told.

"Cleveland!" she exclaimed. "This is L.A., this is local boy David Lee Roth, formerly of that small local band Van Halen. Maybe you've heard of them? Who cares about Cleveland?"

Spoken by someone who "grew up" working for radio stations in the large cities of San Francisco and Los Angeles. In the majority of the United States, staffs at stations are still small, and the opportunities for someone who wants to break in like Sue did still exist. The "I'll do anything" (within reason and the limits of the law) attitude is still applicable, as I learned from disc jockey Dave "Sandman" Barravechia, who holds forth at station WZLE in—can you guess?—Cleveland. In these days of talk radio domination of the airwaves, there isn't much room for anyone who doesn't aspire to be an "on-air personality," but that doesn't mean programs aren't scripted. You can use your writing talents to get started in radio, possibly writing Public Service Announcements, or "PSAs." You might also try writing commercials for your local station.

"At WZLE we have scripts for PSAs, scripts used in commercial production, as well as promos," Dave informed me. "At our station, our production director is in charge of everything that has to do with our commercials. Sometimes our sales people write scripts for commercials because they know better what their clients want to say. As far as PSAs and promos, our program director picks out which events to promote."

What's the secret of a good radio script? Dave had the answer for that as well.

"When a script is written to be spoken over the air, the more succinct the better," he said. "They are as short as they can be while getting the point across. It takes a lot of practice and training to be able to use a few words and get a big message across. If someone wanted to get into this area of radio, I would suggest that the best training they could get would be from any radio journalism classes they could enroll in." He offers a word of caution, though. "It's hard to make a living in radio," Dave says. "You have to develop several skills in order to be successful. Only a small percentage make it to the big-time in radio."

There is no set format for radio scripts. They vary from station to station. If you write a sample script to show the program director or production director, remember to make it a large typeface and at least double-spaced, so it's very readable.

If you write a sample script and don't know where to take it, just drive down to your local station, go to the reception desk (if they have one), and ask. Radio stations are still, by and large, relaxed operations, even in larger markets. In the radio shows I do to promote my books, I have yet to encounter anything but a friendly atmosphere.

If you want to write for radio in a larger market, there is also hope for you. Do you think Howard Stern makes up all those loony things you hear on his show?

Even Rush Limbaugh isn't clever enough to do that.

"Howard Stern even talks about his writers," Sue Steinberg says. "All those wonderful bits that seem like they're so spontaneous and ad libbed are well-rehearsed. If someone is trying to break into writing for radio, they should write bits, and it's usually topical bits. What's going on in the news, what's happening politically. If you're in Cleveland and you know the Rock 'N Roll Hall of Fame is there, write about it, because that personalizes it. It's knowing your market, which goes back to being in touch with the listener, that intimacy thing."

Back to Those Golden Days of Yesteryear

Is radio drama dead forever? Maybe not. At the Gene Autry Museum in Los Angeles, original radio Westerns have been broadcast in recent years. With the parts read by well-known actors like Bruce Boxleitner and Melissa Gilbert, the shows featured live audiences, a studio band, and are broadcast live. There's a wonder and...well, what can I say but "intimacy" to it that's like nothing else. Watching *The Tonight Show* live isn't as good, and I've done both. The actor's expressions, the timing of the band, and the sound effects created by the "Foley artist" all make for a tremendous evening of entertainment unlike anything else.

If you've never heard any old-time radio shows and don't know where to find them or scripts for them, have a look at The Generic Radio Workshop and Vintage Radio Script Library at www.genericradio.com. Also see www.simplyscripts.com/radio.html and Radio Theater on the Web at www.greatnorthernaudio.com/audio_theater/radio_theater.html.

In major markets like Los Angeles and New York, radio dramas come and go. It might not be the same in your locality, but who's to say you couldn't put something together? A piano player, someone doing the sound effects, some actors who can deliver lines well, and a microphone are all you need.

Except for a script, of course, which is your job. Looking for a format to use? The format I gave you for a stage play will work just fine, with one big difference—SOUND EFFECTS. There are no stage directions in radio scripts, only sound directions. Put them in CAPS so they won't be missed when the Foley artist starts figuring out what tools of the trade to use to make the right sound at the appropriate moment. Take a look at the links above and you'll see more radio scripts than you can imagine. Radio was almost as busy as television in its Golden Age.

Who knows where you can go with a good radio script? Why, you might even come up with a silly title like *A Prairie Home Companion*, talk about a fictional place named Lake Wobegon, have yodelers and banjo players on the same show, and get someone interested in listening. It worked for a guy named Garrison Keillor at National Public Radio.

In radio, the theater of the mind, anything is possible.

The Last Word

If you aspire to do more than just write radio scripts, or write and produce radio shows, such as becoming an on-air radio personality, you could also start just about anywhere. Rush Limbaugh, of Excellence in Broadcasting and Republican Revolution fame, got his break in Sacramento, California. While you're working on the proper intonations of voice and delivery, do yourself a favor and get a subscription to *Talkers* magazine. It is a trade publication covering the explosive area of broadcasting that seems to be at every other stopping point on the radio dial these days. You can't find *Talkers* on your local newsstand—it's subscription only—but you can reach editor Michael Harrison at:

TALKERS Magazine
650 Belmont Avenue
Springfield, MA 01108
(413) 739-8255 phone
(413) 746-6786 fax
www.talkers.com.

Just how far can you go, starting in radio? All the way to the top, and not just in radio. Consider best-selling author Mary Higgins Clark, who became a radio scriptwriter after being widowed. She had been fascinated by radio dramas as a child; after losing her husband she turned to writing for radio to support her family. The four-minute programs she created were broadcast five times a week on 500 stations, hosted by major celebrities. If you don't think there's room for such a program these days, you haven't heard Paul Harvey lately. (As of this writing, he was still alive and talking, although his son seems to be handling a lot of the broadcast. And now you know the rest of the story.)

It wasn't hearing something of hers on the radio that amazed the author of *Loves Music, Loves to Dance*. What stunned Ms. Clark was hearing one of her books for the first time on an audiotape in the car. She was so absorbed she went through a stop sign. Of course, the tape was playing through her radio speakers.

If you're looking for a place to get your writing career started in a big way, try your local radio station. I'll be interested to hear how you do.

Chapter Thirteen

Business Bucks, Bucks, Bucks

WHY SHOULD A CHAPTER ON BUSINESS WRITING FOLLOW ONE on radio? Because they go hand in hand. Radio depends on its sponsors more heavily than any medium except "free" television, and vice versa.

If you have ever worked in a corporate atmosphere, it probably shouldn't surprise you when I say that business writing is where the most money is spent on writers. The amount of copy written for advertising overwhelms us all on a daily basis. If you don't want to be a copy writer, how about penning a business plan, a year-end report, a newsletter, a technical manual, an audio-visual script, a Web site, or even a corporate speech? If you can write well, you can make a mid to high level five-figure or even six-figure income. If, that is, you know how and where to market your valuable services.

The Key to the Kingdom

When I met Stef and Mary Donev, they were a good example of a successful business writing team. They'd done everything from year-end reports (both written and video) to scripts for shows at theme parks. Of all the things mentioned above, they had never done a business plan or Web site, but don't fret—I have. Since I first interviewed them, they have gone on to write a number of books and have become experts in disaster relief. For example, at this writing, they provide Off-hours Earthquake Media Information for the California Institute of Technology in Pasadena, California.

In comparing notes about writing for businesses, I found we shared a similar approach. Their secret was to not approach a job as writers.

"We're problem solvers," Stef told me.

"And business people first," Mary added. "Then we're writers."

I asked them to explain, which they did, in spades. The basic problem each business has, Stef told me, was that no one there could do the job, so that's why they hire freelancers. He and Mary told me about one instance when they were contacted about a tractor manufacturer.

"So what do you folks know about tractors?" the CEO asked them in the first meeting.

"Nothing," Stef replied quickly. "That's your job."

"We're writers," Mary told the executive. "You're the expert on tractors. You tell us what your problem is and we'll figure out how to put it in writing the way you want."

No, they didn't offend the man. They got the job. Remember what I told you earlier about all writing taking the reader or viewer some place that he or she cannot go, has not gone, or hasn't seen from your unique perspective? That principle still applies in writing for business. You might not smile when you think of Alka-Seltzer, but the phrase, "Plop, plop, fizz, fizz, oh what a relief it is" will put a smile on your face. That's a unique perspective. I don't know the copy writer who came up with that, but I'd be willing to bet he or she had the problem of "How do we sell Alka-Seltzer in a new and fresh way?"

In interviewing Stef and Mary about their decades of experience writing for businesses, I found that, no matter what the business was, no matter what kind of personalities they encountered, there were some things that kept coming up, time after time. Combining their tips with my own experience, I sketched out an approach that has worked for them and for me:

(1) Don't expect to get the job overnight, but be prepared to do it overnight, once called. Lasting relationships of any kind are cultivated over time. It was five years between a couple of jobs I did for one company; it just worked out that way due to my schedule and their need for my services. When they needed me, though, they needed me to get the job done "yesterday." Stef and Mary Donev told me of a job they got writing scripts for a major theme park

attraction that came after a year of Mary calling the company and offering their services once a month. They never got so much as a returned phone call. Then one day a call came and they were asked, "Could you be here at two o'clock?" They wrote the script in a week and it was being performed as soon as it was finished. That's not an uncommon type of occurrence in the world of big business.

(2) Know your audience. If you are meeting with the head of an organization, do your research. If possible, find out what publications the organization puts out, what kinds of ads they place in newspapers and magazines (if any), and how their business is doing. Any new client appreciates someone who is prepared and ready. The story about the Donevs and the theme park is a good example.

(3) Isolate the problem. After you get down to business, find out what it is your client is trying to accomplish. It may be obvious, or it may not. Sometimes, the client won't know exactly what it is they want. You might even encounter someone who will say "So what is it that you can do for me?" right away. Others will know specifically what it is they need, but don't know how to or don't have the time to accomplish it.

(4) Be flexible. If you come up with some ideas, don't marry them. Be willing to throw it all away. If you are billing by the hour, it won't matter, anyway. Don't let your pride get hurt if one of your precious ideas gets discarded. On the other hand, be willing to stand up for something that you think will work. Maybe the client simply isn't seeing what you see, and can be convinced. Still, it's their business on the line. Truth be known, your business is, too. Word of mouth is a large part of Stef and Mary's business, which has grown steadily over the years due to pleased clients who tell other businesses about the fine job the Donevs have done. People who are flexible and friendly are a lot more fun to work with, and people remember them.

(5) Look for the hidden agenda. A client may be embarrassed by the job done by an in-house employee who blew it. Stef and Mary told me about one client who wanted to present a new product on video. An employee who thought he was the next Spielberg hired a couple of actors and shot a video, which was shown to the Donevs without

the employee present. It was an awful, boring fifteen minutes' worth
of "talking heads." One actor explained the new product to another,
with the "student" looking on wide-eyed and asking obvious, leading
questions. Doing a new, effective video was the obvious problem.
The hidden agenda was doing it without embarrassing the company's
employee. So they used the basic story of the video and presented
it in a more engaging fashion. Thus everyone won and the Donevs
did not make any enemies.

(6) Don't talk money until you've worked out the job. Some clients may
ask you that immediately. Usually, this means they have limited funds
to work with. Most companies budget out their year in January,
which makes that a good time to promote for new clients. If you're
being asked to do a job in November and you're asked how much
you charge up front, it could mean that the funds to pay you are limited. On the other hand, it could mean that the person dealing with
you needs to get some figures in order to report back to a higher-up
what the job is going to cost, at least roughly. Don't hesitate to quote
your price once you've gone over the job and established a rapport,
however. If you seem uncertain when talking money, that can easily
be seen as personal uncertainty about your abilities to perform.

What should you charge? Naturally, it will vary from region to region. The
Donevs have clients all over the nation, but most of their jobs are for people
in Southern California, where they live. Since they live on a mountain north
of Los Angeles, they've acquired clients in the L.A. basin and in smaller
cities north of the mountains. Their non-L.A. clients, they told me, roughly
pay only half what clients in Los Angeles will pay, but they're usually much
more relaxed and easy to work with, which provides its own compensation.

Here's a good shortcut to determine your rates. Get the latest edition
of *Writer's Market* and look for the chapter on rates. It's usually called
"How Much Should I Charge?" or something like that. After you read that
and have an index, look in the Yellow Pages. See if you can find anyone
listed under advertising, copy writing, public relations, or any other listing
applicable to what you want to write. Call them, pretending to be a potential
client, and ask what they charge. If they say, "Well, that depends on the
job" (and they probably will), be ready to tell them about a specific job you

have in mind. A forty-eight-page full-color catalog, for example. Again, this will depend on what you want to write, so you'll have to figure this out. If you can find several numbers in the phone book that might answer your question, call them all and compare notes. Then compare that to the suggested rates in *Writer's Market*, and you'll have a good idea what to charge.

If you can't find anyone it the phone book, that's to your advantage. That means your client can't find anyone, either, so they probably don't know what the "going rate" is, until you tell them.

If you can't figure out what rate to ask for, see if you can find something listed in *Writer's Market* that is similar to the job you want to do. It's unlikely you can find your area of writing listed, however.

The Requirements of Business

In the headlong rush to get products to market and ace out the competition, corporate executives usually don't have the time to think through the minute details of what they present to the public. That's why advertising agencies make so much money. Some executives are generally nervous as well, which is why they rarely entrust their entire company communications to a single person, or a team of persons. This often works to their detriment, and financial depletion, which gets passed on to the consumer. Let me give you some examples.

I was once hired by a major Los Angeles bank to write a manual to be used by their executives to schedule employee work hours during the 1984 Summer Olympic Games. The Games were an astounding success, in case you didn't know. Even more remarkably, the air in Los Angeles was relatively free from smog, and traffic on the freeways was manageable, even during rush hour. Why? Because all major businesses staggered their hours. Some banks would open at six o'clock in the morning and close at two P.M., for example, while others would open at eleven and stay open until seven. My job was to tell the execs of the bank how to figure this out. I was given a computer study that had taken a year to compile. I had to learn the bank's in-house word processing program to use in writing the manual. (This was before personal computer use was widespread.) In all, I spent three months on the bank payroll and came up with a pretty decent manual. After the bank execs got through tearing apart what I'd done, they ended up using only *two pages* of what I'd written, and they were happy with my work!

Another time, I worked a full quarter of a year for a major health food company, running a marketing department and using all the talents I had developed over the years: Supervising three other writers and a large art department, I got out a monthly magazine, a monthly newsletter, several brochures, a new company business plan, and several translations of the new corporate video. In addition, I wrote all the collateral materials for the yearly convention of 2,000+ people, hired the event coordinator, picked the major talent (Marie Osmond), wrote the program for the convention, supervised the events, and wrote and produced the multi-media slide show presentation that was the hit of the convention. Quite a bit of work in three months, if I do say so myself, for a company that was at the time grossing $28 million a month. Money was no object when it came to putting on the yearly convention, and there's the rub.

The new corporate video, already finished by an expensive outside advertising agency at the time I came on board, cost $350,000 for a twenty-minute program. Since the company was operating in ten foreign countries, it had to be translated into versions usable in those countries, including an "Australian English" version which wouldn't offend the distributors "down under." I hired a trusted associate to direct that work (under my supervision). Meanwhile, among all my other duties, I wrote the slide show that was the opening presentation of the convention. It was such a hit that the distributors from around the world wanted it, instead of the new video, to use in selling the company's products! It cost less than $40,000. The last time I inquired, over 100,000 copies of the slide show, converted into video, had been sold to distributors. (Unfortunately, I got no royalties, but I was well paid for my time.)

Then there's the Pax TV network. I almost moved to Florida to be the head writer for the company Web site. I was paid a lot of money to write a lot of articles until a new executive hired by the former NBC executive running the network overruled the executive I was working for, and all my work went unused. That's the point I told them I wasn't interested in the job.

Does this give you an idea of how businesses throw money around? Any freelance writer should know that most businesses have a good deal of money to spend, particularly at the first of the year when their budgets are approved, and just before major company events like stockholder meetings and yearly conventions. With that in mind, let's delve into some of the products you might produce for a business.

The Corporate Speech

When you think of speeches made by former President George Bush, is there any phrase that comes to mind? Chances are good it's "a thousand points of light." When you think of President John Kennedy, do you hear "Ask not what your country can do for you, but what you can do for your country"? These phrases added to their speakers' fame, but they were both written by well-paid speechwriters. Similarly, few corporate heads write their own speeches. Instead, they find the best writers possible to put words in their mouths. As an example, Emmy award-winning David Axelrod, whom I mentioned in the TV chapter, has written speeches for executives at companies like Dow Jones and Gallo Wineries.

The first freelance writing money I ever made, other than for articles, was $75 for a speech I wrote for a corporate "roast." There is no set format for a speech, and each person you write a speech for can vary considerably, but I can give you a few tips:

(1) Double or triple-space the text, and print it in large type. (If you have a computer with scalable fonts, the last part is easy.) The extra spacing gives the exec room to make notes. Large type makes the speech easy to read. If the company and executive are sophisticated enough to use a TelePrompter during the speech, they'll still probably want a printed version of the text.

(2) Spend a lot of time determining who the executive's audience is, including details about specific individuals. For example, when I wrote the "roast" speech, I dug up "inside information" about the person being roasted from his friends in the company. The speech was a hit.

(3) Once you know the audience, get to know the speaker. Ask him or her about speeches they've given in the past, what worked and what didn't. They might volunteer this information without your asking, but probably won't. Do your best to get them relaxed and in your confidence, and you'll get to the heart of the matter. You'll cut past the superficiality and find out what truly motivates this

person to do a good job. If you can get to the core of their passion and then translate that into a speech, chances are you'll have a lasting client.

(4) Be prepared to rewrite endlessly, but don't give up your integrity. If you've worked and worked a speech but the executive still isn't satisfied, even though you think it's a fine speech, it might be time for you to hold your ground and state the reasons why you think the speech is fine. You're hired to do a job, but you shouldn't be required to be a doormat for anyone's ego (or anxiety).

(5) Draw from the masters. It's no accident that good speeches contain quotes from leading figures of history. If you've never heard of *Bartlett's Quotations* or similar books, you'd better spend some time at the library before you attempt to write a speech. Knowing that author Kurt Vonnegut called New York City "Skyscraper National Park" (in his 1976 novel *Slapstick*) can not only bring a laugh but make the speaker appear to be well-read and humorous, thereby putting his audience into better rapport as he launches into the important parts of his talk.

How much should you charge for a speech? Again, it will vary by the market in which you live, but you can always refer to *Writer's Market*. Another great resource is the BizTech Division of the National Writers Union, which "represents Business, Technical, and other writers who work for employers and clients as freelance contractors or temps." (See http://nwu.org/bite/bitehome.htm for more information—the BizTech division was formerly called the "BITE Division.")

The Company Newsletter

With easy-to-use desktop publishing software, there is little excuse for any company, no matter how small, to not offer a newsletter to clients and prospective clients. The opportunity this offers freelancers is that the majority of people who run companies haven't a clue when it comes to laying out or writing a newsletter, computer or otherwise. If you're looking to simply write a company newsletter and not also create it via desktop publishing, chances are good you'll be left in the dust. There are simply too many people out there who can do it all.

So get over the "I'm just a writer" syndrome quickly, if you want to do newsletters. If you own a computer and can learn a program as common as Microsoft Word, you can put together a professional newsletter, using ready-made newsletter templates that come with the programs. If you're more adventurous and learn programs like Adobe Photoshop or Quark Express, you'll be able to create a publication rivaling those of Fortune 500 companies. Other than that, the written content of a company newsletter varies little from what you would write in an article. The important point is that you maintain a cheery, "good news" type of attitude, usually in a conservative tone.

To build a good business of doing newsletters for companies, I'd advise you to have the following:

(1) A computer with plenty of memory and a good desktop publishing program;

(2) A good color printer;

(3) A scanner (for incorporating photos and artwork into the newsletter);

(4) Fax facilities (even if on the computer—many older and international businesses still send faxes); and

(5) A decent digital camera and the ability to take good pictures. If you don't have a digital camera and prefer film, that's fine, but you'll be working in digital.

Just remember that your job is to make people feel good about the company, and you'll be on your way. My best example of this is my "Press Gang" newsletter, which I used to send out on a regular (though not monthly) basis. It was not hard for people to think about hiring me as a writer, because I continually kept them abreast of what I was doing. Inevitably, when someone called me about a job, it began with "I read in your newsletter." Later, I did an e-mail newsletter on a more regular basis, which went to about half the people in my database.

Newsletters are their own separate art. You'll find lots of advice on them in your local library, and they are often a good way to develop stable business for yourself as a freelancer. If you've never done one, use your computer to develop one, then send that out to prospective clients as an example of what you can do. If you can afford it, get the ability to export your newsletter in Adobe Acrobat format, which seems to be fairly universal around the world. With a nice newsletter, you'll get some business.

The Company Brochure

Just as the most common word processing programs offer newsletter templates, many have brochure templates as well. That aside, you should view a brochure as a continuing revelation. The cover should intrigue the reader, either with a statement or a posed question. "Why are Krazy Kornflakes the best on the market?" for example. "Because Chucky Jackson says they are!" exclaims the copy inside the next fold, which is under a picture of a grinning eight-year-old happily eating his corn flakes. "And Chucky isn't alone," leads off the paragraph at the top of the next fold, which launches into a description of a bar-graph comparison of kids across the country who sampled all the leading brands of corn flakes. The last fold of this imaginary brochure might describe, in confident detail, the solid history of the Krazy Kornflake company, a family-owned business dedicated to happy, healthy youngsters everywhere since it was founded fifty years ago by Korny K. Krazy. You get the idea.

The good thing about writing brochures is that they're done a lot more often than newsletters. You don't have to be able to create them via desktop publishing, but why not? Don't limit yourself to being a mere copywriter and your bank account will also be less limited.

If you don't know Powerpoint presentations or another similar way to do an electronic presentation, invest in a class and software and learn. You'd be surprised how often this will come in handy in working with businesses, and in building your own freelance business. You'll also be surprised at how few executives have a clue about creating such things.

The Year-End Report

It used to be that a year-end report was done only by highly paid advertising agencies, or in-house communications departments. That changed with desktop publishing. These reports are created for the benefit of stockholders, both existing and prospective. These days, they come in several forms: in print, on video, and sometimes in EPKs (electronic press kits). Like newsletters, they are an art in themselves; they present the full corporate image to the public. Therefore, they are scrutinized to the minutest detail. Since they vary from company, and since you'll be competing with big advertising companies who want the business, I won't attempt to provide any kind of standard format.

Instead, I'll offer some common sense. If you want to do a year-end report, contact a company you have your eye on and ask them to send you their latest report. They'll do it right away. Study it and see if you can find ways to improve upon it. If you can, write out those improvements, be it better copy or better ideas or both. If possible, lay out a sample page on your desktop publishing program and study how it can be improved.

If it's a video year-end report, you'll need to know video-scripting format, which we'll get into later.

I don't know anyone who makes a living doing company year-ends, but I'm sure there are people out there who do. I would advise you to learn about them as merely one more piece of the business writing pie.

The Business Plan

You can buy software that walks you through creating a business plan. It's not that hard to find a template for one on the Internet. Barring that, if you're writing one for a company and have never done one, head for your local library. If the company doesn't have a business plan and doesn't offer you a sample of the kind of business plan they want, they are as clueless as you are. A great source of information is:

Small Business Administration
409 Third Street, SW
Washington, DC 20416
1-800-U-ASK-SBA
www.sba.gov

You can also check the phone book for an SBA office near you or find one on the Internet at www.sba.gov. Since complete books have been written on writing business plans, I won't attempt that here.

The Business Guide

Businesses that depend on independent distributors for their marketing, such as Amway, have business guides that lay out the ground rules for each individual representative of the company. These are policies that have been developed over time and include "boiler plate" legal language that protects the company in case a distributor goofs. The company can always claim "Well, it was right there in the business guide and the distributor signed a statement agreeing to uphold same." To give you some idea of the content of such a guide, I'll give you a sample of the chapter headlines of one I worked on:

  I. Basic Principles

  II. Eligibility To Become A [Company Name] Distributor

  III. Rights Granted

  IV. Independent Business Relationship

  V. Compliance By [Company Name] Distributors With All Applicable Income Tax, And Other Sales Laws

  VI. Authorized Sales Region/International Business

  VII. Pricing

  VIII. Representations Made By [Company Name] Distributors

  IX. Labeling And Packaging

  X. Advertising And Use Of Name

  XI. Cancellation, Resignation, Termination, Death, Or Incapacity

  XII. Excuse For Non-Performance [This was basically a disclaimer saying neither the company nor any distributor was responsible for delays and failures in performance caused by circumstances beyond their control, such as strikes, labor difficulties, riot, war, fire, death, curtailment of supplies, or government decrees.]

  XIII. Assignment And Delegation [This section explained how no distributor could assign his or delegate his or her rights as a distributor without the prior written consent of the company.]

  XIV. Limited Warranty [Covered what the company would exchange or refund and what it would not.]

  XV. Infringement [A statement that the company had not infringed on any patents, trademarks, trade names, or copyrights.]

  XVI. Copyrighted Materials [A statement that all company literature and programs were copyrighted and could not be duplicated without written consent of the company.]

  XVII. Exclusive Rules [A statement that the Business Guide, Distributor Application and Agreement, "and the instruments and documents referred to herein constitute the entire understanding of the parties with respect to the subject matter." Also, that the Business Guide and Distributor Agreement could be amended at any time by any instrument in writing signed by an officer of the company.]

XVIII. Waiver [It follows, in full.]

The failure of [the company] to exercise any rights stated in the Business Guide, Distributor Application Agreement or to insist upon strict compliance by a distributor with any obligation or provision thereunder shall not constitute a waiver of [the company's] right to demand exact compliance therewith. Waiver by [the company] can only be effected in writing by an authorized officer of [the company].

I hope this gives you an idea why business guides are written under legal supervision. In the case of the above guide, I got constant complaints from distributors while I worked for the company that the guide was impossible to comprehend. Well, naturally! That's the way the in-house company lawyer wanted it. In trying to make the guide more readable and understandable, however, I encountered something that opened my eyes to corporate politics. Despite everything else I had to do during my three-month stay to get the company through its annual convention, I also was asked to supervise the revision of the business guide. Being a "give it to me, I can handle it" type of guy, I took the project on. Then I hit a brick wall named Cynthia, the in-house lawyer. It seemed that it took forever to get her legal stamp of approval on anything, much less a lengthy document like the business guide. So I did some snooping, hanging around in her outer office making small talk with the secretary, while I inquired on the progress of various documents.

I discovered that Cynthia wasn't doing much work at all. Repeatedly, I heard her talking with friends on the phone about beauty appointments, entertainment events, her new Mercedes, etc. Cynthia had it made and was taking advantage of the situation. I found out that she didn't want things to move quickly because she'd get all the work done and might be out of her cushy full-time job. A man in the same position, of the same parasitical mentality, would have acted the same. Needless to say, she and I didn't get along, and I made it known to the owners of the company what her real performance was all about. But guess what? They didn't do anything, because they were involved in illegal tax evasion that eventually got them indicted in one of the largest tax evasion cases in California history. It reminded me of the joke about people stranded on a desert island who try to make the swim to another island to retrieve a boat. The only one who makes it past the sharks is the lawyer. The sharks part for the lawyer—professional courtesy. Unless you're just itching to become the most profound business writer of all time, I'd advise you to stay away from things like business guides. It won't be worth the headache. A business plan is completely different. Leave the legal writing to the lawyers—when and if they can get around to it.

The Personnel Manual

Any company with more than a dozen employees should have a personnel manual. Don't count on the Director of Personnel to write it; those people are usually equipped with a psychology degree and very little common sense. Basically, personnel manuals handle two basic areas for a company: (1) a description of company regulations and practices for the benefit of employees; (2) something in writing to fall back on, should a supervisor need to discipline an employee.

Will most employees read a personnel manual? Probably not, but that won't stop companies from having them written. There is no established standard for personnel manuals, but all of the following should be covered in detail:

- Basic company policies, such as physical exams or drug tests required for employment;
- Work hours, overtime, holidays, vacations, sick days, personal days, jury duty, and leaves of absence;
- Salaries and benefits, performance review, merit increases, benefits, educational assistance, and severance pay;
- Profit sharing and pension plans;
- An equal opportunity statement;
- Safety regulations and advice;
- A confidentiality clause regarding company events;
- Causes for discipline, discipline guidelines, and grievance relief; and
- Any other information relevant to that particular company.

Again, much of this is the domain of lawyers. The above is to simply give you some idea of what a personnel manual contains, if you've never seen one. How much should you charge? I advise you to stay away from a flat fee. Because you'll very likely be dealing with lawyers to get the thing to a final approved version, do what they do, and charge by the hour.

The Technical Manual

Unless you've been living in a cave in the Gobi Desert, I'm sure you've had some experience with a technical manual. That book that attempts to tell you how your computer works, perhaps, or the booklet that came with your DVD player. Well, someone has to write those things, and that's where freelancers come in. I've done a few of them, including the first one for Miracle Ear, the almost invisible hearing aid that Ronald Reagan made famous when he was President. No, I didn't write a manual on how to use the hearing aid. I wrote a manual for the Franchise Consulting Group in Los Angeles, which had contracted with Miracle Ear to develop a manual explaining to new franchise owners how to set up and promote their hearing-aid business. I did not write the "boiler plate" legal language of the manual, just the step-by-step "now you do this" type of thing, which came from my interviewing people in the company.

How do you format a technical manual? You wing it. There's no standard. Just try to make it as simple as possible, and write in a language that is suitable for someone with a fifth-grade U.S. education. This is no slam against owners of hearing-aid franchises—writing for the fifth grade is the accepted standard "language" for most business writing. In any of the business manuals I've written, I've tried to approach the problem as if I were the recipient.

Don't assume they know, or can logically figure out, anything. Take it step by step in the logical progression of use of the item or operation of the business.

Sometimes, this approach can drive you crazy. When I wrote a manual about the operation of an indoor amusement park for kids, I never saw the park (which was located in Houston, Texas). I had lots of audiotapes from the various personnel at the park that operated different parts of the operation on a daily basis. I organized their advice into a manual, which was then gone over by the owner, who corrected what I'd written, and I continued to massage the writing until everyone was satisfied. The manual became the "bible" for all other franchises of the park around the country, although I never set foot in a single one!

One drawback you'll run into, if you try to get into the technical manual business, is a problem of degrees. If you see an ad for "Technical Writer" in your local newspaper, most likely they'll ask for someone with years of experience, and you may need to know specialized programs to get the job. Occasionally, proficiency in Word will do. You might be able to convince them you can write anything and get the job, but in some cases, if you don't have specific technical know-how, you'll be up a creek. For example, if you have to write a manual on the operation of a new piece of high-tech equipment, but cannot read an electronic schematic, you're wasting everyone's time.

If, on the other hand, you have a degree in electrical engineering or computer science and can also put words on paper in a way that explains complex things in a simple, straightforward manner, you may be able to make a very good living as a highly paid technical writer.

And sometimes you don't even need a degree. A case in point is Andy Shafran, whom I ran across on CompuServe. Andy interviewed me one night for a book he was doing about (can you guess?) CompuServe. What struck me about Andy was that he was being paid to write the book while he was still in college! How did he get such a job? I'll let him explain.

"About a year ago I saw a public job posting on CompuServe for a new author to write an entry level Lotus Notes book. I called, faxed my resume, and was generally annoying to the acquisitions editors at Que [the publisher] until they finally said 'Enough already, take the damn contract and write the book.' It wasn't exactly like that, but I was persistent. I was very careful to meet all of my deadlines. A month after the project was complete, I called them up and reminded my editor I was interested in writing more. They shuffled me some smaller contracts, which became progressively bigger and bigger.

"Then someone at Alpha Books (they work in the same building as Que) called me up and said he had heard about me. He wanted to know if I would write *The Complete Idiot's Guide to CompuServe*. It was a book that paid royalties (my first one), so I jumped on it. I now have too many writing offers to handle. Since I am a full-time college student, I can only do one project at a time. It's too bad; otherwise, I'd have written several more by now."

Andy told me he thought it was "pretty uncommon to be offered an entire book on your first time out," and right he was, in most cases. The exception is in technical writing, where it doesn't make any difference about your background, *if you know the technical area well and can write about it so people can understand it*. Obviously, Andy has that ability in spades. A senior at Ohio State when we met, Andy got college credit for the Lotus Notes book. If he had any secrets, it was to "be flexible in writing styles— humorous, dry, casual all have different places and are all important." And "my girlfriend is an English major, for what it's worth." That meant he had someone to check his punctuation, spelling, and grammar. Of course, it didn't hurt that Andy's father owned a computer store, and that he "grew up on Kaypros, Apple IIs, and CP/Ms" and bought his own PC ten years before and continually upgraded it. Then of course there's the fact that he was a Computer Science Engineering major and continually read tons of computer magazines.

You have to admire a guy like Andy. It was obvious he was the type of person who would write his own ticket as a technical writer, or anything else he tried to do. He got rich during the years when that type of how-to computer book first started coming out.

The Business Script

You don't need a technical background like Andy's to write business scripts. You just need a good visual sense, an inclination to want to make films, and the ability to duplicate on paper the vision of your client. You'll hear the business script described in many different ways: the audiovisual script, the educational video script, the presentation script, etc. That doesn't change the fact that it is a script written with one thing in mind: the education of its audience. Since one of the primary hurdles (if not the main hurdle) any business faces is getting the public to understand its product and what it can do for them, and since a visual presentation does that better than any-thing other than hands-on experience, I've saved my favorite and most lucrative form of business writing for last.

I've enjoyed all the videos I've written, which have enjoyed a good deal of success. The first "how-to" video I attempted was a golf video for women, which ended up as *Jan Stephenson's "How to Golf."* You won't find my name on this certified gold video, because I sold out my interest and walked away from the project after a disagreement with the producers, but I put the project together, wrote the first draft of the script, and was paid handsomely for my efforts. I already mentioned the multi-media slide show I wrote which became a corporate video after being more popular than a slick program that was much more expensively produced. Another how-to I wrote, *A Woman's Guide to Firearms*, won the Silver Medal at the New York International Film Festival, over hundreds of other entries. (Before you start thinking I'm a card-carrying member of the Aryan Nation, let me explain that the latter video was made for use in safety instruction.)

So I think I know something about this type of writing. Still, before I tried to write one, I didn't know the first thing about writing this type of program. Whatever it is you do for a business client—a TV commercial, a slide show, a video year-end report or a how-to video—you'll use the same script format. It's considerably different from any other filmed or video-taped program format. At the same time, it's a very simple format:

Work-Related Accidents: Something To Avoid

VIDEO	AUDIO
1. Jack walks toward the Ajax Building, eating a banana. He tosses the banana peel behind him, paying little attention to the people following a short distance behind.	1. <u>Announcer (O.C.)</u>: It's a normal workday for Jack, your happy working stiff, but it's
2. Sally co-worker laughs with her friend Ethel, not watching where she's stepping.	about to turn unhappy for Sally, thanks to
3. Close on Sally's foot, as she slips on the banana peel.	Jack's carelessness.
4. Slow motion as Sally's feet go out from under her and she falls.	2. Sally Agghhhh!!!

5. Close on Jack's concerned face. Camera pulls back to reveal an ambulance, lights flashing, as it pulls away carrying Sally.	3. <u>Announcer (O.C.)</u> All it would have taken was one step to the trash can. Right, Jack?

00:18

Breaking down that opening sequence, you notice that the video column on the left is written single-spaced, just like a screenplay. The audio portion is written double-spaced, like the dialogue in a sitcom. At the bottom on the right you saw "00:18." That's the timing of the scene in seconds. Each page of an audio-visual script is timed in this fashion. Additionally, with each successive page, you "add up" the elapsed time and indicate it in this fashion:

<u>00:30</u>
01:00

The bottom number would be the total for two pages, or one minute. If the script was a thirty-minute script, the bottom of the last page might read:

<u>00:30</u>
30:00

Some sources suggest a straight line across the top of the script:

VIDEO	AUDIO

Personally, I think that's a matter of style. You won't lose a job over it. Similarly, I've seen books advising you to put a line of technical information across the top of each page, but you needn't worry about that. A mere

PAGE 1 (etc.)

is sufficient. The only thing that really matters is the two-column format, the way your dialogue matches the action depicted, and the timing of the scenes (which is based on the way the dialogue reads, so you can put yourself on a stopwatch and time it). Also, you must underline each successive person who speaks. The "O.C." stands for "Off-Camera," meaning that we don't see the announcer. "O.S." meaning "Off-Screen" would also be acceptable, as would "V.O." for "Voice-Over." Remember what I said earlier about leaving out camera angles in a screenplay, since that was the director's job? This doesn't apply nearly as much in an audio-visual script.If you need to say "High Angle, looking out over the valley," go ahead and do so, if it emphasizes your point. Remember my advice about keeping film scenes to three minutes or under? With audio-visual scripts, fifteen seconds is a good limit.

And as you might have suspected, there is software for this kind of script writing. I suggest a search at www.writersstore.com for the latest and best.

Don't worry about putting something in a script that you think might require too much expense. There is a thing called "stock footage." If you want a plane taking off from a major airport, an affordable film clip of same can probably be purchased and incorporated into your video from a company that specializes in supplying generic footage. If you're not sure about this, ask the people you're working with.

Remember to tell a story, even in the smallest film. Another good rule when it comes to something for a business is the "three times to be sure they'll get it" maxim. You've probably heard it before: tell 'em what you're going to tell 'em, tell it to 'em, then tell 'em what you've told 'em. There's something about a thing repeated three times that manages to get through to people. But you won't do it with "talking heads" sitting there repeating it, over and over and over. Action, action, action, whenever you can and within your budget.

Should you attempt to be a filmmaker, or just write scripts? That's up to you. If you're trying to get brochure and newsletter business, I'd advise you to become a full-fledged desktop publishing operation. If you're at all technically inclined, it is now possible to shoot perfectly acceptable business video on many high-end consumer camcorders and edit on your computer, adding the voiceovers, sound, and special effects yourself. That requires a good deal of dedication and expense, however, so unless it's just something you have a great desire and ability to do, you might be better off sticking to writing. After all, I don't expect a sudden upsurge in corporate literacy any time in the near future. There's too many lawyers involved, and they don't want people getting too smart, do they?

I hope you have a great time writing for business. It's a continually challenging environment. Just remember to go at it as a problem-solver first and a writer second. Solve some problems, write some things that increase business for your clients, and you'll never be out of work!

Chapter Fourteen

Telling the World About It: Newspapers, Advertising & Public Relations

I F YOU EVER PUBLISH A BOOK AND TRY TO PROMOTE IT, YOU WILL
learn some big lessons fast. The first one is that your publisher will most
likely not roll out a broad national campaign on your book. You won't get
flown across the country to stay in the finest hotels, appear on *Regis &
Kelly* or *The View* on ABC, and you won't meet with the President in the
Oval Office to discuss the social merit of your tome. Of course, all that
could happen, but don't count on it. Prospective authors I meet always
seem a bit saddened by this revelation. That's when I tell them about how
motivational guru Wayne Dyer put a trunk load of books in his car and
traveled the country talking about it, eventually pushing the book to
#1 best-seller status. I also relate the story of 1960s poet Rod McKuen,
who approached Random House founder Bennett Cerf at a talk the
publisher gave in the San Francisco area. Would Cerf be interested in
publishing a book of poetry, McKuen asked? Cerf declined, stating there
wasn't much money to be made in poetry.

"Strange," replied McKuen. "I wonder how I managed to sell 35,000
copies of my book?"

"Let me see it!" Cerf exclaimed.

I wasn't there, but it went something like that.

As you become more established as a writer, you will begin to see how
intricately connected the worlds of advertising, newspapers, television, the
Internet, and public relations are. Originally, I intended to write separate

chapters for each of these areas of opportunity for writers. Then I realized that advertising is the stuff of college degrees, even though it is based primarily on good copy writing and excellent execution of bright ideas. The same goes for public relations, although most public relations specialists can't write their way out of a paper bag. Both professions tend to get inflated reputations, perhaps due to the enormous amounts of hot air circulating through their offices.

In this chapter, I'll discuss good copy and good public relations, as well as how a newspaper works. Despite our "Information Age" when computers and television seem all pervasive, a great number of people in the broad world read their local newspaper each day. They still depend upon it for information on where to shop, what's available to buy, and where to go for good meals, entertainment, etc. The Internet hasn't taken over completely. It's my feeling that, if you understand how newspapers work, you'll have a basic grounding in writing good copy and know how to promote anything you choose to tell the world about, including your latest creation.

Knocking Around the Newspaper

I first interviewed Craig Howson about the newspaper business a decade ago but what he told me then still applies today, particularly with regard to getting started in your local community. Howson grew up in Prescott, Arizona. He held a number of jobs at the *Prescott Courier* at one time or another, beginning as a reporter. He was news editor, editor of the Sunday paper, business editor, feature editor, and city editor. After leaving the *Courier*, he became editor of the *Aspen Daily News* in that colorful Colorado ski town where I've had the pleasure of speaking many times. Then he moved on to editing magazines. A part-time job at a Prescott radio station led to being news editor at the station. After getting to know the local newspaper reporters, he landed a job at the paper. Craig took the print job because he felt his future in radio was limited. He didn't have a "major market voice."

"I also got tired of working by myself," Craig told me. "At the *Courier* I was meeting people all the time. I started as county government and education reporter. Our county was bigger than eight states, and Prescott is the county seat. I love politics, and there was a lot of politics there."

In the first five years, Craig moved up the ladder, covering just about every job on the paper, eventually supervising three other writers. "I did just as much writing as all the other people did," he adds. "I did all the layout for the pages, edited copy, that sort of thing. Basically, anything I wanted to do was a story. We redesigned the paper. It was a lot of fun."

After a change in editor and publisher, Craig became city editor. Staff got cut to the bone, and experienced reporters were replaced to cut costs. Craig saw changes he didn't like.

"Every real estate agent in town had his own column," he said.

Not willing to push journalistic integrity aside, he moved on to the magazine RCR (Radio Communications Report) which covered the then emerging mobile phone industry. From there he became the editor in Aspen. The last time I heard from Craig he was freelancing, but he felt his newspaper experience was tremendous. If you learn to write for a newspaper, he told me, you can write anything. Plus, the sense of intimate involvement in the current events is immense.

"I was there when the Space Shuttle blew up, and when Reagan got shot," Craig said. "One time [in Aspen], we had a city councilman who had just lost an election walked into the lobby and shot and killed himself. It was the first and only time I ever got to literally yell, 'Stop the presses!' I was the only one in the newsroom, and the presses were just starting to crank up when the receptionist came back and said 'Kirkpatrick just shot himself.' The thing I miss about working on a paper is that when you see something on television, like the O. J. trial, you kind of miss being in the middle of it all, because you get to see things nobody else gets to see. There is a lot more material that comes in than is ever printed, because you just don't have room for it all, but you see it. When Reagan got shot, I wrote the Brady headline five or six times, because the guy lived and died. Brady Alive, Brady Dead, Brady Alive, they couldn't make up their minds."

A downside of the job was the heavy personal involvement.

"When I went out to dinner, everyone knew who I was," Craig confided. "I did a series on teen suicides, and I knew a couple of the families. I played tennis with the mothers of a couple of the victims. Another was the kid of a woman I dated. You're a lot closer to your readers, a lot closer to your community in a way a lot of big city papers just aren't. You could walk right into our newsroom any time you wanted. You're just closer to people. You feel what they feel. It's the part of the job I really liked and the part that made me get out of it. It got to the point that if an accident report came in I was

terrified that I'd send a reporter out there and find out the victim was
somebody I knew."

Another drawback was the hours—all the hours in the day.

"I basically worked twenty-four hours a day, seven days a week," Craig
recalled. "My camera was always in my car. I didn't have a private life to
speak of. I remember going home from dinner one night with a girl and a
fire engine goes rolling by. There was a house on fire—I had to cover it and
shoot pictures. Pissed her off, but that was my job. It was my responsibility
to shoot pictures of the fire."

Last but not least, the money was "terrible," according to Craig. Which
was another reason he moved on to other things. Nevertheless, he wouldn't
trade his newspaper experience for anything.

"Knowing where to dig up information, knowing there's more than one
angle to something, knowing that everybody's got an ax to grind, learning to
be creative and think on your feet—all these things have stood me in really
good stead. I'm a journalist and I always will be. A part of me will always be
a newspaper guy."

Is a newspaper job still worth pursuing, given the pervasiveness of
the Internet? My opinion would be yes, as long as there are newspapers
around, and you want to write for them. Veteran newsman Gene Koprowski
offered this advice on breaking in to newspaper writing, no matter how big
the paper.

"I can guarantee you a freelance job at any big city daily," he told me,
"if you do the following. Call the high school sports editor. This is a beat
that is understaffed, underpaid, and under-appreciated, but their output is
probably the reason most suburbanites buy the big-city daily in the first
place. Best of all, there's not much competition for the positions. Everyone
is trying to break into the news or features department, but the editors
there are jaded and rude."

Gene stands by his advice because it worked for him.

"Call the high school sports editor and tell him you would like to
cover one game, say basketball or football, a week. The pay is lousy and
so are the hours, but if you need professional clips from a major daily, this
is the fastest way to break into the profession. Take your clips from your
college paper, local paper, or whatever, and use them as a marketing tool
to approach the prep editor. Tell him you know the coach at your old high

school. Create your own story. In a month, you will have four clips from a major daily. And once that happens, you open up opportunities at other papers, magazines, and newsletters for higher paying, higher profile jobs. I did this myself. I covered prep sports—about which I know very little—for just a few weeks before the editor asked me to write an opinion piece for the paper. The opinion piece caught the attention of the local CBS affiliate, and they called me for an interview. This kind of stuff is great for your career."

These days, that kind of work might catch the attention of someone on the Internet, and the next thing you know you could be working for ESPN.com.

Seasoned reporter John D. Reger, who was a journalism major at Long Beach State, told me his first news job was covering high school sports and "some colleges and pros." Something that opened his eyes was the relationship between advertising and newspapers, and how integrity could be compromised.

"It's a business," John said of newspapers. "You can't ever forget that. The papers are not like *Lou Grant* [the old TV sitcom starring Ed Asner]. They are run by bean counters. If you are lucky, you will get to practice a slight variation of the journalism they taught you in college. I once wanted to write a column about a car dealer who was planning to buy a minor league hockey team. He only threw his name in to get the free publicity and had no intention of buying the team. The team ended up disbanding because any really interested parties left when they thought the car dealer was going to buy it. Well, I wanted to blast the car dealer, but was told by my editor that he [the car dealer] was a personal friend of the publisher and bought four full-page ads a day. He was off limits. He could rape little girls and it wouldn't get in the paper."

If the above story seems cynical to you, be advised that reporters from any urban paper around the world have similar stories. Craig Howson was right; you do see things as a journalist that most of the public rarely sees. I first learned how intimately connected advertising and the print media was when writing for *Palm Springs Life* magazine. The thick glossy Southern California monthly had a regular Beverly Hills section, which made some sense because so many of their readers' primary residences were in Beverly Hills, with second homes in Palm Springs.

"I want you to write some advertorials," editor Walter Bowart told me. "Four of them this issue."

"No problem," I replied. "What's an advertorial?"

It didn't take long to find out. Merchants would buy full-page ads and have complimentary articles written about them. Since I was adept at finding the good side to anyone, I was perfect to write advertorials, which come from combining the words "advertising" and "editorial." In fact, I wrote them for a Century City newspaper and several other Southern California publications.

Is this a compromise of journalistic integrity?

I never saw it that way. I never lied about anyone, or painted a false picture. If I was writing about a rare coin dealer on Rodeo Drive, I talked about the fact that he could actually read the Coptic language that an ancient document was written in. In journalistic terms, this type of article is often called a "puff" piece, which was fine with me. I didn't mind saying something nice about someone when it was paying my rent and allowing me to pursue loftier aspirations.

The above stories should give you some ideas of how to break into newspaper writing. If you haven't studied journalism and don't know where to start in writing for a paper, just remember the basics I talked about in the chapter on articles: who, what, when, where, why, and possibly how. If you cover those bases in your article, you'll do all right. If you want to know the proper formats to use, refer to my articles chapter. The only addition is that it used to be a common practice at newspapers to end an article with the following:

- 30 -

You don't have to do that these days, but it's a fun thing to know. Rather than waste your time with other ideas, let me refer you to the book which reporters around the United States use regularly. It's the *Associated Press Stylebook and Briefing on Media Law*, available at your local bookstore and library. Some large big city papers, like the *Los Angeles Times*, have their own stylebook. *The Chicago Manual of Style* is also popular, but the AP book is more broadly used than any other because it also pays attention to covering yourself legally in our "sue-happy" society.

Making Money Twice

Once you've published some articles in the local paper, it might occur to you to get them reprinted in other markets. One writer I knew who worked for a small newspaper in West Virginia was thrilled the first time one of his stories got "picked up" by the Associated Press and reprinted around the country. When that began happening on a regular basis, he found out that his editor was selling the stories to the AP but keeping the money for himself. Needless to say, the fur flew.

Whether you are on the staff of a paper or not, you can resell your stories via syndication. When you see "AP," "UPI," or "Reuters" alongside a story, it means it's come from somewhere other than the newspaper in which you're reading the piece. *Writer's Market* once devoted an entire section devoted to newspaper syndicates, with pages of advice on who bought what and from whom, but no more. Newspapers are generally on the decline in major markets, thanks to the Internet, and syndicators only take on columns from writers who have national recognition already. If you sell an article locally which you feel may have national or even international appeal, however, you still might sell it to *Reader's Digest*. As long as your local interest story might have interest nationally or internationally, there's always a chance, and with the Internet, you could make people aware of it on your own.

One last thing about newspaper writing. If you've ever had a letter to the editor published, you've probably known the thrill of "wow, they thought I had something worthwhile to say!" Along that line, why not try writing an "op ed" piece? In case you don't know, that stands for "opinion editorial." Contact your local paper, ask how long an op ed piece should be, then write it. Whether you want to have your say about the injustices meted out by the local dogcatcher or how you think a toxic landfill any-where is a bad idea, you just might get published. If your piece is about a subject that is also "hot" in other parts of the country, chances are good that you can sell the article again. Unfortunately, you'll probably have to do the marketing yourself.

Now that we've generally covered the world of newspaper writing, let's get into the world that supports every newspaper. Namely, that bastion of the free enterprise system—advertising.

Advertising: Awful or Amazing?

There is a way to succeed in advertising without really crying. (Sorry for that pun on an old phrase, but I couldn't resist.) You don't have to have a degree to get hired by an advertising agency, but in most instances it's required. If you don't believe me, check the ads in the Sunday paper. Also, don't expect to make much money starting out, and be willing to work anywhere you're placed, such as the mailroom or reception. Ad agencies are by nature neurotic beasts.

When I first began attempting to make a living as a freelance writer, I did word processing. One of my temporary assignments landed me in the office of the head man at Foote, Cone & Belding, one of the larger ad agencies in the country at the time (and the place Helen Gurley Brown worked before she wrote *Sex and the Single Girl* and became the legendary editor of *Cosmopolitan* magazine). After completing one of the letters I was dictated and handing it to my employer to sign, I told him of my writing aspirations and asked him how I could break into advertising.

"Write something," he told me. "And let me see it."

So I did. I wrote several fictional TV commercials and some magazine ad copy and brought it back to him, weeks after my assignment at the agency had ended. To my surprise, I was ushered right into his office, by his new secretary. Had I made that good of an impression?

I had indeed, merely because I'd done what he asked.

"You came back," he told me. "You did what I asked. Most people never make it to that step."

I'd like to report that I went on to make a huge six-figure income coming up with catchy phrases, but it didn't happen that way. After that seasoned ad veteran dissected my creations, I didn't continue to follow up. It wasn't that I didn't appreciate the attention, it was just that I got lucky elsewhere. Not long after that, I won money on a game show and landed the job of managing editor on a new start-up business magazine in Los Angeles. With my income taken care of for a time, I abandoned word processing and my advertising aspirations.

No one has ever been able to draw a distinct relation between advertising and public consumption, although millions are spent daily in all forms of the media to achieve exactly that. Advertising people measure their effectiveness in things like "impressions." I learned that from a slick ad exec who had a plaque on his wall which read: "If you can't dazzle 'em with brilliance, baffle 'em with bullshit."

Believe me, he practiced what he advertised.

Here's an example of an impression. Let's say a radio station manages to come up with some figures that say they reach an average of three million people each hour. Or a magazine with a circulation of 300,000 figures that each copy of the magazine passes through five people's hands before being discarded, resulting in 1.5 million actual public contacts. The radio station and the magazine would deliver three million and 1.5 million "impressions," respectively.

Although newspapers might be in decline, radio is not, particularly with the advent of satellite radio and the ability to "broadcast" on Internet "stations." It deserves your attention.

What's a good ad? One that someone remembers. After all, you might only get one chance to sell someone on your product, or one impression. Will they remember it, and thereby seek it out in the market? That's what you want them to do.

One ad exec I knew built a huge business in Dallas, Texas. He was the #1 man at the largest agency in town, with major clients like the Dallas Cowboys football team and the Dr Pepper soft drink company. One of his main tricks was something he'd learned from an old ad veteran. When he created a new TV ad, he didn't hire an expensive composer to come up with new, memorable music. Instead, he used songs everyone knew which were in the public domain, meaning he didn't have to pay anyone a royalty. Here's a fictional example of an ad he might have created using this method. The tune is "The Battle Hymn of the Republic," although the words are a little different.

> *They're just the greatest football team that anyone has seen*
> *The Cowboys are a legend, the stuff of Texas dreams*
> *Go down to the stadium and watch America's team*
> *The 'Pokes go marching on!*

'Pokes, of course, being short for "cowpokes," which is one of the nicknames for the Cowboys in the Dallas area.

Like I said, I didn't go on to a great future in advertising, but you get the idea. You know the tune, and you remember the commercial. That's why celebrities get so much mileage out of advertising. Michael Jordan, perhaps the greatest basketball player of all time, not only promoted McDonalds, he got his own burger named after him. Will it help a kid play better hoops? No way, but it will make them feel like it will. That's what advertising is all about—emotions and feelings first, and facts second. If you don't believe that, the next time you listen to a car commercial, see if you can't recognize the voice. Isn't that movie star Michael Douglas touting that luxury car? It sure is. You don't see his face, but you're familiar with (and therefore, advertising logic says you feel comfortable with), the voice. Maybe he won't go so far as actress/model Brooke Shields and become an on-camera spokesperson for Ford, but why not make a good bit of extra cash by going into a sound studio to do a thirty-second voiceover?

As I said, I won't attempt to delve very far into the world of advertising in this book. There's simply far too much to cover, whether I interviewed experts or not. If you want to make money writing advertising copy, find a local agency and offer your services, just like Gene Koprowski did in approaching the sports editor of a newspaper. Advertising, even for someone with a college degree, is an area where the apprentice "I'll do any job while learning" approach still works. Whether it's awful or amazing, it's a part of our lives that will never go away. If you lean toward Madison Avenue with your writing aspirations, be prepared to make a full-time pursuit of it.

Remember the story about the car dealer who bought four pages of ads in the paper each day? It's doubtful he really could get away with rape, but the relationship between advertisers and the media is intense and ongoing. A top TV writer/producer once told me that he was once working on a show at a network when Johnson & Johnson pulled ads from 500 separate programs in a year's time, because they didn't approve of the content. If you don't think that had some impact, we're not living on the same planet. It's like Craig Howson said—what is seen behind the scenes at a newspaper and what actually goes out to the public is far, far different than most people imagine. That includes the stories behind those ads on the back page.

It's a PR World

Did you know that reporters didn't write many of the shorter stories in the newspaper? Oftentimes, particularly in smaller papers, the stories are merely reprinted from a press release, sent to the paper by a public relations specialist. When I say, it's a PR world, I mean a Public Relations world. In Hollywood, it's not uncommon for a movie or TV star to pay a PR firm $5,000 a month or more to get them favorable press. When someone holds a press conference, they don't just sit in front of a microphone and make an announcement. How do the reporters know to get there? Did they all get a phone call? Probably not. They probably responded to a press release, which more than likely was faxed to them, but could have been mailed.

What's a press release? Is that when Skip Press gets out of jail? (Hey, did you expect me to resist making that joke?)

A press release covers the newspaper stock in trade: who, what, when, where, and why. It can come from the person who is seeking the publicity, but that's generally not a good idea. It's a strange thing with the press, but they like to learn about something from someone other than the true source. That's why press agents stay in business. It's the old "Hey, did ya hear?" kind of mentality. Most people I know who are wise to this but can't afford to hire a PR firm get around this by typing out their own press release and sending it out as though it came from someone else. It needs to be printed on some form of stationery that denotes a business, not a person. If you are promoting a book, it could be your publisher's stationery. At the top, in large, bold type, the type of news you are providing should be prominent. Also at the top should be the phrase FOR IMMEDIATE RELEASE at the left side. At the right, indicate the date, so the reporter knows when you sent it out. If possible, keep the press release to one page. It's good to double-space it, for readability. At the bottom, after you've said what you have to say, give a name of a person to contact and a phone number. That's so the reporter can just pick up the phone and call with any pertinent questions.

Below is an abbreviated example of a press release on a book of mine. It was printed on the stationery of the publisher, B&B Publishing. To keep it on one page, it was single-spaced.

BOOK NEWS from B&B

FOR IMMEDIATE RELEASE   DECEMBER 1994

AWESOME ALMANAC CALIFORNIA

B&B Publishing, Inc. is proud to announce the publication of a new title in the AWESOME ALMANAC series of state trivia books—AWESOME ALMANAC *California*! This book closely follows AWESOME ALMANAC *Florida* that was published in November. All the "awesome books—Indiana, Illinois, Michigan, Minnesota, and Wisconsin—have been well received. B&B will continue to add to the series with Ohio, New York, and Texas scheduled for Spring 1995 release.

Award-winning writer Skip Press, a California resident, is author of the California book. He brings a unique and entertaining tone to this fun and fact-filled book.

Each AWESOME ALMANAC contains comprehensive coverage of the best, the worst, the most, the least, the good, the bad, the famous, the infamous, and much more. They are loaded with essential as well as fun information. New features include a subject index, bibliography, and detailed state map.

Here are some comments we have received on earlier books in the series:

(quotes follow)

AWESOME ALMANAC California
by Skip Press
$14.95 list
Trade paperback - 7 3/8" x 10 1/4" 206 pages
ISBN 1-880190-21-4
Publication date: December 1, 1994

The AWESOME ALMANAC series is published by B&B Publishing, Inc. Distributed by Login Publishers Consortium.

For further information contact Katy O'Shea (414) 275-9474.

The press release also gave my phone number, if anyone wanted to call me to schedule an interview. Since B&B was in Walworth, Wisconsin, and I'm in Southern California, and since Katy O'Shea at B&B would have to relay phone calls to me, anyway, I let them list my phone number on the press release, to save time for everyone.

Get the idea? If your press release were about an event rather than a specific product, you write it so that any reporter reading it could simply use your paragraphs intact, with the most important information in up front. For example:

ANYTOWN ELECTION NEWS!

FOR IMMEDIATE RELEASE   Today

George Gump will announce his entry into the mayoral race today with a press conference scheduled for 9:00 A.M. Gump states a simple reason for running for mayor.

"I'm sick of being sick of the sickos in city government," says Gump, a local veterinarian since 1969. "If you're not part of the cure, you're part of the disease, and I'm just the man to clean up the epidemic of stupidity we've had to endure in Anytown for the last couple of years."

Gump brings a convincing bag of political knowledge and common sense into the race. He won the first race he ever entered, Anytown's Donkey Derby, in 1979. The winning attitude has always...

At the bottom of this fictional release would be the name of someone who is serving as George's campaign manager, probably his wife or his mother, given what we know about George, along with the address of his campaign headquarters and the phone number. A fax number, e-mail address, and Web site should also be listed, as appropriate. Basically, answer all the questions you can in the press release, but say only enough to get the recipient intrigued enough to call the person listed. After all, that's the point.

A press release can be a potent tool for anyone wanting media coverage, but a press kit is the full package. For one how-to video I did, I not only wrote the script, co-produced the production, and played one of the roles,

I also got the job of putting together the press kit, even though we had hired a PR firm at $3,500 a month to put our tape on the map. A press kit basically consists of the following:

- A press release describing the main event, such as the release of the video, book, or whatever

- A bio of the principal people involved

- A synopsis of the production, movie, book, or whatever

- A photo or photos of the principal people involved

- Photocopies of any other pertinent and notable press that has been received, such as a good review

- If you have the facilities to make an electronic press kit (EPK) you should also include a CD or DVD of same

In the tape I mentioned, I wrote the bios on the main actors, even though they had starred in movies and our narrator was the star of a popular TV series. I didn't know enough at the time to tell the PR firm to do it themselves, since we were paying them. I was young and gullible enough to do their work for them. They got our show reviewed in *People* magazine, so maybe they were worth it, but sometimes I wonder. A DVD of the show is still being sold today, so maybe the content alone and self-generated publicity would have been enough.

A bio is a short biography about a person or a production. It shouldn't be any longer than three pages, double-spaced. One I wrote about world champion boxer Carlos Palomino, for example, was a page and a half. If you can keep it to one page, all the better. I usually take the approach of current event (the show or event), followed by the past (what the person has done of note), then more information on the current event, wrapping up with future plans. It's a past, present, future structure that seems to work pretty well.

The synopsis is merely the beginning, middle, and end, making it sound as compelling as possible. It's more of an advertising piece than a scholarly dissertation or critical review.

If you include photos, get them taken by a professional photographer, and use black and white. Remember, they go mostly to newspapers, who will usually run the photo you send, rather than send out their own photographer and incur extra expense.

A word of caution in photocopying articles—clear it with the people who printed them. This is rarely done, even by top PR agencies, but they break copyright laws when they photocopy and broadly distribute hundreds or thousands of reviews, articles, or whatever without obtaining permission first. Note: This also applies to electronic articles found online.

As with much other advice in this book, I'm not claiming to be a scholarly professor of every detail of public relations. I just wanted you to have an idea of what goes out to the media, to get their attention.

You might have been wondering if could you make a living writing for public relations firms. I doubt it, unless you were on staff. You could pick up some extra cash writing bios, however. I've done that in the past from time to time. When I was doing it, fifty dollars for a short bio was the norm. Check your *Writer's Market* for currently acceptable rates.

The funny thing about a great number of PR people I've met is that they couldn't write to save their lives. Remember that as a freelancer. PR people *need* you. They are particularly friendly if they think you can be a regular source of articles about their clients, but they can turn into completely cold fish if you suddenly aren't able to do anything for them immediately. It's the kind of thing that gives "PR" a bad name.

I was once the editor of a decent-sized entertainment magazine in Hollywood. When I came on board, a lady at the legendary PR firm of Rogers & Cowan treated me like I was made of pure gold. She told me that she thought I had a special touch, that I would put the magazine on the map, make it take off like a rocket. And she got me to put one of her clients on a cover. Love you, love you, love you, dah-ling!

When I left the magazine to try and produce a film script I'd written, the lady wouldn't return a single phone call, period. I was completely persona non grata. I was stunned at the treatment. Good old naive me again. Similarly, when I wrote all the entertainment-related articles for *Boys' Life* magazine for over a year, one PR firm in Los Angeles treated me like a king. I got one of their clients a cover story simply because the editor liked the photo so much. When I quit writing for the magazine, it was like the PR firm didn't even know me.

Other PR people in my experience have been downright nasty, when I tell them I'm writing something about their client. I've hardly written a bad word about anyone in my life, yet when I was writing a book about a popular singer and merely wanted a single question answered by the PR person (when an album came out), it took me three weeks and a personal letter to the owner of the agency to get the question answered. As it turned out, the singer was writing her own biography, and thought my book might be competition. Petty? Damn right it was, and my book was for young adults and sold only to high schools, which I made pains to explain up front, but it didn't make any difference.

There have been a few bright spots in my dealings with PR people. Marvin Levy, staff PR at DreamWorks (and before that, Steven Spielberg's company Amblin Productions), has always treated me with respect, taken my phone calls, and answered my questions, even when I wasn't writing anything about his boss, or one of his boss's shows.

For reasons given above, I wouldn't advise anyone to try and make a living in public relations, if they have higher writing aspirations. Why? Because basically, you'll be asked to put on a front, bend the truth a little, puff up people who may not deserve it. One PR person I know started out as a serious journalist. He did good interviews with top musicians, and made a living as a freelancer. Now he concentrates on "lines and inches" all day. Lines about his clients, and column inches of print about them, in publications. That's the focus of his life now. It's sad. Still, many newspapers articles start only because of materials received from PR people. If the subject of the press release is a big advertiser in the paper, do you think they'll get any attention?

Now you have some idea of how the newspaper-advertising-public relations machine works. Many fine writers started at a newspaper. You can make a lot more money in advertising, but you might feel a bit hollow at the end of the day. Public relations? I barely consider it writing, but it is essential that you know how that game works, when you're out promoting something worthwhile that you've written. After all, one day you might plan to tell the world about something you've done, maybe even something that makes the world a better place.

Blog It!

If you don't know about the power of Weblogs, you weren't paying attention during the 2004 U.S. Presidential election. "Blogs" made a big difference as the political wars of the Democrats and Republicans played out. These self-maintained and quickly updated Web sites that link to various articles and references on the Internet allowed "viral" infections of data that might show up on a cable news show within minutes of appearing on the Internet. While traditional journalists and TV newspeople at first derided the bloggers, they soon were forced to accept them and even quote them, due to the vast popularity of these self-published sites. My author friend W. T. Quick (see www.iw3p.com) coined the term "the blogosphere" to describe how quickly Weblogs pervaded media consciousness.

If you want to start your own Weblog, it's easy. Just surf over to www.blogger.com and follow the instructions. Who knows? Before you can drive to the store and back, you might find something you wrote being quoted on a cable newscast. Stranger things have happened.

Knocking It Out of the Park: How to Get Your Own Big League Publicity

I speak on a lot of different panels, most of them in Hollywood but also around the United States. At the 2005 Do It Yourself Convention ("Do It Yourself in Film, Music and Books"—see www.diyconvention.com) I had the pleasure of sharing a panel with several successful people including songwriter/author Seth Swirsky (see www.seth.com). Seth was a very successful songwriter before becoming an author. His music successes include "Did You Give Enough Love?" by Celine Dion, a #1 single in Canada for the album "Celine Dion," and "Instant Pleasure" by Rufus Wainwright for the movie "Big Daddy" (1998).

Seth's career as an author was not something he planned, but his book *Baseball Letters* became a big hit. While on the panel with him, I learned that he accomplished some amazing things, PR-wise, so I asked him to describe how he used networking skills to work his way onto major morning talk shows like *Good Morning America*.

"First, I truly believed in my book," Seth said. "I felt strongly, that if people saw it, they would love it. I say this not in a conceited way, but to magnify the point, that you *must* really believe strongly in your work. Only then will you have the ability to knock down all the doors. Once you have this strong belief in your book, you must be able to describe it in a few short sentences to prospective producers of radio and television shows that you think may have you on. I practiced my pitch by calling my friends and describing my book to them until I felt comfortable that I had narrowed my pitch down to the least amount of words. By the end of a week of practice my pitch went something like this:

> When the baseball strike of 1994 occurred, my first son Julian was born. I thought, if baseball never comes back, I want to write some letters to some players that I can show my son someday. The result was my book *Baseball Letters* which is made up of the actual handwritten letters to me from people like Cal Ripken Jr., Ted Williams and dozens of others.

Seth summed up his pitch by describing it as "folksy with a beginning, a middle, and end." In other words, exactly what most network morning talk shows love to feature. And once he had that pitch perfected, he used what he calls "The Folder" to get the word out.

"Every time I told people that I was making this book, many would say 'I have a friend who works for CBS who would love this' or 'I know a guy who knows a guy at ESPN who is really into baseball...' Without fail, I would get a pen and a piece of paper and write down these people's names (who offered to get my book to their friends when it came out). When I got home, I just stuck all these scrap pieces of paper, with telephone numbers in a folder called *Baseball Letters* Publicity. Even though my book was months from coming out, I made a point of always solidifying every 'lead.' If someone offered to get my book to someone who might like it, I wrote it down. This is extremely important to an author. Authors need every bit of help they can get if their name isn't Grisham or some other top literary name.

"On top of this, every time I read a magazine that I thought might feature my book if pitched properly, I cut out the person who wrote the article I liked and put it in the folder. Not just the mainstream magazines, but airline magazines, hometown newspapers from where I grew up, college newspapers from where I went to college—whatever had a shot to write a piece on my book if I pitched it correctly, went into the folder. Two months before my book was slated to come out, I took out the folder and made a master list of all of the contacts that friends had offered and ideas of good places to send my book."

Seth also knew something that few new authors realize:

"You must start pitching your book two months in advance. Your book company will give it three to four weeks from the release date and then it's history. In short, *you must be your own publicist*. If they get you on a talk show, that's an added bonus. That is the mindset you *must* have. Only your hard work getting publicity will determine the ultimate success of your book."

Next, Seth made a master list. In Column A went the person's name. Column B had the media outlet they worked with. Column C had their e-mail address, phone number, etc., and Column D was his own comments section, for use when he called and followed up.

"It is a simple system that works," he revealed. "Then, I started a non-stop campaign of calling each contact, giving my twenty-second pitch (that's about all you have, so it better be tight). When I felt like I hooked a producer (it *is* like fishing) and he said he wanted a copy of the book, this is what I did next:

"(a) I overnighted him a copy so he got it by 10 the next morning. If your book arrives by 4, the next afternoon, he may have forgotten about your conversation, that's how fast the world is moving these days. And what did you save by not having it arrive when it could get into his "rotation"? 6 bucks? Cost ineffective! Included with the book you send, should be a personal letter, reminding him of your conversation, thanking him for his valuable time and again, quickly, outlining your project. In short, keep selling.

"(b) O.K. A producer has interest in your book. Now, you *must* follow-up. You must remain in his 'rotation.' In other words, where he's actively thinking of how, where and when to book you on his show. You must give him a few days to consider your book and proposal for his show. You should 'follow-up' (that's the term to use because they respect that you're working for your own book) about 4 or 5 days later. Write a short e-mail. Keep your publicity effort in motion, always moving forward."

Seth estimates that he had an astonishing ninety percent success rate with the media he went after. Why?

"I was impassioned about my project, conveying in my pitch that they had to have me on with my unusual book. But the thing that got me in

Newsweek's Christmas "What to Buy for Christmas" issue, a review in *People* magazine, a large profile piece in *USA Today*, on *Good Morning America*, three times on the "Today" show, etc., was *follow-up* and then more *follow-up*. Persistent, ongoing (for months if need be), polite, professional *follow-up*. It's the difference between the men and the boys."

Seth told me that he is certain his system will work for promoting any book. Once you can answer what is unique about your book, that is the beginning of getting your pitch together. He began learning how to do this in his first job out of college, as a songplugger at Chappell Music Publishing in New York City. His job was to take a song that one of the staff songwriters wrote and match it with a popular singer, like Barbra Streisand. If Ms. Streisand recorded the song, that's how Chappell and the songwriter made money. He learned that he had to do a tremendous amount of follow-up once he pitched the song to the artist's representative, manager, or record company.

"I learned the right rhythms of when to follow-up and when to lay off," he confided. "If you follow up too soon and too often, you're perceived to be a pain in the you know what to the people you want to like your project. But, if you wait too long after you've sent your material, you're forgotten. It's an art to know when to push or to pull. I came up with the 3 P's—three words that describe my strategy: Passion, Persistence, and Patience. Your passion for your work must show, you must be persistent in pitching your work and following-up, and you must be patient as well, knowing most good things (like a big TV interview) don't happen overnight.

"I believe that all a person has to do to succeed in anything in life is to get a pen and write down what you want. Outside of things like 'I want to own a yacht in a year' you can achieve it, if you are willing to flow the Three P's."

I don't know about you, but this P (the Press who wrote this book) thinks Seth Swirsky has some smart advice, and I plan to use it.

We've covered a lot in this chapter, but I hope you've gleaned some useful information on how the world learns about your work, and how to get it to them. If you have a lot of success using anything you've read here, let me know, won't you?

Chapter Fifteen

It's a Funny Life, and Sometimes a Comic One

A S YOU MIGHT HAVE SURMISED FROM THE NATURE OF THIS BOOK and all the personal writing stories I've related, I'm a person who is interested in just about everything. I've always had the attitude that if it was something that could be written, I could write it. As I was finishing up this book, I sold a comic book. I never tried very hard to sell a comic book, but I had a collection that would have made me rich if I'd been allowed to keep it! The original Spider-Man, for example.

This is a chapter for "everything else." If you want to write and sell calendars, greeting cards, jokes, recipes, or novelty books, this chapter is for you. I can't see making a living at any of the above, but you might be one of the rare ones who does.

Bob Lovka was the perfect person to speak to about "everything else" because he worked for a company who published just that. For years, Bob was the Senior Editor, Adult Trade, Humor & Creative Development for Price Stern Sloan Incorporated, a Los Angeles publishing house that is a division of the Putnam Berkeley Group, Inc. Price Stern Sloan relocated to New York in 1997 and Bob left the company, but at the time of the interview he knew this part of publishing as well as anyone.

Like me, Bob came to Los Angeles not knowing anyone. Also like me, he got a job by answering an ad. He was hired by a gift company to write things like posters and bumper stickers. By his own admission, he went in and lied his head off about his capabilities. He got the job first, then figured out how to do it. Could he do a few "on spec"? Sure. He wrote a few, they hired him, and he was a working writer.

From there, Bob branched out to comedy skits, writing for a TV show called *Bedtime Stories*. Small world. My youngest brother Tim and his first wife were early big winners on the show. I only found out Bob was connected with the show when interviewing him for the book.

In Bob's office were dozens of books his company had published, some board games, and calendars galore. He told me he was looking for a good calendar, in case I had any ideas. If there was one unifying element of all the various items, it was humor. In the world of "specialty" publishing, humor is king. If you have a good sense of humor and can write, you can do well. If you can also draw, like Gary Larson of *The Far Side* fame or the late Charles Schultz of *Peanuts*, you might become a millionaire seemingly overnight.

Seeing all the funny things around the office prompted me to ask Bob that eternal question: "So what's funny?"

"It's just a feeling inside that something is going to work," Bob ventured. "It just makes you laugh."

At that point of the conversation we were joined by Leonard Stern, the comedy-writing genius behind the company. Leonard was a writer on many early TV hits, such as *The Honeymooners* with Jackie Gleason (remade as a feature film in 2005). Being the persistently inquisitive pest that I am, I asked Leonard the same question I had asked Bob.

"Jackie Gleason was asked why the Honeymooners and *I Love Lucy* succeeded and lasted so long," Leonard said, "and he always had the answer, 'Because they're funny.' Most contemporary comedy hasn't been, but it's starting to reemerge. In those days, it was funny without being acrimonious or cynical or skeptical, so it was pure fun. I don't know if you can teach somebody to be funny, but if somebody has a sense of humor or odd perspective, they just look at things and think of things in a different way." Then Leonard really got down to business, telling me how comedians were different when he started out. He feels that comedians these days are less funny because they write their own material.

"You don't have the equivalent of S. J. Perelman writing for the Marx Brothers," I offered as an example. (And if you don't know the Marx Brothers, wow, have you missed it.)

"Right, no one is making demands of them, other than themselves, and their standards are lower than they think they are. But I still don't know why something is funny. I've been asking my peers that forever. From age twelve I was able to write jokes. Whether it's a compensation or a gift, I can't answer. That's the hardest question to answer. I don't know how it's defined by anyone. You go by instinct and history."

With an eye toward history, I asked Leonard if the difference between popular comedians who came from the world of stand-up, as opposed to comedians who came from the world of vaudeville (such as Bob Hope) made a difference.

"I think stand-up is devoid of character," Leonard told me. "And vaudeville was based on character, on creating a personality. Milton Berle was a joke teller, but he also was a sketch comic—he changed his identities. Some like Gleason were poor monologists, but were marvelous when they got into character."

Leonard was not without hope for modern devoid of character humor. He cited Jerry Seinfeld's success, as well as that of Tim "Home Improvement" Allen, whose fame was founded on his character "Tool Man." We talked of how Phil Silvers' great character of "Sgt. Bilko" in a 1950s TV series was being redone as a feature by Steve Martin. We mused that maybe character was coming back.

"There was a spirit of fun that took on a life of its own," Bob added. "It's got something you can identify with, that little exaggerated view, that skewered view that's still within the realm of reality. That's something in all these great classic things that you have an empathy and a feeling for. A real persona, a real situation tweaked just enough to make it recognizable. That's where the best comedy comes from. It's a communication."

Bob told me that, despite all the talk of market research that one continually hears about, the basic decisions of what his company published had mostly to do with gut instinct.

This surprised me, because Price Stern Sloan was at the time perhaps the most recognized publisher on the West Coast. I asked him to give me an example of a book they had published on instinct—just because they thought it was funny. He offered me *Sheldon & Mrs. Levine*, a satirical take-off on best-sellers at that time, the ornate Griffin & Sabine books. *Sheldon* was written by the writing team of Sam Bobrick and Julie Stein.

When I saw Sam's name, I wasn't surprised Price Stern Sloan had published the book. Sam was a funny and highly accomplished playwright who made a fortune when he created a long-running teenage sitcom that became an industry all its own called *Saved by the Bell*.

Small world again. One of the young adult novels I had written for hire was a *Saved by the Bell: The College Years* paperback novel, under a pseudonym.

Why did they publish *Sheldon & Mrs. Levine*? Because it was funny, Bob told me, and indeed it was. It was hilarious, matter of fact, chronicling a Jewish mother who won't leave her son alone. But don't get the wrong idea. Even if they hadn't known who Sam was, Bob said, someone at the company would have read the book. If it could make it up the chain of command with everyone thinking it was funny, they'd publish it. The only exception in their submission policy was drama.

"We don't do dramatic novels," Bob emphasized. "Don't send 'em."

OK, so maybe I haven't told you what's funny, but I've given you some idea of the inner workings of a comedy and comedic publishing. Mark Twain said that all comedy was based on sorrow. If you think of Charlie Chaplin's "Little Tramp" character, or the troubles endured by Laurel & Hardy or The Three Stooges, you see the wisdom of Twain's observation. Having written a book on Twain, I know that he suffered a good deal of personal pain, yet managed to turn it to humor. And aren't the twin faces of the theater one smiling and one crying?

So let me make that distinction for you once again:

If you want to sell your comedic writing, you'll go a lot farther with humor than you will with what often gets called comedy. What's the difference? Humor is socially acceptable. A chuckle, maybe even a guffaw results from humor. You wouldn't be surprised if a comedian was banned from the radio, as George Carlin was when his famous "seven words you can't say on radio" [all profanities] bit came out on a comedy album. You would be surprised, though, if you heard that a humorist had been banned from airplay, wouldn't you? Humor is rarely mean-spirited, while "comedy" often is. Also, comedy can vary widely by culture, while humor is universal. Example: A popular Japanese TV show was based on a group of people surprising someone who is sleeping and screaming as loud as they can, shocking the person awake. The Japanese like scatological humor, while that's still taboo on American network television. That's comedy. One of the most popular Japanese TV commercials of all time, on the other hand, featured two small children taking a bath together. A large bubble appears on the surface of the water and bursts, causing one child to look at the other, wide-eyed. Obviously, one child passed gas, but which one? When Johnny Carson played the commercial on *The Tonight Show* a few years before he turned the show over to Jay Leno, it got one of the most gigantic laughs ever, and was the most popular of all the foreign commercials he showed that night.

That's humor. If you have to pick between writing comedy and writing humor, pick humor. Humor touches on the universality of the human condition everywhere, and is not limited to time or culture.

Now that we've covered some basics, let's go into some of areas where you might sell humorous writing.

Just Joking Around

When I wrote a book on Joan Rivers and her daughter Melissa, I was amazed at how she had struggled to make it as one of the first female stand-up comedians, writing for the old *Candid Camera* TV show, and only getting her break and first appearance on *The Tonight Show* by getting the producer to book her not as a comedienne but as a comedy writer. Joan was determined and never gave up, no matter what the setbacks. Her story is most common in the world of stand-up comedy.

I once contemplated doing stand-up because it was the obvious route to getting one's own TV show. I haunted the Comedy Store on Sunset Boulevard in Los Angeles on Monday nights, watching Robin Williams, Martin Short, Jim Stahl, and others in the Comedy Store Players make people laugh with improvisational comedy night after night. I remember how my jaw dropped open the first time I heard the routine of Andrew Dice Clay. Jim Carrey amazed me with his physical contortions and bizarre routines—and this was long before he became a movie superstar. I never did figure out if Andy "Man on the Moon" Kaufman was putting on an act or truly hated women when he invited women onstage to wrestle him. Sam Kinison never screamed at me personally, but he did catch me off-guard once as we had a drink at the bar and talked about his days back in Oklahoma, when he was a Baptist minister!

What kept me from pursuing stand-up was the amount of time it took: years on the road to get good enough to become a regular at the Comedy Store or the Improvisation. I watched too many comedians struggling with drugs, and didn't laugh when Taylor Negron would joke onstage "Comedy isn't pretty."

Do you want to write and sell jokes? You won't make much money. Try $25 to $50 for a joke, if you're really good. How many of those can you write in a day? Can you do it every day, for a week? Can you write not one but three very good fifteen-minute routines? That's what you'll need if you get booked on *The Tonight Show*. Why? Because if you're a hit, they'll want you back in a few weeks, then a few weeks after that. You can't do the same routines each time, can you? And if you make it there, you'll get booked in Vegas, where the real money is. And if you do well in Vegas, chances are a network executive will be talking to you about your own sitcom. If, that is, your special on HBO is a hit.

If you want to be a comedy writer, but don't do your own stand-up, you're probably not going to make a living. There are simply too many jokes out there. If you're really good, though, you might land a job as a staff writer for Jay Leno, or David Letterman. Guess what the odds of that are?

That's about all I can tell you on writing jokes. If you're serious about it, move to New York or (preferably) Los Angeles and start making the rounds. Hang out at the comedy clubs, offer some sample jokes to some comedians, and see what you can do. It's that simple and that difficult. I suggest Los Angeles over New York for two reasons: (1) that's where the TV shows are filmed; and (2) it's easier to stay alive while starving in a warm weather climate. Format? Whatever you can type out on a 3×5 card. Milton Berle, the comedy pack rat of all-time, has file cabinets full.

Or, you might wait until a TV show like *Last Comic Standing* holds auditions in your town. You know what they say about he who hesitates, don't you? In a comedy club, he's the guy they throw stuff at.

If you're funny and you're in Hollywood, you can make a lot of money writing comedy. Mid-January, 2005, Universal bought a comedy spec (written on the speculation that it will be bought) screenplay called *The Break Up* by Jay Lavender and Jeremy Garelick for more than two million dollars. Vince Vaughan was slated to star. That kind of money would make me laugh, how about you?

The Comic Book and Graphic Novel Route to Real Money

Let's say you have a wacky mind but you don't plan on writing funny books, are not a stand-up comedian, and you haven't yet written a comedy screenplay. How about writing comic books or graphic novels? That's a misnomer any more, because most of them aren't comic. Many stars who began as comedians, however, have made box-office history starring in films that started out as comic books. Jim Carrey in *The Mask*, for example. Michael Keaton in *Batman* for another. When I was a kid, we would have called a graphic novel "a big comic book," but things are more serious these days. The recent *Batman* movies at Warner Brothers only became a possibility for a live-action movie after the astounding success of a graphic novel called *The Dark Night Returns* by Frank Miller.

As I was finishing this book, my son Haley and I saw the movie *Constantine* starring Keanu Reeves. It was adapted from the comic book *Hellblazer* written by Jamie Delano and Garth Ennis. We were eagerly awaiting the debut of Frank Miller's *Sin City*, another movie from a comic book, starring Bruce Willis and a boatload of stars. Miller was responsible for the 2004 movie *Elektra* (a comic book character), *The Punisher* (comic book), and many other films. He is someone to be emulated if you want to work in both the comics/graphic novel world and in Hollywood. He also wrote two *Robocop* movies.

When I was writing the last edition of this book, I sold my first comic book. It was basically a fluke because which happened only because of my friendship with Dave Simons, a well-known comic book artist and illustrator with whom I collaborated. Our *Tribe 13* never made a splash, but it was fun to do.

Another writer who became a big success in writing comics fell into the profession by chance. Peter J. Quinones had friends who were trying to break into the field as artists. A friend named Glenn Johnson read a fantasy novel Peter was writing and created four "beautiful pages of artwork" to accompany it.

"At that moment," Peter remembered, "I decided I really wanted to see my words illustrated. I'd grown up reading comics and had always made up stories. And, being a member of the TV generation, I was used to thinking visually."

Peter and Glenn took the four illustrated pages to ComicCon, a yearly convention for the comic book trade that takes place in San Diego, California. They found a publisher who liked the artwork and asked if Peter could tell the story in thirty-two pages.

"Yeah, no problem," he replied, even though he had originally envisioned it as a ten-part, ten-pages-per-chapter work.

The book was published in 3-D, and was a hit. Small, independent publishers gave Peter more work, and he learned his craft, little by little. To him, those early books were his resumes. One of them was noticed by an artist who went on to become one of the top illustrators for Marvel, who picked up a project they created together. There was no set format and no one to teach Peter—he merely learned by doing, which he says has not changed to this day.

"You have to work for a lot of independents to learn your craft," he advises. "It helps if you're in New York. You don't have to live in a major metro area, but just make sure you go to the conventions. The only person who can buy your work is an editor. If you don't go to their office (and odds are they wouldn't see you if you did), you can go to conventions. However, what you want to give them is a published work. My experience has been that they don't really read your proposals. They can't really tell if you can pace a book, do dialogue, etc. It's like in Hollywood. You have to have the right format, and the best format is a published comic book."

Most of Peter's stories—which he presented in one-page synopsis form—were connected with an artist like Glenn Johnson, Kelley Jones, or Ron Lim. So he recommended hooking up with an artist right from the start. What if you don't know one? Go to a comic convention and meet some.

"Usually you are also helping the artist," Peter said. "You give him a story to draw, so that he's not just submitting pin-ups."

Selling comic books, like selling jokes, is really that simple. You go where the people are and give them a sample of what you can do. If you don't live in Southern California or New York, spend your vacation this year at some place where a major comic book convention is taking place, and start making the rounds. It is probably the only way you'll ever get started in that business.

Just don't think it's only beginning writers who want to do comic books. Mickey Spillane, the 1995 Grand Master of the Mystery Writers of America, sold his first story in 1935, then went on to create the legendary Mike Hammer detective character. Mike Hammer was originally Mike Danger, which Mickey intended to be a comic book. In 1993, he was approached by a Boca Raton, Florida company who wanted to put Mike Hammer out as a comic book. Mickey turned them down until they suggested using Mike Danger.

That's why May of 1995 saw the Big Entertainment Tekno Comix version of *Mike Danger* on the newsstands, "with plans to move into the television science-fiction market eventually," according to Spillane. You can take the comic books away from the kid, but you can never shake them out of him.

As I was writing this book, two friends of mine were selling almost a project a week to American movie studios. Jennie Lew Tugend produced the *Free Willy* movies and many others, and her producing partner Lauren Weissman once ran Jane Fonda's company. They joined forces to sell American rights to the media product of a major Japanese company that produced books, novels, movies, and the manga and anime so popular today. I wrote a chapter about it in my *Ultimate Writer's Guide to Hollywood*. If you can do a comic book or graphic novel, you're basically creating a "storyboard" template for a movie. That can have great appeal in selling the movie rights, no matter what language it's written in.

Greetings and Gewgaws

Do you want to write greeting cards? Do you want to be the next Hallmark? You don't have to move next door to a greeting card factory, but you would be better off if you are affiliated with an artist. Like writing for comedians, you probably won't make a living writing greeting cards. One successful greeting card writer I knew had a full-time job as a secretary at a firm where my wife worked. Her advice to me about selling greeting card slogans was "Write something that makes people laugh." But don't get too encouraged. Carole King, an "idea person" at Hallmark, told me that it was a fluke if they published something other than a card created by a staff writer. I've known people who made a success of greeting cards, but only because they self-published them. One of the major Internet success stories early on was Blue Mountain Arts electronic greeting cards. You never know when something will hit big with the public. Maybe you'll come up with it. Greeting cards for cell phones, anyone?

A gewgaw is a trifle or bauble. Like a desk calendar, for example, the kind of thing Bob Lovka published when he found one funny. Or the "Golf Tip a Day" calendar Price Stern Sloan was so successful with. No matter what the Internet does, people will continue having desks.

If you want to be a success with the more obscure areas of writing, I'd advise you to come up with a character or characters. Which means you either should be an artist as well as a writer, or hook up with an artist who can't write that well. I once introduced the daughter of a highly successful cartoonist to the owner of a syndicate. She and her brother had revived a comic strip their father had made famous, and they weren't happy with the syndicate who was distributing the strip. I learned that she wrote the strip, while her brother drew it. Their father had done both, but the two of them together couldn't match his brilliant wit. As I listened to her tell me about her supposed marketing troubles, I looked over the strips she and her brother had done, and knew immediately why they weren't doing as well. It wasn't the syndicate, but the approach. For her father, the characters were like his own children. He had a lot more affection for them than his real-life daughter and son had. He maintained a humorous approach, a bemused, good-natured parent who sees all the flaws but still loves the young-uns. The new version of the strip, on the other hand, had a comedy approach, trying to tell jokes and make social points that seemed at times irrelevant.

In contrast, how many *The Far Side* calendars have you seen on office desks? (Maybe there's one on yours.) Bizarre as Gary Larson's humor may be, the people in his cartoons seem to all be from the same unique world. They're like strange children that he manages to love, and thus get us to love, who remind us of ourselves in a way that makes us laugh. Because of that, we buy T-shirts, calendars, coffee mugs, and books about *The Far Side*. We buy the humor, and when one humorist fades away, another one pops up. *Dilbert*, for example.

I previously mentioned the cartoon that appeared on my personal stationery of Mark Twain trying to pick: "Boysenberry Finn? Strawberry Finn? Blueberry Finn? Cranberry Finn?" Having the cartoon on my stationery got me noticed, made people laugh, and swayed them toward giving me writing jobs. One guy made a deal with myself and John Caldwell to put the cartoon on T-shirts and sell them, with us getting a percentage. We made the deal, he sold a lot of T-shirts, and the last time I called to ask about my check, his phone was disconnected, with no forwarding number.

It's a funny life. If any of the above stories and advice on "other" areas of writing have helped you, I'm glad. I hope you pursue them vigorously if so inclined. Lord knows we could use a few more laughs in this world.

There's really only one other area of writing to cover, and that's the subject of our next chapter. It's the world of self-publishing, which can make you mad, make you millions, or maybe only make you famous. Wouldn't the latter be all right?

Chapter Sixteen

Doin' It Your Own Darn Self

ORIGINALLY, I INTENDED TO CALL THIS CHAPTER "LAST BUT Not Lost." I changed my mind because I realized the "lost" might be taken as a slight on people who decide to self-publish, and nobody wants to be thought of as coming in last. See? After all this time and after all this book, I can still be flexible. There may be hope for me yet!

If you decided to publish your own book, you wouldn't be in bad company. Maybe you read the book *The Celestine Prophecy*. It was originally self-published, as I mentioned earlier. I'm sure the story about poet Rod McKuen publishing his own book of poetry and selling 35,000 or so copies before being picked up by Bennett Cerf and Random House got your attention. If not, reading one of M. J. Rose's self-published erotica books would (www.mjrose.com).

If you can't get anyone to do it for you, do it yourself. It's amazing how many people have made a success with that attitude. Perhaps you've heard of that fellow Mark Twain, or that playwright named Shakespeare? How about Benjamin Franklin? Self-publishers all.

I've known a number of people who self-publish books, some with fine success and some with not so fine. Let's just say they could have spent their money more wisely.

One of the better aspects of the Information Age is that people can more easily exchange notes, keep in touch with each other, and make their books look just like those from big publishers.

I pose this question to you—can you tell the difference between a self-published book and a non-self-published book? If you can, you know something I don't know. In this day of "trade paperbacks" and perfect binding (paperback books held together with glue as opposed to stitching), the only way someone will know you self-published your book is if it's stapled together and has hand-written photocopied pages instead of nice type. Even then, if you have worthwhile information or entertainment within those pages, you probably can sell what you've written.

The biggest problem you'll run up against, believe it or not, is bookstores. I'm not talking about unique stores that are a mainstay of the community. I'm talking about the chain store down at the mall, or even the book section at Wal-Mart. For mass-market booksellers, public profile is the key. If the author's name is John Grisham and the title is *Runaway Jury*, that doesn't take much advertising to move. The public perception of that book is instantaneous.

If you've written *Bed & Breakfasts of Montana*, however, don't count on the Borders bookstore in El Paso to order mass quantities. You're going to have to advertise that in *Bed & Breakfast* magazine (if there is one) and sell it through travel agents and the like. A major publisher just doesn't have the time, and chances are good that you'll have to self-publish that book. It's not a dead certainty, but it's a pretty good bet.

So what if you either want to self-publish or can't find anyone to publish your book? Should you go to a "vanity press," a publisher who takes your money, prints up copies of your book, and says, "Thank you very much, you're a fine person"? I would eschew you from doing so. Notice I got very scholarly there—I said "eschew," meaning DON'T! Unless you have money to burn and/or just don't want to put in the work of marketing that book you slaved to write, stay away from vanity presses. They'll tell you about people who have self-published and gone on to great success (like I did), but they won't show you many books that *they* published for authors that went on to great success.

You might have the wherewithal to publish your book electronically. The second edition of this book was published electronically in Adobe Acrobat format. The Acrobat Reader is a free download across all computer platforms and I enjoyed getting small checks from something that could be sent to someone via e-mail if necessary.

One fellow I know started his own electronic paperback and audio book company and has done most of his marketing via the Internet. See www.fictionworks.com for a look into the universe of words created by Ray Hoy and his creative friends. You can even get a free ebook, the thriller *Early Frost* by John Tyler. Who knows, he might even publish your book.

What is a Hit Book, Anyway?

Before I go any further, what constitutes a successful book? Believe it or not, for a hardcover book 5,000 copies is respectable. Double that for softcover. If you as an author can turn out books that generate that kind of sales for your first book, your publisher will continue to work with you. You won't be on any best-seller lists, but you'll get another contract, or several. I know, because I've done it, and talked to many authors who have done the same.

5,000 books? Hah, you say. I could sell that many with my laptop tied behind my book. You probably could. Guess what? Even if you find someone to publish your book, you'll still have to do the bulk of the promotional work, to get that book to sell. Unless, of course, you come up with some wonderful book that gets you a chunky six-figure advance from a major New York house. Then the publisher will buy those big ads, spring for the PR firm to get you booked on the talk shows, and pay for your air and hotel bills. But how often does that happen, realistically, for a first-time author?

Shake a Long Tail: Finding Special Audiences

I knew an author who sold over 50,000 copies of his line of children's books at street fairs and personal appearances before the Internet really took off. The father of a friend of mine sold as many books about Southwest cooking at county fairs and other folksy outlets.

After the first print edition of this book came out, I met a fellow named John Ross, who wrote the novel *Unintended Consequences*. John paid a printer in his hometown of St. Louis to print his book and take orders, and when I met John he had sold over 25,000 copies at $29.95 per copy. Some months later, he was set to appear on ABC television in *Prime Time Live*. What John did was create a fictional story that appealed to a specialized audience, gun owners. *Unintended Consequences* is about a law-abiding gun dealer who is victimized by government agents and retaliates in a virtual war. He also brings up factual issues that are not commonly known in the book. For example, the 1969 U.S. Gun Control Act was copied from a 1933 Nazi law banning gun ownership in Germany. It's a chilling bit of information, woven into a good story, and the book is a blueprint for anyone who thinks his or her own work might not fit in with traditional publishing. Even more remarkable about John's book is that he marketed it solely through word of mouth and ads in specialized magazines.

With all three of these examples there is a common thread: If you know about and effectively market to a specialized audience, you can sell enough books to have what a major publisher would consider a hit—that's roughly anything above 10,000 copies.

The phrase "The Long Tail" is a Hollywood buzz phrase as I write this book. It was first coined by *Wired* magazine editor-in-chief Chris Anderson in a 2004 article to describe how major money is made from minor media projects by certain business entities like Amazon.com or Netflix. From the article:

> There are any number of equally attractive genres and subgenres neglected by the traditional DVD channels: foreign films, anime, independent movies, British television dramas, old American TV sitcoms. These underserved markets make up a big chunk of Netflix rentals. Bollywood [ed: the Indian movie community] alone accounts for nearly 100,000 rentals each month. The availability of offbeat content drives new customers to Netflix—and anything that cuts the cost of customer acquisition is gold for a subscription business. Thus the company's first lesson: Embrace niches. Netflix has made a good business out of what's unprofitable fare in movie theaters and video rental shops because it can aggregate dispersed audiences.

You can shake this "long tail" of the customer base that would support your product if you are smart enough to (a) know they exist and (b) write a book or create a media product and help them find out it exists. For example, I called in to a national radio show one day and the host asked what I did. "I'm an author," I said. I was asked what I'd written, and I named the first edition of this book. We sold 5,000 copies in the next week

or so. I didn't have a public relations person behind me, but the radio
show was heard by millions of people. You simply have to be clever in
using what resources you have available to let people know you have
something available.

More often than not, Hollywood movie producers on the west coast
of the U.S. and New York publishers on the east coast of the U. S. don't
really understand that beliefs and needs of people in the middle of their
country. Since the mega-success of the Left Behind Christian novel series,
however, they've been catching up. Here's an example. You may have
never tuned into TV preacher Joel Osteen's TV show services, but a lot of
people have. That's why his book *Your Best Life Now* landed at the top
of the Wal-Mart.com best-seller list before it was even released in 2004.
Warner Books shipped 2.2 million copies in less than two months. Osteen's
book was one of the bright stars of the fourth quarter sales of bookseller
Books-A-Million. I'm sure someone at that company said "Praise the Lord!"
over sales like that.

So what's your niche?

A Poynter to Ponder

There are a number of self-publishing experts around the country who
can help you figure out what to do. One of them is Dan Poynter of
Santa Barbara, California. Dan travels the country giving lectures like
"How to Write and Publish Books" and touring with other information
professionals who advise you on all aspects of book marketing, promotion,
and distribution. In a mailed packet from Dan, I learned about a fifty-page
report about college publishing, an Internet book listing service, how paper
prices rose forty-eight percent, the number for the Publishers Marketing
Association, publications that were advertising for books to review, and an
affordable book promotion service. On his Web site you'll find resources
like *Mr. Self-Publishing's Notebook*, a collection of all the materials from
the Publishing Poynters newsletter, "245 pages of book tips, resources,
freebies and humor on a CD in MS-Word and PDF (can be read by
both the PC and the Mac)" for $19.95. The newsletter itself is a free
twice-monthly e-zine; sign up onsite.

Dan Poynter is only one of many information providers who have grown
up around self-publishing, but I've always found his mailings interesting, and

his advice good. And no, I don't get a single thing from him for mentioning him in my book. Contact him at:

Para Publishing
PO Box 8206-240
Santa Barbara, CA 93118-8206
(805) 968-7277 phone
(805) 968-1379 fax
info@ParaPublishing.com
www.ParaPublishing.com

Setting Your Price

For an example of a nice self-publishing start-up, take a look a www.stuntpublishing.com. The company was launched by television producer Michael Kewley to produce "books that are simple, clean and bold." Kewley worked in film and television for twenty-five years with credits like Supervising Producer on *Law & Order: Criminal Intent* on NBC, so he might have more resources than the normal aspiring self-publisher, but successful people are great to emulate.

I'll leave it to you to figure out the details of your book if you decide to go the self-publishing route. The Stunt Publishing site might help in figuring out how much to charge; I cited it because so many new writers I've taught gravitate toward children's books.

Meanwhile, here are some things you need to know. Publishers call the costs of production of a book "PP&B," meaning paper, printing, and binding. Of course, they also factor author advances and royalties, promotional costs and staff salaries into this figure. Bookstores usually get the books for at least forty percent off the list price. One book I did was sold to the distributor for 1/3 the list price of the book, or about $5 per unit. (The list price was $14.95.) I know this because my publisher asked to renegotiate my royalty contract. Landing the big distributor allowed a lot more books to be sold, but at the old royalty rate I had negotiated for myself it made it pretty darn tight on the publisher's end. Being a good guy who was willing to bet on long-range, high volume sales, I struck a new deal and the publisher gave me the exact details on everything (which publishers don't normally do). Since the book was in its second printing after only a couple of months on the market, it was an educated guess on my part that I was making the right move.

You'll know how many hours it took you to write your book. You'll know the costs that went into producing the manuscript. (If you don't, your business sense is lacking and I hope you inherited money to live on.) You can find out how much it will cost for "PP&B." Remember to factor in promotional costs, which includes mailings, phone expenses, and travel. If you have a normal size book, you can mail it in a two-day overnight Post Office "Priority Mail" hard envelope, so take that into account. To get someone to talk about your book in the newspaper, or to put you on their radio or TV show, you're going to have to send him or her a copy of the book. You might get by with forwarding an electronic version of your book, but people get a little tired of looking at computer screens these days, and ebook readers are still not as popular as people initially predicted they would become.

Add all these things up and divide the total cost by the amount of books you plan to print in your first run. After someone revives you with smelling salts or whatever, you can add the profit margin you think you can get away with to the average cost per book, and that will be your cover price. Why do you need to know this? Because most likely you'll print a "trade paperback" and you'll print the suggested retail price right on the cover. You have to print it on the cover so the bookstore can slap their less than that price label on the cover and their customers think they're getting a big bargain. That's the way it works.

If you're still unclear what a trade paperback is, go to a bookstore and ask to see one.

Where This Leaves You

The good news about self-publishing is this: No one has to know you self-published, and they won't know unless you tell them. I'm assuming you won't make the mistake of calling your publishing outfit "John Doe Publishers" if your name happens to be John Doe. Don't call it "My Own Dang Self Publishing Company," either. If you can't come up with a decent enough name, ask a friend or relative to do so.

A word of caution, however. Be sure you incorporate your publishing company. Why? Because if you make some claim in your book, or offer some advice which some kook later decides to use as the grounds for a lawsuit, the entity of your company will get sued, not you personally.

This might not seem important to you until the day you are served legal papers at your front door.

Now, how could I write a book about writing in the Information Age without mentioning good old Andy Warhol, who self-published a magazine called *Interview* which went on to become as famous as its founder. You know Andy, don't you? The guy who said "In the future we'll all be famous for fifteen seconds." You know, the guy who painted canvases of Campbell soup cans. Quite an entrepreneur, that Andy.

Once you have a book in hand, whether someone else published it or you did it your own dang self, you'll be facing that cold, cruel PR world that I spoke of earlier. It doesn't have to be a cold, cruel world but I've been writing for a long time now and I'm kind of tired, so you'll have to indulge me for a few final moments.

I'm hoping that you've written a nonfiction book. I'm hoping that it's something that's a current hot topic, or at least a book about something we all need to know more about, or wouldn't mind knowing more about. A cookbook, perhaps, or a book of poetry. "But you left those out!" I hear you scream.

Well, sure I did. Just put your name and address at the top left of the page and double-space your recipe and/or poem and send it in. Now are you happy? Anyway, once you have a book in hand you'll need to know how to let people know about it. If you did what I suggested, and got some journalism experience under your belt or on your resume, if you joined those writing groups I suggested, you'll have developed some media contacts and will have an idea of where to go to get your work noticed.

Feeling lonely? Visit the newsgroup alt.publish.books and do some reading (see www.google.com if you don't know about newsgroups). Krissy Brady's online magazine (www.bradymagazine.com) was started to offer aspiring writers and self-publishers a place to commune. Jenna Glatzer's Absolute Write (www.absolutewrite.com) is an even bigger place to hang out and learn—she even covers greeting cards and poetry!

If you've produced a book and want some ideas about how to promote it, visit the Wheatmark site at www.wheatmark.com to see how they can help you. And if you want to reach talk shows, check out the Radio-TV

Interview Report, "the magazine 4,000 producers read to find guests" at www.rtir.com. The company says it is "the world's largest database of authors and experts who are available for live and telephone interviews on a wide range of subjects."

You can do very well at self-publishing, but it might take some time to be able to make a living at it unless you figure out a way to get your work known by the public. Whether your visibility comes through major media, the Internet, or word of mouth at public venues, ultimately it will be up to you how well you do, both in creating and selling your work.

Just remember to never forget the "little person" because we are all little at least once. There was a famous Chinese poet whose lines were clever enough he became China's most revered philosopher. His name was Lao Tzu, and he always tried out his poems on the little old lady selling flowers down at the corner. His name means "Old Master" and he was the father of Taoism as the author of the *Tao Te Ching*. Was it true that he lived to be almost 200 years old? We may never know, but the wisdom of his words have survived the ages. Consider this:

> *The Great Tao flows everywhere.*
> *It may go left or right.*
> *All things depend on it for life, and it does not turn away*
>   *from them.*
> *It accomplishes its tasks, but does not claim credit for it.*
> *It clothes and feeds all things, but does not claim to be*
>   *master over them.*
> *Always without desires, it may be called the Small.*
> *All things come to it and it does not master them;*
> *it may be called The Great.*

When your life is over, your words may live on. If they are helpful words, they may live forever. I hope that, by sharing this book with you, I have helped you in some small way to create something great. If you find that I have, please do the same for some other writers, and we'll have a better world. Keep writing, keep learning, and good luck.

THE END

Index